Strengthening
the Financial Sector
in the Adjustment Process

A15046 715375

Roberto Frenkel
Editor
CEDES, Argentina

D1736204

Published by the Inter-American Development Bank
Distributed by The Johns Hopkins University Press

Washington, D.C.
1994

The views and opinions expressed in this publication are those of the authors and do not necessarily reflect the official position of the Inter-American Development Bank.

Strengthening the Financial Sector in the Adjustment Process

Distributed by
The Johns Hopkins University Press
2715 North Charles Street
Baltimore, MD 21218-4319

Library of Congress Catalog Card Number: 94-78308
ISBN: 0-940602-78-4

AUTHORS

Bonomo, Marco Antônio
Economist, Economics Department, Pontificia Universidade Católica, Rio de Janeiro.

Carneiro, Dionísio Dias
Economist, Economics Department, Pontificia Universidade Católica, Rio de Janeiro.

Dominioni, Daniel
Economist, Centro de Investigaciones Económicas (CINVE), Montevideo.

Fernández, Raúl
Economist, Centro de Estudios de Estado y Sociedad (CEDES), Buenos Aires.

Frenkel, Roberto
Economics Director of the Centro de Estudios de Estado y Sociedad (CEDES), Buenos Aires.

Garcia, Márcio Gomes Pinto
Economist, Economics Department of the Pontificia Universidade Católica, Rio de Janeiro.

Lora, Eduardo
Economist, Fundación para la Educación Superior y el Desarrollo (FEDESARROLLO), Bogotá.

Noya, Nelson
Economist, Centro de Investigaciones Económicas (CINVE), Montevideo.

Rozenwurcel, Guillermo
Economist, Centro de Estudios de Estado y Sociedad (CEDES), Buenos Aires.

Werneck, Rogério L. Furquim
Economist, Economics Department of the Pontificia Universidade Católica, Rio de Janeiro.

Zuleta, Luis Alberto
Economist, Fundación para la Educación Superior y el Desarrollo (FEDESARROLLO), Bogotá.

Zuluaga, Sandra
Economist, Fundación para la Educación Superior y el Desarrollo (FEDESARROLLO), Bogotá.

FOREWORD

This is the eighth book of a series published under the Centers for Research in Applied Economics Project sponsored by the Inter-American Development Bank. In keeping with the centers' objective of addressing the major economic and social problems affecting Latin America and the Caribbean, this volume examines the importance of developing a strong financial sector to meet the many demands that accompany the adjustment process. The four case studies included in this book examine the structure and activities of the financial sector in Argentina, Brazil, Colombia, and Uruguay. Together with an overview chapter by Roberto Frenkel, the project's coordinator, the studies focus on current developments in the financial sector of these countries, including analysis of recent policy shifts, an evaluation of each system's performance in the face of economic adjustment, and recommendations concerning future policy.

The studies affirm that the recent trend toward economic liberalization has increased the financial strength of these countries. Three of the countries in particular, Argentina, Colombia, and Uruguay, have made great strides toward economic liberalization: eliminating interest rate controls, encouraging more foreign participation in the financial sector, lifting barriers to the formation of new financial institutions, and privatizing a number of state-owned enterprises. This approach to economic management, along with a more efficient system of regulation for the financial markets, has been positive for the investment climate in Latin America. As a result, capital has been pouring in from abroad over the last few years, brightening the prospects for long-term development finance. However, these capital flows must be viewed as a mixed blessing for the financial sectors of the region, because they could also contribute to macroeconomic imbalances in the form of rapid monetary growth, appreciating exchange rates (both nominal and real), and increasing quasi-fiscal deficits. Because of these dangers, some of the financial sector reforms have been rolled back as reserve requirements on deposits have been increased and interest rate controls put in place.

The studies also confirm the important role played by the public sector in determining the success of financial reforms. Fiscal deficits, in particular, have been found to have a profoundly negative impact on the development of a healthy financial sector. By absorbing the nation's supply of loanable funds, a government that runs a fiscal deficit effectively denies commercial banks the opportunity to make anything other than short-term loans. Consequently, only public financial institutions are capable of meeting the medium- and long-term financing needs of small and medium-sized businesses, homeowners, and exporters. Thus, if public sector deficits can be brought under control, then the high and volatile inflation rates that accompany them should also stabilize, thereby boosting the consistently low national savings rates in the region.

Furthermore, although macroeconomic stabilization is an obvious requirement for a strong financial sector, there are two specific and related financial sector reforms that will, in turn, expedite economic stability. The first of these is to grant greater independence to central bank authorities. The second reform that is needed is the privatization of public financial institutions, a step that will almost certainly guarantee greater financial discipline throughout the system. These reforms should be accompanied by the development of a strong regulatory framework to avoid some of the excesses that have been experienced in some countries of the region. By adjusting to the needs of these newly liberalized economies, the financial sector can position itself to benefit greatly from the improved investment climate.

Nohra Rey de Marulanda
Manager, Economic and Social
Development Department

CONTENTS

CHAPTER ONE

STRENGTHENING
THE FINANCIAL SECTOR
IN THE ADJUSTMENT PROCESS: AN OVERVIEW

Roberto Frenkel[1]

This study focuses on the role of the financial system in the development process in Argentina, Brazil, Colombia, and Uruguay. Its point of departure is a definition of the ideal role the sector ought to play in that process: a properly functioning and efficient system should intermediate a sizable portion of the savings generated in the country, do so at low cost, and help bring about a better allocation of those resources. The study's terms of reference were aimed at identifying the problems which in each case place obstacles in the way of that financial intermediation and at outlining reforms designed to remove the obstacles.

The study chose a broad starting point to encourage a discussion of the financial sector in terms of its contribution to development under each economy's current operating conditions. This approach was selected in order to avoid imposing an *a priori* model of the financial system and a single agenda of desirable reforms on the country researchers. Although the study is justified by the general observation that the national financial systems are not fulfilling the ideal role described earlier, the project had to take account of the whole range of national situations and ensure that they constitute the main ingredient of the suggested policies.

The study was designed in accordance with the types of problems peculiar to the sector or with those stemming from the macroeconomic situation and policies. Such problems can be viewed as obstacles to the sector's function of fostering saving and investment. One part focuses on the sector's microeconomy, its particular characteristics, structure and costs, the regulations governing its operation, and its efficiency. Another part concerns the sector's role in macrofi-

[1] The author is grateful for the comments received from the Network of Applied Economic Research Centers (Inter-American Development Bank, Washington, D.C., July 1993) and those made by an anonymous IDB reviewer.

nancial relations. The purpose of this part of the study is to highlight financial problems that derive from the country's macroeconomic situation, condition its current operation, or seem likely to arise in the near future. The final part of the study contains a discussion and assessment of the ongoing reforms and the proposals made by local authors based on their analyses.

The chapter consists of five sections. The first four summarize the results of the study and the policies suggested in each case by the authors of the country studies. The more important points and policy suggestions attempt to reflect those formulated by the authors of the country studies. The conclusions offered in the last section bring those elements together.

Argentina

In Argentina, the implementation of a successful stabilization program is the main starting point for observing the development of the financial sector. A first step in the reversal of earlier negative financial trends was taken with the BONEX plan of early 1990. This operation compulsorily rescheduled the fiscal and quasi-fiscal domestic public debt. This was done through the forced exchange of public securities in domestic currency and most of the financial system's deposits (which basically constituted short-term financing of the public sector, given the high reserve requirements and the unavailabilities imposed by the central bank) for external bonds (public 10-year securities in dollars). The intervention affected the public's assets, including current accounts, to a value of approximately $8 billion. The intervention generated monetary conditions that made it possible to curb hyperinflation in March 1990. Although inflation continued high that year, the financial system began to adjust to the extreme demonetization of the economy, and as early as mid-1990 deposits were trending upward. The improvement of the financial system was consolidated when the Convertibility Plan was implemented in April 1991. Since then a significant inflow of external capital has caused a significant increase in the monetization of the economy. In addition, unlike what happened after the external debt crisis in the early eighties, the newly available funds flowed mainly to the private sector. The study of Argentina centers on the evolution and prospects of the financial sector in the context of the current Convertibility Plan.

Large Size of the Financial System in Relation to Low Monetization

Seen from a sectoral perspective, the operation of the financial system, despite the small volume of funds it intermediates, shows a relatively high number of firms and branches. At the end of 1991 it was made up of 218 financial firms with 4,138 branches. Of that total, 168 were banks with 4,063 branches, and 50 were nonbanks with 75 branches.

There are slightly under 8,000 inhabitants per banking firm, a "banking density" comparable to that of the industrial countries but inconsistent with the degree of monetization, which is much lower than in those countries. In fact, notwithstanding the substantial growth in deposits sparked by the Convertibility Plan, at year-end 1992 the total amount attracted by each branch barely topped $6 million. These comparisons suggest that the bloated size of the Argentine financial system, a longstanding phenomenon perpetuated by the 1977 financial reform, remains a problem.

The number of persons employed in the system tends to underscore that assessment, although a significant adjustment has been evident since 1990. In 1989 some 149,000 people were working in the financial system. Slightly over 55 percent of that total were in the official banking system, 43 percent in the private system and the remaining 2 percent in nonbanks. At year-end 1991, however, the total number employed in the sector stood at around 122,000, or 18 percent less than two years earlier.

In any event, by the end of 1992 the volume of deposits attracted per employee was estimated at only $205,000, a figure consistent with the low levels of business per branch already noted. Without a doubt this very low level of productivity goes far to explain the high cost of loans and other services offered by the domestic financial system.

Participation of the Public Banking System

The other distinguishing feature of the financial structure is the high relative participation of the public banking system. In the period from 1983 to 1992 it accounted for, on average, 50 percent of the deposits and 63 percent of the loans. This major share of total loans underscores the important role the central bank's policy on cash reserves and rediscounts has had in the intermediation activity carried out by the financial system.

From the inception of the remonetization process initiated in early 1990, and to a considerable extent as a consequence of the structural reform undertaken in the national public banking system, the role of the official banking system has tended to shrink with respect to both deposits and loans. For the moment, however, that has not altered its predominant position in the system: in June 1992 it still accounted for 43.8 percent of the deposits and 54.7 percent of the loans. The continuing gap between loans and deposits which these figures also reflect is attributable to intervention by the central bank. Although since the Convertibility Plan the granting of new rediscounts has been very restricted and new loans and deposits have tended to balance each other, the problem of carryover persists: in early 1992 central bank financing represented 32 percent of the deposits of the national public banking system and 53 percent of those of the provincial banking system.

Monetization, Capital Flows and National Saving

Although the remonetization triggered by the Convertibility Plan was swift and very substantial, the level from which it took off—following hyperinflation—was exceptionally low. Furthermore, the economy's liquidity indexes are still at a much lower level than those observed not only in industrialized countries but also in other economies at a similar level of development, and they are indeed appreciably lower than before the financial crisis of the early eighties. In addition—and this is one of the central problems of the Argentine economy at present—private saving has followed a downward trend since the Convertibility Plan came into effect, as a result of which the returning flow of capital from abroad is the only source fueling the remonetization process.

Obviously, this situation cannot last. In the first place, although privatizations have been operating as an important autonomous factor in attracting capital to Argentina, and some important public enterprises are yet to be privatized (in particular Yacimientos Petrolíferos Fiscales, the state oil company), the end of the process is not very far away.

The other factor determining the inflow of capital has been the progressive adjustment of private sector portfolios to the new conditions created by the Convertibility Plan. This factor cannot remain in operation indefinitely either.

To date, capital inputs have been fueled by a surge in credit and sharply reduced domestic interest rates, thus ensuring their increasingly swift domestic absorption. This has led on the one hand to a substantial revival of productive activity, but on the other to inflation remaining well above international levels, causing the exchange rate to fall even farther behind than it did prior to the Convertibility Plan, and leading to a deterioration of the trade balance and current account of the balance of payments.

High Differences in Lending Rates

An appreciable difference between domestic and external borrowing rates has existed since the inception of convertibility. As a result of borrowing rates at higher than international levels and very high albeit declining spreads, lending rates in the local financial system remained excessively high, especially in real terms. Among other things, this made evident the persistence of high intermediation costs for financial organizations and clouded the outlook for the recovery of private investment. Another factor also influencing that variable was the persistence of a marked preference for short terms of deposits in the financial system ("short-termitis"). The two factors, added to the virtual absence of public investment and the stagnation of exports, determined that consumer spending would lead the recent recovery. Although the investment rate rose over its 1990 minimum, it remains among the low levels of the past decade.

Expansion of the Dollarized Segment

Another remarkable aspect of the increase in financial intermediation since the implementation of the Convertibility Plan has been the rapid growth of a dollarized segment. While at the end of 1988 the financial system had only $1.2 billion in deposits (less than 12 percent of total deposits), more than $11 billion were in deposit by December 1992 (almost 45 percent of the total). As a counterpart, approximately 40 percent of the financial system's total credit and half the credit to the private sector are denominated in dollars. The bimonetary configuration is similar to those of Bolivia and Uruguay. A majority share of dollar credits is earmarked for the purchase of consumer goods, immovable property, and the production of nontradable goods, whose earnings are not dollarized and depend on domestic absorption. This characteristic is combined with the macroeconomic prospects in order to determine the existence of a systemic risk of insolvency.

Fragility, Risk of Insolvency and Financial Deepening

For strictly sectoral reasons as well as macroeconomic ones associated chiefly with uncertainty about the continued external financing of a heavily deficit-burdened current account, the financial system still displays some of its past fragility. First, its financial depth is lower than where it stood prior to the debt crisis. Second, the average term of deposit, in both domestic and foreign currency, remains exceedingly short. Third, the intermediation spreads between lending and borrowing rates are very high, particularly in national currency transactions. Two other elements of a different nature contribute to the weakness of the financial system. The first is the fact that the public banking system continues, as noted, to channel a large share of the resources intermediated by the system and is undergoing a profound crisis. The second is the fact that the loan portfolio of the financial institutions, including the dollar-denominated part of it, as also noted, is highly concentrated in the nontradable goods sectors.

All of this notwithstanding, since 1991 the financial system has recovered much of its function as administrator of the community's means of payment. This is particularly significant inasmuch as two bouts of hyperinflation, one in 1989 and the other in 1990, threatened its very existence. However, the system is still failing to fulfill its role of providing funds for investment on the scale and under the conditions required for the reconversion of the productive structure and the resumption of growth. Another continuing problem is market segmentation, which imposes severe credit rationing on small and medium-sized enterprises and on the country's less developed interior regions. In addition, the combination of the characteristics of the system that began to take shape in 1991 and the macroeconomic problems facing the Convertibility Plan make for fairly high risks of illiquidity and insolvency.

Ongoing Reforms

The stabilization period has been active in the area of reform. Reforms of the national public and provincial banking systems are underway, and since late 1992 measures have been adopted to improve credit assistance to small and medium-sized enterprise. In addition, new legislation passed by Congress but not yet applied grants the central bank a considerable amount of autonomy.

The reforms approved and pending are helpful to the system but do not appear to carry enough weight by themselves to overcome the obstacles still hindering its essential functions. Furthermore, the course of the system does not indicate that the previously mentioned shortcomings of the market are being corrected.

The widespread imposition of regulations with respect to terms, rates, or allocation of credit is not only undesirable but also seemingly impossible. "Liberalization" was a process largely imposed by events, and the opening of the financial markets is a longstanding phenomenon in the Argentine economy, probably irreversible, which largely accepts the spreads of the possible regulations. This observation, however, must not be taken to suggest passive policies.

Strengthening the Public Banking System

The proposed approaches point in two main directions. One entails the strengthening of a properly rationalized and reorganized public banking system. The proposals encompass the national and provincial banking systems.

When the process of reforming the national public banking system is completed, only one retail bank in that category will be left. That is the Banco de la Nación Argentina, which will primarily serve the small and medium-sized enterprises of all sectors. There will also be two wholesale banks, the Banco de Inversión y Comercio Exterior (BICE), which has not yet started operations, and the Banco Hipotecario Nacional. In the case of the Banco de la Nación Argentina, the achievement of the objectives set for it will depend on an improvement in the efficiency with which it is managed and its continued ability to recover its business; heretofore its efforts have been concentrated on large enterprises or directed at extra-economic aims. With respect to the Banco Hipotecario and BICE, the uncertainties pertain to the extent to which funds will be available to them. That availability depends directly on access to funds from abroad and placement of their securities in the local market, and in neither case does rapid expansion in the short term appear possible. Disregarding considerations of conditions in the international capital market, dependency on international financing puts the achievement of their objectives at risk. The limited financial deepening, high costs, short terms, marked segmentation, and the concentration of credit point to a role for the public sector in changing repayment terms and in ensuring access to credit for investment. Experience fully justifies the decision not to use rediscounts of the central bank for those purposes, but, in addition to external funds, those institutions should be capitalized with resources duly included in the budget. Cofinancing with the private sector for long-term projects ought also to be explored.

Intervention to Reduce the Risk of Financial Crisis

The second direction aims at finding better alternatives to cushion the adverse effects of macroeconomic disturbances on the financial system. One of the proposals entails strengthening ongoing efforts to make bank supervision more efficient. Two other approaches would entail changing current courses of action. The first would restore the central bank's function as lender of last resort, which is excluded in the recently approved legislation. The second would set up a deposit guarantee system.

Brazil

In Brazil the persistence of high inflation rates directs the study to the relationship between the evolution of the financial system and the inflationary process. Although high inflation was widespread in Latin America in the eighties, the Brazilian experience is unique in certain aspects. A salient feature is the financial system's role in providing domestic assets accepted by the public as substitutes for money. This adaptation has enabled the Brazilian economy to avoid, until now, the sharp demonetization experienced by other Latin American economies undergoing similar inflation, and to partially curb capital flight and the dollarization of the public's assets. While on the one hand evidence indicates that the dimensions of the system and financial activity are excessive, on the other, credit to the nonfinancial private sector fell from around 35 percent of GDP at the end of the seventies to 12 percent of GDP in 1992.

Dimensions of the System

The financial reforms of the mid-sixties created a system based on institutional specialization. The system grew rapidly, but in a much less segmented form than foreseen in the original legal design. Financial institutions belonging to the same conglomerate made joint use of a physical and organizational infrastructure while maintaining separate accounting systems to comply with regulations. A new reform in 1988 gave this process legal recognition with the creation of a multiple bank, and conditions for inflow into the system were deregulated. At present, multiple banks perform the major part of financial activity. The three largest banks are public and in 1991 handled 66 percent of the credits and 46 percent of the deposits of the system. The degree of concentration is also high among the private banks.

The inflation tax and the role of providing liquidity with illiquid public securities caused the system to expand greatly. The 1980 census recorded 638,000 bank employees. From 1980 to 1987 the system's aggregate value grew at an estimated rate of 7 percent annually (from 8 percent of GDP to 14 percent of GDP), and employment in the system probably doubled in that period. While credit shrank from the mid-seventies to the present time, as noted, revenues from financial intermediation resulted more and more from offerings to the public of indexed financial assets secured against government bonds. By means of formal and informal buyback agreements, the central bank permitted the banks to create short-term deposits with daily cash flow which cover the purchase of long-term government bonds. The available evidence indicates that the system's average spread tended to increase in that process, hand-in-hand with the rise in the mean and the variability of the exchange rate. The spread also tended to fluctuate more between institutions, which indicates that risk increased along with average profitability.

Persistence of Some Positive Features

The adaptation of the financial system to providing cash flow and intermediating government borrowings is very profound. However, the Brazilian system preserved some positive features that stand out in comparison with the other cases. One of these features is the survival, in an environment of high inflation, of a segment of long-term credit for investment in fixed assets. This is provided almost exclusively by the Development Bank (BNDES), a public bank supported with fiscal funds. The bank's total lending as well as the flow of new loans attain high levels in macroeconomic terms. This institution has qualified staff and has been ably performing its function of selecting projects and allocating resources, despite the macroeconomic and political instability of recent years.

Another feature, which may be positive if efforts to stabilize the Brazilian economy succeed, is the system's high degree of specialization. For example, the futures and options market grew strongly, devoting itself mainly to trading financial assets. The number of transactions this market took ranked sixth in the world in 1992. Clearly this hyperdevelopment is largely caused by high, variable inflation, but the innovations could be instrumental in reducing intermediation costs in a more stable context.

The Problem of the State Banks

Some of the most serious problems in the structure and operation of the Brazilian financial system stem from the size and behavior of the banks belonging to the states. The chief reason for this difficulty is that the central bank lacks the authority to close down these institutions when they are technically bankrupt. The problems with these banks began in 1982 when they were used to finance state governments facing general elections. Since then these banks have been regular funding sources for their states and municipalities. This is possible thanks to a loophole in the law. While other banks are legally restricted to having not more than 10 times their net worth in state and municipal bonds, the banks of the state can be funded without limits against this type of assets. Attempts to close this legal loophole have thus far come to naught. When one of these banks gets into difficulties, the central bank is pressured into bailing it out. This is usually done by swapping state and municipal securities for federal securities of equal par value but higher market value. In addition, these banks have several times exceeded the limits of risk diversification under central bank rules which set the maximum concentration of credit or guarantees on a single client at 30 percent of net worth. By virtue of those mechanisms, the banks of the state almost possess the ability to issue money.

Adaptation to High Inflation and "Financialization"

The evolution of the system in recent years took place against a background of high inflation (about 20 percent a month) whose disruptive effects accentuated the failures of successive attempts at stabilization. The salient characteristic of this evolution is the association developed between the financial system and the government to devise substitutes for money and prevent the public from fleeing domestic assets. The association came about in the mid-sixties with the government's decision to create a public securities market in order to avoid resorting to the monetary financing of the public deficit. Indexing was first applied to debts with the treasury, then to mortgages and payments thereon, and finally spread gradually to all contracts. Over the years the central bank successfully performed the task of underwriting public debt paper, at the same time providing substitutes for money: first placing the papers directly in the nonfinancial sector and later ensuring the liquidity of government financial assets retained as a counterpart of private deposits in private financial institutions. In some cases the latter offer indexed substitutes of deposits on current account covering government assets of up to twenty years' maturity. The process led to a merging of financial activity in the daily transaction of public papers of any maturity that could be used as bank reserves and are frequently transacted between banks and the central bank, guarantor of the liquidity which sustains the system. The incentive of reducing the burden of the inflation tax prompts the nonfinancial sector to merge resources into cash management, producing what has been called "financialization" of all activities.

The process just described has thus far averted the massive dollarization of the public's financial assets witnessed in other instances of high inflation, but it has been unable to escape the distortions and inefficiencies that result from boosting financial activity in order to minimize the inflation tax. From the second half of the eighties these costs rose not only because of the accelerating inflation rate but also because of a new phenomenon: uncertainty about the permanence of the rules. Since the Cruzado Plan there have been several interventions in financial contracts for various reasons, particularly the attempt to curb inertial inflation by preventing indexation. This new factor also affected the function of the financial system by contributing to shorter contracts and higher premiums demanded by possessors of wealth in order to hold on to domestic assets.

Effects of the Failure of the Stabilization Plans

Five "shock" stabilization programs have been tried and have failed since 1986. All included significant changes in the rules of the financial sector based on the intention of stopping indexation and making possible an active monetary policy after the shock. The last two were the Collor Plans. The first Collor Plan began with the greatest intervention in private contracts ever carried out in Brazil. Private financial assets amounting to 10 percent of GDP were frozen (M4 plummeted from 15.7 percent of GDP before to 5.2 percent of GDP after the shock). As had happened on previous occasions, exceptions tended to restore liquidity in the following months. The experiment with active monetary policy in the second half of 1990 put an end to the automatic buyback of federal government bonds by the central bank. Indexed bonds were replaced by traditional discounted treasury notes. This gave the central bank greater control over the money supply. The experiment ended abruptly in December 1990 when it became clear that the political power to let some heavily indebted state banks go bankrupt was lacking. The case underscored how heavily political exigencies can weigh on attempts at reform.

The second Collor Plan, in February 1991, radically changed the rules of indexation by prohibiting the application of past inflation indexes in the short term and replacing that indexation with a benchmark interest rate determined each month by the central bank on the basis of the market rates of thirty-day certificates of deposit. The new legislation also introduced the so-called Fondos de Aplicação Financeira (Financial Application Funds), managed by banks, which can be final holders of public bonds. Shares in these funds replaced indexed cash accounts, which were prohibited. Issuance of other short-term financial assets was also permitted, with great flexibility for closed-end funds.

Beginning in 1991, the restoration of monetization was carried out in the context of a very conservative monetary policy with high interest rates. All in all, the restoration of the demand for domestic assets which ensued is quite remarkable if one also considers the severe political crisis of 1992. Nevertheless, the Collor Plans left memories of massive intervention that are rekindled each time "financial reform" is bruited as a possibility. This possibility is associated with speculations on what shape the next stabilization policy might assume.

Financial Reforms and Policies for Stabilization

The future course of the Brazilian experience of megainflation and the outlook for the financial sector remain matters of conjecture, as they depend so heavily on the policy of stabilization. The advent of a hyperinflation process originating with a massive flight of domestic financial assets cannot be ruled out. Repudiation of the public debt would extend to private assets and trigger withdrawals from the funds, undermining confidence in the banks. Proposals exist to dollarize financial assets, based on the belief that the loss of confidence would only affect cruzeiro-denominated assets. Similar reasoning lies behind the idea of dollarizing the public debt by using central bank reserves as collateral. These proposals have in common the assumption that the survival of the banking system in the face of massive flight depends on the government's permitting the dollarization of financial activity.

Policy suggestions formulated in the study go beyond conjectures on the immediate future and the characteristics of the next stabilization policy: they address the financial system following stabilization. The proposals are based on two factors that can ensure a positive future role for the financial system in reviving growth. The first is that, from the point of view of the supply of financial intermediation, the system is currently stronger and more specialized than in the past. The second is that, from the point of view of the demand for funding, credit has fallen to such low levels that the expansion of credit is pivotal to investment and consumption. The suggested policy guidelines have two aims: to make the stabilization policy more likely to succeed and to strengthen the financial system that will emerge from the present crisis.

One policy proposal would give greater independence to the central bank. Since 1992 Congress has been discussing ways to grant such greater independence, the necessity of which is acknowledged. Two different proposals are under discussion, and it is probable that new legislation will be approved in the near future. It is clear that the legal form will not be sufficient to guarantee the result, but it is considered an important step in the right direction. In the short term the effective independence and authority appear indispensable for resolving the problem deriving from the operation of the public banks.

The second proposal addresses the operation of the official banking system. The behavior of these banks was one of the principal reasons behind the failure of the stabilization policies. Between mid-1991 and mid-1992 the central bank had obtained sufficient political support to control those banks, but with the political crisis the difficulties grew and they are still present. Most of the state banks are overstaffed and a sizable part of their portfolios is irrecoverable. This situation stems mainly from excessive credit to governments of states and municipalities or their enterprises and agencies. Restructuring coupled with greater control of the central bank is one possible approach to tackling the problem. A more far-reaching solution may be offered by privatization. This idea would encounter strong resistance in political quarters and from labor unions. The federal government could initiate the process by taking measures with respect to its own agencies and then turn its attention to the states.

Impacts and Probable Problems Associated with Stabilization

A number of probable impacts and policy themes appear related to the effects and consequences of the stabilization policy and of the low inflation rate resulting from it. The treatment of the public debt establishes a dividing line between the possible stabilization policies. Although it represents little more than 10 percent of GDP, the servicing of that debt consumes a sizable part of the public budget because interest rates have been extremely high, partly owing to the premiums for the risk of nonperformance, which have risen sharply since 1990. Discussions about the treatment of the public debt during the stabilization period are perceived as an indicator of nonperformance risk; this creates a vicious cycle as interest rates rise and more discussion about the "solution" of the problem ensues. One of the most feared interventions is the obligatory swapping of very short-term assets for longer-term assets. The debate concerning the order between stabilization and restructuring of the public debt is currently underway. A new intervention could cause a series of bankruptcies and profoundly affect the financial sector.

Even if no rejection or forced refinancing of the public debt materializes, the intermediation of government bonds would, after the stabilization, cease to be the chief banking activity as it was in the eighties. Stabilization would also impose the restructuring of the system of branches set up to capture the inflation tax. A phenomenon of this kind came about following the Cruzado Plan, when the system adjusted very flexibly, closing hundreds of branches and massively cutting staff. This restructuring tended to remain, despite subsequent acceleration of inflation. It is probable that the large public banks will have the greatest difficulties adapting in the face of low inflation.

The deregulation of external financial flows is a subject that has attracted increasing attention in Brazil. The greater part of the current debate centers on the sequence between deregulation and stabilization, rather than the policy in itself. In 1991 and 1992 Brazil received a substantial flow of external capital, thanks chiefly to the repatriation of funds motivated by the lowering of international interest rates and by high domestic rates. Management of the impact of these flows on the financial sector and of their effects on monetary policy is a relatively new item on the Brazilian agenda and would have an important place in stabilization.

Long-term Credit: Strengthening BNDES Financing
Through Private Cofinancing

One last aspect of financial sector reform relates to the creation of long-term capital market. The modest results achieved in the past were swept away by accelerating inflation. It is widely acknowledged that little can be done in this regard before stabilization becomes a reality. However, under stable conditions it will probably, even from an optimistic perspective, take the state some time to recover its historic role of providing long-term funding for private investment. A suggestion in this respect is to use the good performance of BNDES, limited in its fiscal coverage, to cofinance projects with the private banking system.

Colombia

In the mid-eighties the Colombian financial system underwent a severe crisis which was aggravated by the macroeconomic maladjustments of the time. To deal with that crisis the government took over several institutions, and the crisis was overcome through measures to improve the system's reliability and prof-itability and to correct the main problems regarding the quality of its commercial assets. The Colombian financial system is nevertheless poorly developed and has a segmented structure based on specialized lending operations, with some-what diversified borrowing operations. These issues were addressed by reform policies beginning in 1990, when a law went into effect completing a liberaliza-tion process that had been in progress for some time and introducing more unity into the system. However, the new structure is ambiguous and the liberalization came into conflict with macroeconomic policies. The policies suggested in the study center primarily on those questions.

Structure of the System

The Colombian financial system is built around 24 commercial banks, which operate primarily as short-term financial intermediaries. Five of them are official banks, including two that were nationalized during the financial crisis and whose reprivatization is planned. The privatization process launched in 1990 has reduced the public sector's share in the banking system from 60 percent of the assets in 1989 to 44 percent in December 1991 and 37 percent at year-end 1992. The banks' assets amount to 22 percent of GDP, of which approximately 45 per-cent is allocated in loans. The banks' coverage is fairly diversified. The main borrowing components are checking accounts (29 percent), certificates of deposit (20 percent), and savings deposits (10 percent). The banks are the only entities authorized to operate checking accounts. Although funding sources are fairly stable, the banks do not effect many changes in repayment terms.

Attempts to create an investment banking system date back to the twenties and thirties. The official banks devoted to mortgage financing and agricultural development—the Central Hipotecario and the Caja Agraria, respectively—date from that period. The sixties saw the creation of finance corporations designed to foster the capital market and long-term investment. Twenty-two finance corporations are currently in existence, six of them official. In general, the banks own the corporations as part of financial conglomerates. In these cases they have merged their investment business into enterprises of the conglomerate. The finance corporations' assets amount to approximately 5 percent of GDP, of which close to 70 percent is allocated to loans. About 44 percent of the corporations' coverage comes from certificates of deposit and 22 percent comes from resources of the Banco de la República (central bank). Funds from the public are spotty and unstable. Hence the granting of long-term credit has depended mainly on resources from the central bank and international organizations. These are the only entities to make capital investments, but the fact that these investments amount to only about 5 percent of their assets shows how far they are from achieving their original goals.

The savings and loan corporations date from the early seventies. They have had exclusive authorization to operate in indexed fashion (in "constant purchasing power units"). Nine institutions, three of them official, fit this description. They have a comprehensive network of branches and carry close to five million accounts. The corporations are owned by financial groups or conglomerates active chiefly in the construction and insurance industries. Their assets represent slightly over 8 percent of GDP. Seventy percent of the assets are allocated to loans. Practically all the resources come from savings deposits indexed by means of the periodic revaluation of the "constant purchasing power unit."

Other specialized segments of the system are, relatively speaking, of lesser importance: the commercial finance companies, lending primarily to consumers and businesses; companies specializing in leasing with purchase options; bonded warehouses; and trust companies. Apart from these institutions there are more than 1,000 first-degree savings and loan cooperatives that are supervised by a body separate from the financial authorities. The cooperatives have a total capital comparable with that of the savings and loan corporations.

Leaving aside the cooperatives and special funds, the Colombian financial system has 160 entities, of which 23 are public. The assets of the system represent approximately 50 percent of GDP and are distributed almost equally among public and private entities. In addition to the large public banks mentioned, the share of the official sector is scattered through all the segments as a result of preventive nationalizations carried out in response to the crisis of the eighties. The privatizations mentioned previously only diminished public participation in the commercial bank segment.

Segmentation and Low Financial Deepening

The system is highly segmented and the degree of financial deepening is low. The private sector's financial assets stand at 38 percent of GDP. Of this total, eight points are central bank liabilities, thirteen are commercial bank liabilities, nine are liabilities of the savings and loan corporations and the rest are spread among the other entities. Monetary assets represent 14 percent of GDP and savings instruments 20 percent. The financial analysis represented by these figures has remained constant since the mid-eighties.

Financial interrelations in the Colombian economy are concentrated in two groups, one made up of the external and public sectors, and the other of all the financial intermediaries and the private sector. The public sector holds a net debt equivalent to almost 40 percent of GDP, the majority of which is financed with external credit. Lending by the banks and the other financial organizations mentioned is directed primarily to the private sector, and much of the borrowing is also from that sector. In sum, the Colombian financial system is poorly developed and segmented and plays an unimportant role in the financing of private and public investment.

Interest Rates and Intermediation Spreads

Interest rates on bank certificates of deposit remained more or less stable in nominal terms between the second half of the eighties and 1991. Until 1990 this involved a slightly decreasing real rate, as inflation climbed from less than 20 percent at the beginning of the decade to 30 percent at its close. In 1991 the real rate was approximately 12 percent. In 1992 the rates were reduced about 10 points by an administrative measure, which drove down the real rate to approximately 2 percent. Interest on savings accounts, controlled until 1991, remained at very low or negative real rates. The correction rate of the indexed savings rates of the savings corporations has been almost constantly below the rate of inflation because of caps and methods of calculation. However, if one adds the interest rate to the correction rate the returns on these accounts are about the same as inflation. The yield on certificates of deposit was low but positive throughout, although it turned negative in 1992.

Ordinary bank lending rates surpassed 20 percent in real terms until 1985. From 1986 until 1991, nominal lending rates remained more or less stable, which meant that real rates fluctuated by about 20 percent. The reduction of the nominal rate to 37.5 percent in 1992 raised the real lending rate to 8 percent. The real lending rate of the savings and loan corporations was in the order of 8 percent.

The gross financial intermediation spread, taking into account the banks' actual financial cost, was stable at 17 percent until 1992, when it fell to 13 percent. The spread held constant despite reductions in operating, cash reserve, and mandatory investment costs. In addition, lending rates are much more inertial than borrowing rates in short periods. This evidence suggests that the market is not competitive and its pricing practices are characteristic of an oligopolistic market.

Assessment of Ongoing Reforms

The restructuring of the financial sector acquired special importance in 1990 as one of the elements of the ambitious economic modernization program of the new government of César Gaviria. The program further included the freeing of external trade, the elimination of restrictions on foreign trade, the simplification of labor regulations, and the partial freeing of the exchange market by giving the financial system an active role in exchange transactions. The guidelines for reform were laid down by law in 1990. The principal structural reform consisted of adopting the branch banking system as an intermediate step between the multiple bank and specialized bank approaches. The banks, finance corporations, and commercial finance companies were authorized to invest in financial services branches (trust, leasing, and stockbrokerage companies), although credit operations between the parent company and the branch were restricted. The rules regarding mergers, conversions, and break-ups of organizations were eased. Entry into the sector was made possible by meeting capital and professional requirements, and all restrictions on foreign investment were abolished. The same provisions regulated privatizations and laid down rules on disclosure, supervision, and control.

The autonomy of the central bank was established in the 1991 Constitution. The Banco de la República, set up as an autonomous central bank independent of the government, was responsible for monetary, exchange, and credit policies. Its authority is exercised through a board of directors appointed for fixed terms, the general manager, and the Minister of Finance. However, Law 35 of 1993 transferred to the government important functions involving authorization of activities, determination of amounts of capital, and the issuance of prudential standards. That law empowered the Ministry of Finance to intervene in the operation of the system for the setting of maximum individual loans and the imposition of percentages of credit allocations to key sectors (up to 30 percent of assets under conditions of equality for all intermediaries). The central bank is responsible for monetary and financial management, and the Superintendencia Bancaria is in charge of the supervision and administrative regulation of the system.

Until the early seventies practically all interest rates were set by the authorities. Lending rates were the first to be freed. Rates for certificates of deposit of banks and corporations were freed in 1980. The monetary correction applied to all transactions of the savings and loan corporations was partially tied to the interest rate on certificates of deposit in 1984. Yields on certificates of those entities were freed in 1989, and the rest of their operations followed in 1991. Interest rates on their loans were also set free, except for low-income housing (to which they have to earmark 20 percent of the funds they raise). Yields on bank savings accounts were freed at the end of 1990. Notwithstanding the liberation process, which became total in the nineties, interest rates have been the targets of sporadic interventions, the most recent in 1992.

In 1992 various provisions and laws again changed the structure and functions of the entities in a manner inconsistent with the provisions of 1990. For example, the leasing companies were converted into commercial finance companies, which will enable them to attract funds from the public. The savings and loan companies, meanwhile, will be authorized to invest in any type of financial services company and to carry out transactions previously not authorized, such as dealing in foreign currency and granting short-term loans not backed by mortgages. The provisions referred to, among others, were adopted in response to various pressures from the financial institutions to broaden their activities, compensate the loss of some prerogatives, and abolish some of the restrictions on their operations. The result seems to be rather incoherent. No type of institution has the exclusive role of financial conglomerate and crossed investments are a possibility. The system will not prevent the appearance of conflicts of interest and operations are not clearly delimited.

Policies Relating to the Structure of the Sector

With respect to the foregoing and in order to inject more competition into the sector, the study proposes a policy that strengthens the initiatives of the 1990 reform: lift regulatory barriers, open the way to foreign capital investment, ease regulations governing mergers and conversions, determine size by requiring minimum amounts of capital, and spur financial innovation and privatization of state entities. Together with these guidelines, the restructuring of the system should move in the direction of a multiple banking system. The elimination of specializations should make it possible for the institutions to perform all the operations permitted, leaving specialization to those with comparative advantages. The study presents this proposed reform accompanied by a detailed description of the suggested implementation. Other suggestions concerning further sectoral policy are aimed at reducing current cash reserves, strengthening the process of abolishing mandatory investment now underway, and diversifying the instruments of the financial system in the securities market.

Privatizations

As a result of the opportunities afforded by the 1990 reform, four foreign organizations have entered the banking sector (three of them Venezuelan) and five have been privatized. Several mergers and conversions are being studied, as is the creation of new ones, all as part of a competition-oriented environment. Nevertheless, the greatest changes in the structure of property are those relating to the privatizations, which affected both the traditional official banking system and the group of institutions nationalized during the crisis. Still, although the 1990 law gave the government the power to reorganize the public banking system, very little progress has been made in this direction, though several operations are slated for 1993. Law 35 of 1993 included the strengthening of the capital market and support for democratic capitalism among the objectives of the privatizations. These new requirements may complicate the process of privatization, for on previous occasions the bidders clearly preferred total control of the stock of privatized institutions.

Inconsistencies Between the Reforms and Macroeconomic Trends

As noted, in 1990 the last phase of the financial restructuring process was initiated with the approval of a very ambitious legal framework for reform designed to liberalize and deregulate business. In particular, the financial sector was granted a more active role in foreign exchange transactions when the exchange market underwent far-reaching liberalization. It is interesting to observe that despite this development the reform did not permit the dollarization of domestic financial activity. The prohibition on any borrowing in foreign currency was maintained, although credits in foreign currency were permitted on a "house account" basis (which is currently required of banks) or with external resources of correspondents.

In the macroeconomic sphere the reforms gave rise to inconsistencies stemming from the conflict between monetary control objectives and the fiscal and external situations, since the fiscal deficit rose at the same time that an exchange surplus came about. In an attempt to resolve this conflict in practice, financial liberalization was reversed at the beginning of 1991 with the imposition of marginal reserve requirements of 100 percent and an unprecedented hike in the interest rate on central bank securities. These monetary control policies proved unworkable, and the new board of directors, which took office in August, established the objective of reducing interest rates and gradually reducing open market operations. In October, however, the maturity of certificates of exchange issued against foreign currency purchased by the central bank was increased from three to twelve months. These rose from 2.9 percent of the money supply at year-end 1990 to 15.6 percent at year-end 1991 and 27.1 percent in 1992. For similar purposes of sterilization, the banking system was obliged in October and November 1991 to purchase foreign currency on a "house account" basis for an amount equivalent to 30 percent of its foreign exchange borrowings. This amount was raised to 45 percent in 1992. In addition, external financing of the enterprises was authorized in 1992 with the aim of introducing more competition into the system and lowering the interest rate. Finally, in what constituted the step most contrary to the objectives of liberalization, between June and the end of 1992 controls were imposed on interest rates on loans, in the form of a ceiling on the average weighted interest rate for up to 18 months on the loans of each intermediary. The controls brought down the rates, as mentioned earlier, and produced neither rationing nor distortions. The controls appear to have acted by reinforcing the trend to lower rates through the abundance of liquidity and competition with funds of foreign origin.

The conflict between reform of the financial system and stabilization seems to have been mainly a sequencing problem. The early liberalization of the exchange market complicated macroeconomic management because of the presence of high interest rates, the firmness of the current account, and the inflow of capital. The swift accumulation of reserves and the instability of monetary management raised expectations of a real revaluation between mid-1991 and mid-1992. Under these conditions, the expected cost of foreign currency credits was substantially lower than their cost in pesos. Consequently, the financial system's trade portfolio shrank until May 1992. As the expectations of revaluation and an inflow of capital moderated and the interest rate declined, the demand for credit was revived in the second half of 1992. The reorientation of monetary policy has improved the opportunities for reinitiating the reforms. The expansion of savings as a result of the capital inflow facilitates the introduction of new financial instruments such as government and corporate bonds and various borrowing instruments of the banks and other intermediaries. A money supply that attracts funds—through capital inflows and the balance of the current account—makes it easier to keep interest rates low. A start is being made in exploring these possibilities. In 1992 the government floated domestic bonds with three- to seven-year maturities, and the regular floating of treasury securities began in early 1993. However, reserve levels continue high for fear that easing them will cause excessive expansion of the money supply and higher costs for the sterilization efforts that would be required.

The course of the financial system depends on the macroeconomic outlook and on the policies implemented in this area. Moderate expectations of devaluation and the accumulation of reserves will continue to influence the financial system's performance, due principally to the prospects for increased oil exports.

Accordingly, possibilities for developing the system will depend closely on the policies that are adopted to stabilize the current account and the reserves.

Uruguay

The Uruguayan financial system was liberalized in the seventies and underwent a crisis in the early eighties. The financial strength prior to the crisis resulted not from increased savings but from a reallocation of assets following the inflow of capital which had previously fled. When the financial system felt the negative effects in the early eighties, its fragility brought the demise of the national private intermediaries. These events gave rise to a financial system with two peculiar characteristics: it is highly dollarized and the only banks in existence are public or foreign. The Uruguayan study reflects these characteristics of the system.

Structure of the Sector

The Uruguayan financial system is composed of public and private institutions. In addition to the central bank, the public institutions are the Banco de la República Oriental del Uruguay (BROU) and the Banco Hipotecario del Uruguay (BHU).

The BROU is a commercial and development bank and the country's largest institution. It holds 30 percent of the deposits and issues 30 percent of the system's credit. It performs its functions as a development bank by making long-term loans to the productive sectors. It covers its lending with short-term deposits by the public and it has a monopoly on deposits from public enterprises and the government. In addition, it channels international cooperation funds and audits external trade. Until the end of 1992 it enjoyed substantial autonomy from the central bank and was not subject to the reserve and supervision of the private banking system.

The BHU is a development bank that finances housing. Its loans are mostly long-term (15 to 20 years) and indexed according to "readjustable units" tied to the nominal wage index. Some of its funds are borrowings indexed in the same way and others are short-term borrowings. This bank accounts for 10 percent of total deposits and issues 30 percent of the credit.

The system's other institutions are commercial banks, financial houses, and credit cooperatives. There are 23 commercial banks divided, according to their ownership, into foreign capital banks and "managed banks." The banks operate almost exclusively with short-term loans and deposits, without restrictions on their rates, in domestic or foreign currency, and with clients who may or may not reside in Uruguay. The "managed banks" were originally private and were purchased by the state during the crisis to be rehabilitated and privatized. Those currently in existence take in about 8 percent of the system's deposits and issue about 4 percent of the credit. The private banks are branches of parent institutions abroad or corporations whose shares belong to persons not residing in Uruguay (nonresidents). They take in around 40 percent of the system's deposits and issue some 30 percent of the credit.

The financial houses hold deposits of nonresidents exclusively and engage in offshore business, although they can also lend to residents, and they have no exclusive right over extranational transactions, which can also be pursued by the banks. Those transactions are exempted from the mandatory reserve rules and the tax on financial assets. There are 12 of these institutions and all are owned by foreign capital. They hold 10 percent of the system's total deposits and issue 7 percent of the credit. They account for 30 percent of extranational borrowing and loan activities.

There are eight credit cooperatives. These may only carry out intermediation transactions among their members, and they represent approximately 2 percent of the financial market.

Financial Crisis, Disappearance of the Domestic Private Banking System and Expansion of Public Banking

The liberalization and opening of the Uruguayan financial system dates from 1974, as part of an overall liberalization strategy that was particularly swift in that sector. The deregulation of the exchange market and the unlimited opening-up to capital movements were adopted in October 1974. The deregulation of interest rates and the abolition of restrictions on bank lending followed in late 1977. Other measures taken since then and until 1979 were connected with the elimination of the requirement to draw up contracts in domestic currency and with the easing of requirements concerning capital, portfolio ceilings per client, and inputs from new institutions. Financial intermediation increased sharply until 1981 in conjunction with expanding business activity. Credit to the resident private sector climbed from 18 percent to 39 percent of GDP from 1975 to 1981. In that period, gross deposits from foreign operations rose from 11 percent to 33 percent of GDP. This increased financial activity resulted, however, not from an increase in the saving rate but principally from the repatriation of capital and the elimination of the informal dollar markets.

Abandonment in 1982 of the fixed exchange rate or *la tablita* policy had important consequences for the system. Starting in mid-1981 the recession and mistrust of the exchange policy first prompted the public to shift its assets into foreign currency and then, in 1982, triggered capital flight. Even before the recession, enterprises had been overindebted and often delinquent. When the banks saw depositors switch to dollars, they obliged their customers to refinance in that currency a good part of the credits originally contracted for in pesos. This change aggravated insolvency problems when the devaluation came at the end of 1982. With the advent of the crisis, the state sought to save the system through a policy whereby the central bank purchased a substantial volume of nonperforming assets amounting to approximately 8 percent of GDP. The nationally and some regionally owned banks without strong external support did not join in this effort and remained insolvent but in operation well into the eighties, although by the end of the decade they had gone under.

The crisis did not result in the "definanciation" phenomenon observed in other similar cases. The deposits in the system increased in the early eighties. In 1990 they stood almost 50 percent higher than in 1983 and represented (gross, from extranational operations) almost 60 percent of GDP. This was because the central bank practiced an implicit deposit insurance policy that prevented losses and generated confidence, particularly attracting Argentine capital fleeing that country. By contrast, credit to the resident private sector contracted by approximately 30 percent between 1983 and 1990. That contraction was even more pronounced in credit from private banks (50 percent in the same period). One of the reasons for the shrinking credit was that the risk of nonperformance was exacerbated by a restriction of the creditors' power to act, which weakened the value of guarantees and caused uncertainty with respect to property rights. The measures to rehabilitate the system included the mandatory refinancing of loans to businesses, a measure renewed on several occasions, the last time by the 1992 law. While the system's borrowings increased, the public sector (which needed funds) and investments abroad took the place of the private sector in the credit market. The amount under those two headings multiplied sixfold from 1983 to 1990.

In the eighties, the BROU's share of GDP expanded greatly as a result of the same process. Between 1980 and 1990 deposits with this bank grew from 4 percent to 20 percent and its loans to the private sector from 8 percent to 15 percent.

At the end of the eighties the division of roles in the system indicated that the private banks were devoting themselves almost exclusively to business of the wholesale type, with activity concentrated in large deposits and loans, having few customers, a minimal network, and little staff. By contrast, the BROU, the managed banks, and the cooperatives covered retail customers and the large, highly risky enterprises. In 1989 some trends set in that portend a change in this dual configuration, as some private banks turn into retailers. The expansion of credit to consumers and the wholesale trade reflects these changes. However, this process took place while the trend toward a contraction of total private sector credit was continuing. The counterpart of this course of events is that the credit of industry and the agricultural sector continues to fall both in its relative share as well as in real terms, even though the Uruguayan economy grew almost 9 percent in the two-year period 1991–92. Another novel development is the introduction of new instruments, issued by the new banks in the system. These activities and innovations are tending to reduce the financial system's segmentation. However, the new credit is still a minor factor, and it is channeled not to enterprises but to families and small businesses, essentially to finance expanding consumption.

Interest Rates and Intermediation Spreads

In real terms, interest rates on borrowing in dollars and in pesos have been very small or negative since 1985. Lending rates in dollars have also been low—if not negative—in the last few years. Real peso rates, on the other hand, have been high, except for preferred customers. This has been even more evident since 1990, a period when real lending rates in pesos ranged from 8 percent to 45 percent, depending on the type of customer. This increase is attributable in part to the increase in intermediation spreads.

The private banking system's intermediation spreads in dollars have been less than 5 percent in almost the entire period since 1985. They show a slight downward trend and are more stable than spreads in pesos. Intermediation in pesos was always greater, but has been even more so since 1990, with spreads of 17 percent for average customers and 30 percent for the highest-risk ones. In addition, spreads in pesos are more volatile and increase when inflation accelerates. An analysis of the factors explaining this behavior indicates that spreads expanded mainly as a consequence of the increase in BROU rates (which was part of a policy intended to increase BROU's profitability) and of the rising cost of intermediation in the system due to the portfolio shift in the direction of consumer credit (whose selection and administration costs are higher). The observably rising variable operating costs lend support to this hypothesis. Other factors that have affected the behavior of the spreads, though to a lesser extent, are the greater volatility of inflation in the nineties and some changes in the rules governing cash reserves and bidding for drafts. In explaining the level of the lending rates in pesos, this increase in spreads is added to a permanent differential (on the order of 10 percent annually) in the cost of coverage because of the difference between borrowing rates in pesos and dollars.

Dollarization of the System

It has already been mentioned that the extreme dollarization of financial relations is one of the peculiar features of the Uruguayan economy. Of the total financial and monetary assets, including public securities, only around 15 percent have been denominated in domestic currency in recent years. Approximately half of this proportion is the volume of money in circulation plus sight deposits (M1), so that the ratio of assets denominated in dollars to those in pesos is approximately 12 to 1. While total financial assets in relation to GDP remained stable during the crisis and have been rising since 1985, the foreign currency share has grown constantly, accelerating more until 1985 and with new impetus in 1989 and 1990, when the inflation rate fell just short of three digits annually.

The yield differential of assets in domestic currency has been negative almost throughout the period. It was positive only in the period of the *tablita* fixed exchange rate (1978–82), in 1985 and 1986, and since mid-1990 (i.e., in those periods in which an exchange appreciation took place). The above-mentioned changes in the composition of portfolios with assets in dollars came about when the differential was negative and high. By contrast, the positive and stable differentials of the periods of appreciation, ranging from 5 percent to 10 percent, did not cause the de-dollarization of the portfolio. This behavior suggests the irreversibility of the dollarization process.

BROU Reforms

The Banco de la República del Uruguay occupies a prominent place in the reforms now underway or under study. The management of this bank is peculiar. Its assets can be said to consist of two major components. One consists of minor risks, whose credit allocations are based on the evaluation of guarantees. This part is regulated by the bank's technical staff, for whom the guarantee requirement serves as an objective procedure for minimizing losses due to their decisions. The second part is made up of major risks—almost exclusively from enterprises of national groups—whose access to credit is regulated by the board of directors (composed of five members appointed by Parliament at the start of each period of government). Given these criteria, it is not surprising that only the private banking system attends financially to fast-yielding projects with low guarantees. It also explains why the BROU shows a high delinquency rate in its portfolio of large enterprises and a high repayment rate in its more diversified sectors. Despite this deficiency, the BROU is the only available source of long-term credit for the purchase of capital goods.

The bank was recently targeted by a reform designed to bring its treatment into line with the rest of the system. This reform encompassed the mandatory cash reserve regime, including the harmonization of rules governing deposits attracted from the rest of the public sector, the treatment of delinquent accounts, and accounting norms. As a result of the reform and modifications in the system for calculating costs, the bank's lending rates, in pesos and in dollars, rose significantly. This was the desired outcome, for it was assumed that the BROU had the ability to set a lending rate lower than that of the private banking system because it received some taxes and an implicit subsidy by holding public sector deposits and had a lower cash reserve requirement. The study analyzed these factors, and its conclusions suggest that, although it is true that the subsidies from public funds were the chief reason behind the divergence in rates, their elimination does not explain the increase. Instead, the study indicates that the increase seems to have followed an attempt to generally improve the return on investments in order to make up for the loss of the transfers. The increase in the rates in pesos and dollars (2 percent higher than those charged by the private banking system) led to a loss of credit market share, and this tendency is confirmed in all the instruments.

The steps taken in the reform process suggest a lack of any clear idea of what the bank's role should be. Given its relative weight, the diversity of social agents affected by the bank and the political representation of its board of directors, it would be difficult and very time-consuming for the bank to transform itself into a commercial institution seeking to maximize profit.

Financial Fragility and Exchange Rate Risk

The Uruguayan study highlights three items on the agenda affecting the financial sector: (1) the consequences of a stabilization policy, (2) the impact of the public sector's financing needs, and (3) fluctuations of the real exchange rate and exchange risk.

The discussion of stabilization is based on the idea that a stabilization policy would use the exchange rate as a fixed point. This idea is supported by the relatively small volume of domestic currency and by previous experience. The salient points are the dollarization of the financial system and the distribution of the exchange risk. The analysis of stabilization centers on the effects of the real exchange rate which the policy would produce in any case. The first effect refers to the impact of real exchange rate fluctuations on the system's fragility and on business activity. The dollarization of financial relations altered the distribution of exchange risk. Since the financial system intermediates in dollars but assumes no exchange risk, this risk is assumed by businesses. This brings greater macroeconomic instability by transmitting exchange rate fluctuations more directly to credit and business conditions.

The second effect considered pertains to the sizable transfers of wealth caused by variation in the real exchange rate. Unexpected fluctuations alter the ratio between liabilities and the enterprise's own capital and generate transfers of wealth, as do expected ones, through credit rationing in pesos and the absence of futures markets. An estimate of the size of the transfers entailed by real exchange rate fluctuations associated with the stabilization policy can be obtained by calculating the transfers that have taken place in recent years. Since 1987, for example, the trend toward appreciation made it possible for the financial sector to show a capital gain through its borrowings; this gain reached an average of 9 percent of GDP in 1990 and 1991. This was only partially offset by the loss of capital through its lending. The net result in terms of capital profit and loss shows that since 1987 the sector has received transfers of wealth from the nonfinancial sector amounting to more than 5 percent of GDP from 1990 to 1992.

The stabilization policy tends to generate real revaluation and transfers to enterprises initially, although the risk that stabilization will fail is a danger to the system's stability. In a context that provides implicit exchange insurance with respect to dollar deposits, this means that the contingent public sector debt grows at the start of stabilization. The recommendation offered is that fiscal policy should be tighter so that international reserves can be accumulated to cover the contingency of a devaluation.

The difficulties of more restrictive adjustments prompt a search for other risk diversification mechanisms: spur the development of contingent asset markets and impose restrictions on private borrowing in foreign currency. With respect to the former, it appears difficult for those markets to develop without implicit subsidies from the public sector. Restrictions can be introduced through taxes, but this will be difficult to put into practice because of the economy's high degree of liberalization.

Prospects for Less Financial Pressure from the Public Sector

The implementation of a fiscal adjustment that has substantially cut the deficit since 1990 stands out with respect to the probable future impact of the public sector's needs for financing. The public sector was practically in balance in 1991 and 1992. Greater fiscal pressure, an expanding GDP, and the reduction of external debt thanks to the Brady Plan were instrumental in this, but lower international interest rates and the appreciating peso also contributed. The fiscal balance is somewhat shaky because of its dependence on exogenous factors and because it appears unlikely that the economy's growth rate will be sustained and that the level of tax pressure can be kept up. Nevertheless, the reduction of the public debt already achieved makes it safe to assume that there will be no severe pressures from the public sector on the financial system.

Credit to Enterprises Limited by Exchange Rate Risk

The Uruguayan financial system has not channeled much in the way of savings to enterprises since the 1982 crisis. The reasons relate to macroeconomic and microeconomic problems. Among the former is the problem of the distribution of exchange risk, which limits credit in dollars allocated to enterprises, particularly in nontradable sectors. Until 1990 the expansion of the public debt meant strong competition for resources. Banks with problems were taken over by the state and the public banking system acted with little competition, as it was growing in the markets thanks to the security which state backing gave it. In the late eighties the public sector balanced itself, prudential rules were adjusted, the treatment of the public and private banking systems was harmonized and signs emerged of some changes in the banks' behavior. However, all of these factors did not ensure an intermediation directed at the enterprises.

One conclusion drawn from the Uruguayan experience is that, under conditions of economic instability and dollarization, major systemic risks will in the long run bring down the local intermediaries even if prudential regulations are conscientiously applied. The dollarization of the economy creates a structure of incentives in which a banking system that is not public or is not associated with strong international banks will find it impossible to survive very adverse conditions. In the case of Uruguay the demise of the system is important because it has effects on resource allocation: projects with high risks, or high monitoring or selection costs, are shelved.

Policy Proposals

The suggestions offered by the study to reverse the tightening of credit to enterprises cover three areas: (1) modification of the implicit licensing policy, (2) institutional risk of forced nonperformance of contracts, and (3) the role to be played by the public banking system.

The problem of the banking system's security has been dealt with since 1985 with an implicit policy designed to restrict entry. That makes for a system with particularly risk-averse agents. The recent entry of a mixed banking system, with national or regional capital associated with top-rated bank capital, points to the possible existence of a banking system prepared to fund riskier but cost-effective projects. However, although its evaluation is premature, the participation of the "insuring" member may be associated with restrictions of the risk level.

Assumptions concerning the restrictive nature of the current entry conditions are difficult to compare in practice because of the superposition of other factors that are not conducive to efficient intermediation: the institutional risk of forced, legislatively mandated nonperformance of loan contracts. The financial market cannot operate in the absence of clearly defined property rights. Reforms streamlining bankruptcy proceedings and the strengthening of judicial power are important steps. In addition to such proceedings, it is imperative to have institutional restraints designed to prevent the public authorities from breaking contracts by legal means. Such restraint would take the form of an undertaking not to seek modifications of private contracts by invoking the law.

With respect to the conditions governing licenses, it is suggested that the current rules be changed to accept the entry of national private agents. Then, the role of "external insurer" should be replaced by an explicit mandatory deposit insurance mechanism paid for by the national banks, including the public ones.

The third suggestion refers to the restructuring of the public banking system, with particular reference to the BROU. It has been mentioned that no clear guideline concerning its role currently seems to exist. If the current restrictive entry rules are maintained, the bank ought to assume the risks not taken by the transnational banking system. If the entry of a less risk-averse national bank is permitted, its main function will be long-term financing, given the nonexistence of that private market. In any case, its transformation would lead to a focusing of operations on the lending portfolio and to a reduction of its extensive fund-raising network. With respect to management, the role of the board of directors should be limited to supervision and control functions, with practical management left to independent managers and new lending rules curtailing the role of guarantees.

Conclusions

The results of the study confirm its general assumption and its principal motivation: the financial systems of the countries analyzed are far from filling the ideal roles of promoting savings and investment and intermediating efficiently between the two. However, the shortcomings of the institutions and financial markets involved do not seem attributable to any single, easily identifiable cause, such as regulations and controls that hinder financial analysis and impede the development of the system. A comparison of the cases brings out the similarity of structures and situations.

The analyses highlight two sets of factors that explain the structures of the national financial systems and the characteristics of their recent situations. On one hand, there is evidence of the persistent legacy of past processes and policies.[2] On the other, in three of the four cases studied the consequences of cataclysmic macroeconomic changes are of particular importance. Compared with these two determining factors, policies aimed specifically at the financial sector seem to have less critical effects. In many cases those policies consisted of defensive reactions adopted in the short term with the intention of averting what were deemed to be greater evils, and their long-term effects were not foreseen (largely because they were very difficult to predict).

The outstanding example is the Uruguayan financial system. Its two most notable peculiarities are extreme dollarization and a structure in which the national private banking system is absent and intermediation is shared between the public sector and foreign banks. In the distribution of risks of this configura-

---

[2] Each of the national financial systems displays marked local features associated with the historical evolution of the sector. This suggests that in each case the innovations grow out of a more or less traditional matrix of institutions and behavioral patterns. The "historicity" of monetary and financial systems was pointed out by Hicks (1967) as a salient characteristic of this aspect of economic organization.

tion lies an important cause of the Uruguayan system's inability to intermediate significantly between saving and investment. This configuration did not arise out of deliberate policy, rather it is a by-product of the external and financial crisis of the early eighties, the rehabilitation policies designed to reduce its disruptive effects, and the changing preferences of the holders of financial assets in response to the incentives deriving from those processes and policies. The financial system underwent the major change during a period of liberalization and deregulation implemented from 1974 to 1977. What causes can be attributed to those policies? The crisis of the Uruguayan financial system that started in mid-1981 can be explained in part by the fragility brought about by liberalization, coupled with an international economic situation featuring high interest rates and tight credit. It is also obvious that the subsequent course of the crisis grew out of rehabilitation policies that strove to maintain the system's chief methods of operation. However, these facts cannot fully explain the particular aspects of the resulting configuration.

This last observation can be elucidated by comparing the Uruguayan experience with the Chilean one.[3] In that country the financial system had already been liberalized and opened up when the financial and exchange crisis struck, and there too the state provided implicit deposit insurance and bailed out the private banking system on a massive scale. Both approaches to dealing with the crisis also shared a concern for maintaining, during the adjustment process of the eighties, the liberalized and opened structure adopted in the seventies. Nevertheless, the subsequent evolution of the Uruguayan and Chilean financial systems differ markedly and the peculiarities of the Uruguayan system are not manifest in Chile.

The authors of the Uruguayan study stress that the dollarization of savings and financial wealth preceded the opening-up and liberalization in that country. This is a factor that undoubtedly helps to explain the peculiarities. The comparison shows that Chile, unlike Uruguay, had not had massive outflows of capital prior to the crisis. Yet this factor does not give a complete explanation of all the differences.

The foregoing observations are offered in modest recognition of the difficulty of predicting the outcome of financial reform, particularly with respect to policies aimed at liberalizing and opening up the system. In the mid-seventies there was great optimism concerning the effects of these policies. Rapid development, growing efficiency born of greater competition, and higher rates of sav-

---

[3] Analysis and interpretations of the Chilean financial crisis are found in Arellano (1983) and Díaz Alejandro (1985). In McKinnon (1991) and in Fanelli and Frenkel (1993), the Chilean financial crisis is again examined in the light of subsequent international experience. The macroeconomic repercussions and long-term consequences are considered in Held (1990) and in Damill, Fanelli, and Frenkel (1992).

ing and investment were all expected.[4] In Uruguay those effects did not come about, nor did they in Chile or Argentina, which undertook similar efforts at the same time. There is extensive literature that seeks to explain the causes, in a debate that is still underway.[5] Beyond whatever caused the frustration of the reforms' expected results, subsequent developments suggest that a number of powerful forces are impinging on the financial systems. These forces work at different levels, not only of the overall macroeconomic situation (which becomes an immediate reference) but also of the evolution of the real economy, under circumstances that seem difficult to reduce to a simple model. The resulting unpredictability would seem to argue in favor of a "gradualist" approach to any program of reform.

In the cases of Brazil and Argentina, the complexity invoked to explain the configuration of the national financial systems is eclipsed by the magnitude of the effects of macroeconomic instability, current or recent. These effects are clearly the main reasons why such systems are having so little success in their role as facilitators of saving and investment.

In Brazil, more than 10 years of high inflation and the more recent experience of "megainflation" (monthly rates of up to 20 percent combined with anxiety that the rules of the game might be changed unexpectedly) have concentrated a once relatively developed financial system on the administration of liquid assets, and reduced the provision of credit to the private sector to a minimum. The system has grown and is deemed too large to perform its functions in a stable manner. It has also tended to specialize, but in doing so it has steadily drifted farther from its role as intermediary between saving and investment. In Brazil, reformers "have a tiger by the tail": any discussion of financial reform is overshadowed by the sense that the most urgent priority is economic stabilization.

In Argentina, the financial and exchange crisis of the early eighties subsequently combined with high inflation, which was temporarily halted in the middle of the decade but took off again and culminated in two hyperinflationary surges in 1989 and 1990. For the financial sector the process raised the specter of demonetization and disintermediation, caused mainly by capital flight. A mas-

---

4 The theoretical foundation of these policies are found in McKinnon (1973) and Shaw (1973). McKinnon (1991) expresses more modest expectations than those recorded two decades earlier and recommends more heterodox and gradual policies than those put forward in his influential text of 1973. A recent theoretical critique of the theory that underlies liberalization and opening-up policies is found in Stiglitz (1993).

5 In the so-called "Southern Cone experiences," financial liberalization and opening-up were more or less simultaneous with the opening up of trade and deregulation in other sectors. The evaluation of and debate over these experiences gave rise to what is now called "literature on sequencing." See Fanelli and Frenkel (1993) and that work's bibliography.

sive intervention in private contracts occurred with the aim of curbing the hyper-inflation. The financial system did not collapse, however, and intermediation began to grow in mid-1990, although high inflation persisted in that year. Since April 1991 the development of the system has been associated with the course of the stabilization policy implemented at that time. Monetization and intermediation have recovered, though not to their levels prior to the debt crisis, under a completely free and open regime. Although the recovery is an encouraging sign, the financial system does not play an important part in the intermediation between saving and investment. This may be because stabilization and recovery only began recently. Be that as it may, the system's configuration following stabilization is marked by the previous experience: approximately half the system is dollarized, the trend toward dollarization is growing, and access by businesses is segmented. As in the case of Uruguay, past experience weighs on the configuration of the financial system.

The process taking place in the financial sector is intimately linked to macroeconomic trends. Two features should be mentioned in this connection: capital inputs constitute the chief impetus for the expansion, and the latter is led to a marked extent by consumer credit. Thus described, the characteristic features of the system's growth resemble those seen in Argentina, Chile, and Uruguay in the late seventies (McKinnon, 1991; Fanelli and Frenkel, 1993). But comparison with those experiences also brings out some novel characteristics. One is that the main current components of capital flows are repatriation of capital and income from privatizations, instead of bank credits, as was the case in the late seventies (Damill and Fanelli, 1993). The second characteristic is the considerable and growing dollarization of the financial system.[6]

The first novel characteristic referred to above suggests less financial weakness than in the late seventies. The second, on the other hand, implies a reduction in the exchange risk assumed directly by the banks, but not of the system's risk, inasmuch as the major part of the credits in dollars is allocated to nontradable activities with revenues in domestic currency. A systemic weakness therefore exists, and the future of the financial system is closely linked to the course of the

---

[6] In relation to the differences between the present situation and that of the late seventies, it might also be mentioned that the public sector is not running a deficit at this time. Thus the deficit financed by capital revenues is now exclusively private, while financing was divided among the public and private sectors in the late seventies. Two observations need to be made in this regard. The first is that the public sector is financially in balance in its consolidated, current and capital operations, but not in its current transactions. In this way, income from privatizations plays a financial role similar to bank credit in the late seventies. The second observation is that financial balance is what marks the difference between the present Argentine situation and the Argentine situation in the late seventies, but not the Chilean situation. See Fanelli and Frenkel (1993) and the bibliography included therein.

stabilization program, which poses sustainability problems. As in the case of Uruguay, the presence of systemic risks makes it difficult to give the system a greater role in financing investment.

In Argentina and Brazil, macroeconomic change seems to provide the best explanation for the configuration and roles of the system. Both countries also exemplify the manner in which the systems are structuring themselves: with relative independence from specific policies, on account of accumulated past decisions, phenomena imposed by the changing preferences of savers, and the introduction of innovations. Such is the case, for example, with interest rate deregulation in Argentina and the elimination of quantitative restrictions on credit allocation. In Argentina, deregulation dates from the mid-seventies, encouraged first by accelerating inflation and then by the liberalization policy previously mentioned. Regulation of taxes and allotments were reimposed in 1982, this time not as allocation rules but as a means of retrieving businesses and banks from the financial crisis. At a later point, the inefficiency of the controls in the face of market incentives exacerbated by inflation was one of the main reasons for their abolition. In Brazil, the segmentation provided for by the legislation of the mid-sixties was ignored in practice as a multiple banking system was set up that received legal recognition only in 1988. In addition, interest rate controls were clearly unworkable under conditions of high inflation.

In both cases the financial systems are deregulated, and in the Argentine case completely open. In the Brazilian case, transactions with the outside are probably greater than the legislation suggests, and a reform designed to legalize more financial openness appears imminent. It would seem that these features resulted not from deliberate policy but from actual changes in the marketplace. High inflation, capital flight, and the expansion and development of international financial intermediation generate powerful incentives to develop markets more or less recognized or accepted under the formally prevailing rules. Such processes are generally linked with the economic and organizational weakening of the state resulting from a prolonged crisis. Under those circumstances, many regulations fall by the wayside in practice, or, in the worst case, become obvious sources of revenue without any ability to allocate resources. In situations such as these, legal amendments or administrative "deregulation" are little more than acknowledgments of existing reality.

Such processes are phenomena of *de facto* liberalization and opening-up, linked more to capital flight, the prolonged macroeconomic instability of the eighties and the weakening of the state than to a logically thought-out sequence of reforms. By the same token, they are hard to reverse. In some cases the configurations they create seriously hinder the monetary and financial management of the economies in an international environment of abrupt changes. For example, one can cite the different behaviors and effects to which returning flows of capital have led in the nineties. The comparison between the cases of Chile and

Colombia on the one hand, and that of Argentina on the other substantiates that point (Ocampo and Steiner, 1993).

Although Chile and Colombia underwent financial crises in the early eighties—a profound one in the Chilean case—macroeconomic instability (inflation, fiscal imbalance, capital flight) and disorganization of the financial system did not follow to a degree comparable with what occurred in Argentina. In Chile and Colombia the authorities preserved tools and a hold on policy that have enabled them, in the nineties, to establish certain controls and carry out sterilization campaigns designed to moderate the negative effects of the inflow of external capital. These policies have been more or less successful; however, it is not intended to judge their effectiveness but rather to note the possibility of carrying them out. Unlike Chile and Colombia, Argentina responded to the same challenge with an entirely passive policy which produced, among other things, a much greater real appreciation of the currency than in their cases. Our hypothesis suggests that the differences apply not only to the different policies but also to the different degrees of freedom of the monetary and exchange policies allowed in each country by the pre-existing financial configuration.

In more general terms, the difference between Colombia and Argentina, Brazil and Uruguay raises other interesting issues. Although the Colombian economy also suffered the consequences of the debt crisis, it did not, as we mentioned previously, undergo macroeconomic instability processes similar to those of the other three countries. In particular, it did not face an equally great external crisis, while it managed the fiscal crisis reasonably well without throwing the financial system into complete disarray, and the inflation rate never went over 30 percent a year. Even though the financial system also went into crisis in 1982 and the state had to come to its aid, the main solvency problems were overcome in 1985 without triggering major macroeconomic upheavals. However, the Colombian financial system did not play an important role in financing investment. Furthermore, compared with the financial systems of developed countries, the successful Asian economies, (McKinnon, 1991) and the degree of intermediation achieved in the past decade in China (McKinnon, 1993), the Colombian financial system remains shallow. It is at a level similar to that of other Latin American countries in the late sixties, when inflation rates stood, as Colombia's did in the eighties, at around 30 percent annually.

The configuration and shortcomings of the Colombian financial system cannot be attributed, as in the other cases studied, to the macroeconomic cataclysms of the eighties or to the unexpected effects of the liberalization and opening-up policies of the seventies. In many respects, the Colombian financial system of the mid-eighties resembled that of other countries before the reforms and crises mentioned.

Somewhat replicating the vision underlying the reforms of the mid-seventies, the Colombian authorities seem to have attributed the system's underdevelopment to financial repression stemming from the segmentation and regulations imposed on it. Based on this assessment and as part of a more comprehensive liberalization program carried forward with the aim of giving new impetus to growth, a program to deregulate and open up the financial system was put into operation in 1990. The reform process is still in progress and its effects cannot be gauged yet, but some observations on it are in order. First, the activities of intermediaries were not completely deregulated. The previous segmentation made way for a system of affiliates which the authors of the Colombian study consider confused, to say the least. Second, intermediation in foreign currency is not permitted. Third, despite the autonomy legislated by the central bank, the authorities did not abandon the traditional pragmatism of Colombia's economic policy. For instance, they temporarily reinstated controls on interest rates for loans when rates did not respond as might have been expected to monetary policy and competition.

The Colombian system's similarity to that of the other Latin American countries prior to the liberalization and opening-up of the seventies and before the debt crisis casts some doubt on the relevance of the diagnosis of financial repression as the main factor responsible for the low level of sophistication and the system's inability to develop a long-term market—a diagnosis applied previously to some of those economies and now to Colombia.

An examination of some development experiences in countries with sophisticated financial systems that play an important role in the intermediation between saving and investment reveals plentiful evidence to reject a general association between repression and financial underdevelopment. Japan and Taiwan, for example, for decades maintained careful regulation and segmentation policies while they developed intermediation, and they only undertook deregulation and opening-up when they had a large, developed domestic market (McKinnon, 1991). An extreme example of this policy is provided by the recent process of reforms and development in China. The volume of financial saving by households in that country has increased fivefold since the early eighties, reaching 46 percent of GDP in 1991. For that same period, the M2 ratio to GDP quadrupled to 97 percent in 1991. The process of rapid development and massive mobilization of savings was achieved mainly through the state bank and with regulations governing rates and maturities, while private markets were developing vigorously in other areas of economic activity (McKinnon, 1993).

The mass of evidence provided by experiences with successful regulations, added to the failure of some cases of liberalization through shock therapy, emphasizes the weakness of theoretical arguments favoring the financial repression diagnosis. In a recent article, Stiglitz (1993) presents a detailed critical review of those arguments which explicitly outlines the inadequacies of the information available to the agents. This analysis makes clear the weakness of the arguments generally used against government intervention and regulation, with respect to both the behavior of aggregate savings and efficiency in the allocation of credit. Based on analytic conclusions and on the observation of the cases of Japan, Korea, and Taiwan, the author suggests that what he terms "a slight financial repression" should benefit development. In policy terms, Stiglitz's most general conclusion is that shortcomings of the marketplace notwithstanding, and even if government interventions are full of errors, a blanket recommendation to eliminate the regulations would be inappropriate: the aim should be to design the right regulations.

From the point of view of reform policies, the only thing accomplished by criticizing the focus on repression as the chief cause of the underdevelopment of the financial system is to exclude the simplest of the policies—reduce government intervention and regulations to a minimum. But it constitutes only a starting point for the design of effective policies. In addition, the examination of successful policies is undoubtedly useful to gain a better understanding of the financial markets and their possible roles in development. It is also useful as a source of policy suggestions, but no case seems easily transplantable. We have argued above about the historicity of national financial configurations, and those same arguments extend to the design of reform policies.

The strategy of the study was aimed at identifying policy reforms based on their actual characteristics and the current operating conditions of the national financial configurations. Derived from its own analyses, the study's most general conclusion is that the question of liberalization or regulation, couched in general terms, is of little importance for the policy agenda. The financial systems studied failed to play a positive role in development in a context of mostly deregulated and open regimes. We have stressed the fact that most of those configurations were the result of more or less spontaneous market trends and of innovations, rather than of a systematic line of reform policies. We also argue that those developments seem to be difficult to reverse.

The policy recommendations contained in the country studies in no case contemplate any expectations of a "miracle" of rapid financial improvement or the spontaneous establishment of a strong long-term market. The policies suggested call for actions more akin to the painstaking work of a watchmaker than to the relatively simple tasks involved in the abolition of regulations and restrictions. By and large, the policies are aimed at reducing the weakness of the national financial systems and center largely on reorganization, reconstruction and the strengthening of supervisory and regulatory bodies and rules and the financial institutions of the public sector.

In almost all cases, the policies suggested call for redefinition and reinforcement in the area of national and regional public banks. A relatively novel point made with respect to public banks deserves more development than it could receive in this study: in some cases the policies entail the redefinition of relations between the public segment of the system and the political authorities for the sake of greater transparency and democratic control of management.

The specific policy recommendations in all cases stress the close relationship between the outlook for the sector and the country's macroeconomic development. This relationship is more marked in Argentina, Brazil and Uruguay, because of the greater systemic weakness expressed in a close dependence of crucial macroeconomic variables, as is also present in the case of Colombia.

BIBLIOGRAPHY

Arellano, José P. 1983. *De la liberalización a la intervención: el mercado de capitales en Chile: 1974–83.* Estudios CIEPLAN No. 11. Santiago.

Carneiro, Dionísio Dias, Rogério L. F. Werneck, Márcio G. P. Garcia, *et al.* 1993. *Strengthening the Financial Sector in the Brazilian Economy.* Working Papers Series No. 142. Inter-American Development Bank, Washington, D.C.

Damill, Mario, José M. Fanelli and Roberto Frenkel. 1992. *Shocks externos y desequilibrio fiscal. La macroeconomía de América Latina en los ochenta: Chile.* Documento CEDES/77. Centro de Estudios de Estado y Sociedad, Buenos Aires.

Damill, Mario and José M. Fanelli. 1993. *Los capitales extranjeros en las economías latinoamericanas: Argentina.* Working Papers Series No. 145. Inter-American Development Bank, Washington, D.C.

Díaz Alejandro, Carlos. 1985. "Good-bye Financial Repression, Hello Financial Crash." *Journal of Development Economics* (19).

Fanelli, José M. and Roberto Frenkel. 1993. "On Gradualism, Shock Treatment and Sequencing." In *International Monetary and Financial Issues for the 1990s.* Vol. 2. New York: United Nations Conference on Trade and Development.

Held, Gunther. 1990. "Regulación y supervisión de la banca en la experiencia de liberalización financiera de Chile (1974–88)." In *Sistema financiero y asignación de recursos, experiencias latinoamericanas y del Caribe,* eds. C. Massad and G. Held. Buenos Aires: Grupo Editor Latinoamericano.

Hicks, John. 1967. "Monetary Theory and History—an Attempt at Perspective." In *Critical Essays in Monetary Theory.* Oxford: Oxford University Press.

Lora, Eduardo, Luis A. Zuleta and Sandra Zuluaga. 1993. *El fortalecimiento del sector financiero en el proceso de ajuste: Liberalización y regulación. El caso colombiano.* Working Papers Series No. 143. Washington, D.C.: Inter-American Development Bank.

McKinnon, Ronald. 1973. *Money and Capital in Economic Development.* Washington, D.C.: Brookings Institution.

_____. 1991. *The Order of Economic Liberalization Financial Control in the Transition to a Market Economy.* Baltimore and London: The Johns Hopkins University Press.

_____. 1993. "Gradual versus Rapid Liberalization in Socialist Economies: Financial Policies and Macroeconomic Stability in China and Russia Compared." In *Annual Bank Conference on Development Economics.* Washington, D.C.: World Bank.

Noya, Nelson and Daniel Dominioni. 1993. *El fortalecimiento del sector financiero en el proceso de ajuste: Liberalización y regulación. El caso uruguayo.* Working Papers Series No. 144. Washington, D.C.: Inter-American Development Bank.

Ocampo, José A. and Roberto Steiner. 1993. *Los capitales extranjeros en las economías latinoamericanas.* Working Papers Series No. 157. Washington, D.C.: Inter-American Development Bank.

Rozenwurcel, Guillermo and Raúl Fernández. 1993. *El fortalecimiento del sector financiero en el proceso de ajuste: el caso argentino.* Working Papers Series No. 141. Washington, D.C.: Inter-American Development Bank.

Shaw, Edward S. 1973. *Financial Deepening in Economic Development.* New York: Oxford University Press.

Stiglitz, Joseph E. 1993. "The Role of the State in Financial Markets." In *Annual Bank Conference on Development Economics.* Washington, D.C.: World Bank.

CHAPTER TWO

ARGENTINA

Guillermo Rozenwurcel, and Raúl Fernández[1]

The basic financial imbalance of the Argentine economy in the eighties was due to the mismatch between the public sector's considerable needs for domestic financing and the private sector's low voluntary supply of loanable funds. The first situation was due to the steep rise in fiscal deficits, generated in large measure by the greater external commitments and the rationing of the international financial markets in the wake of the debt crisis. The second situation—low supply—was associated with the drastic decline in private savings as available income plunged, as well as with the significant change in the composition of savings in favor of external assets.

Three requirements must be met to eliminate that imbalance and strengthen the domestic financial system: achievement of a sustainable fiscal adjustment, reversal of the demonetization process, and normalization of the country's relations with its external creditors. After the hyperinflationary episodes of 1989 and 1990 were overcome, and especially following the implementation of the convertibility rules at the end of March 1991, the economy made great strides in those three areas. However, it is too early to judge whether the new approach will prove durable.

In this sense, an initial objective of this chapter is to make a detailed assessment of the present condition of the Argentine financial system and its relations with the macroeconomic context. Based on that assessment, its second objective is to evaluate the reforms in progress and to formulate some additional policy proposals. To that end the chapter is organized in three sections. The first analyzes the relations between the financial system and the macroeconomic context. The second describes the main structural and functional features of the financial system. The third section evaluates the ongoing reforms and additional policy proposals. The last point of this section summarizes the paper's principal conclusions.

---

[1] The authors are grateful for the comments of the IDB's anonymous referees and those made by Roberto Frenkel and the other participants in this project.

Table 2.1. Argentina: Surplus and Sectoral Savings Structure, 1980–92
(Percentage of GDP)

Period	Public savings	Private savings	National savings	Primary deficit	Fiscal deficit	Private surplus	Rest of world surplus
1980	1.7	17.7	19.4	3.7	7.2	3.9	3.3
1981	-3.8	17.5	13.7	4.7	12.1	7.5	4.6
1982	-7.0	18.5	11.5	4.6	14.9	9.5	5.4
1983	-5.7	18.8	13.1	8.5	14.5	10.3	4.2
1984	-4.3	14.1	9.8	6.5	11.4	6.7	4.7
1985	0.8	9.7	10.5	0.3	5.7	3.9	1.8
1986	2.5	5.8	8.3	0.5	4.4	0.5	3.9
1987	0.7	6.9	7.6	3.2	6.9	0.7	6.2
1988	-0.6	10.6	10.0	5.7	8.5	4.8	3.7
1989	-0.9	5.0	4.1	1.5	4.8	0.2	4.6
1990	-2.6	12.5	10.0	2.6	5.1	6.9	-1.8
1991	0.1	7.4	7.5	0.1	2.2	0.1	2.0
1992a	2.4	7.7	10.1	-2.2	2.1	-2.2	4.3

Source: Author's calculations based on data from the Secretariat of Finance and the Central Bank of the Republic of Argentina.
a Provinces not included. Provisional data.

The Financial System and Macrofinancial Relations

Supply and Demand for Financing in the Eighties

The purpose of this section is to distinguish, at the macroeconomic level, the sectors that sought financing in the last decade from those that supplied it: in other words, which sectors ran deficits and which ran surpluses. That will make it possible to contextualize the operation and the problems of the financial system that intermediates between them.

Table 2.1 shows figures for the surpluses or deficits of the government, the private sector, and the rest of the world from 1980 forward. The first observation prompted by the table is that the leading recipient of funds has been the public sector. From 1980 to 1991 the fiscal deficit averaged 8.4 percent of GDP, with a downward trend from the middle of the decade. While the average was 12 percent of GDP from 1980 to 1984, it fell to 5.3 percent from 1985 to 1991.

Given the government's heavy demand for loanable funds, it is not surprising that both the private sector and the rest of the world have, in response, been net generators of such funds. As Table 2.1 shows, both sectors funded the public sector in approximately equal shares. The average deficit generated by the private sector in the period under consideration was in the order of 4.6 percent of GDP, while the rest of the world contributed the remaining amount required to cover the government's shortfall.

Unlike the private surplus, which dipped in the middle of the decade, external saving remained relatively stable during the entire adjustment period and was much higher than before the crisis. Nevertheless, the high level of lending through the international capital market took place with practically no voluntary private input. In fact, external saving was contributed largely by multilateral organizations and the more or less forced refinancing of the interest and amortization which the country was unable to pay. Default on interest payments, in particular, was resorted to routinely from 1982 to 1985, and from 1988 to year-end 1992, when relations with private external creditors were normalized under the Brady Plan.

As Table 2.1 also shows, a crucial factor in explaining the increase in the fiscal deficit and the reduction in the private surplus was the plunge in national savings, both public and private. While national savings in the 10 years preceding the debt crisis had averaged 23.5 percent of GDP, they averaged a mere 9.6 percent of GDP from 1981 to 1991, falling to 7.9 percent between 1986 and 1991. The increase in payments to external factors that began with the debt crisis was undoubtedly the single most important factor in explaining this phenomenon.[2]

A good part of the difficulties faced by the domestic financial system, as well as the credit rationing experienced by the private sector, is closely linked to the excessive demand for loanable funds generated by the government.[3] The reason lies not only in the crowding-out effect exerted by that demand, but also by its destabilizing effects on the still fragile financial system.

The difficulties in finding voluntary financing in a context of a falling private surplus and rationed external credit forced the public sector to make routine use of seigniorage to finance its budgetary imbalances.

To illustrate the importance of the inflation tax as a means of financing the deficit, Table 2.2 shows the financial imbalance of the public sector and the private surplus recalculated to account for the depreciation of real balances because of inflation. The corrected fiscal deficit (in terms of the average over the period running from 1980 to 1991) shrinks from 8.4 percent to 4 percent of GDP. By the same token, the private sector surplus drops from 4.6 percent to less than half of 1 percent of GDP. Clearly, this phenomenon was a significant factor in the increasing restriction of liquidity faced by the Argentine economy during the last decade.

Ultimately, the complete analysis of the structure of the sectoral deficit and surplus indicates that the pressure arising from the public sector's need to bor-

---

[2] It should be kept in mind that during the period under consideration, although consumption fell significantly on a per capita basis, compared to GDP it not only did not fall but tended to rise.

[3] Two additional factors of great importance were rationing in the international credit markets and the failure of the financial liberalization experience of the late seventies.

Table 2.2. Argentina: Primary Fiscal Deficit and Private Surplus Net of Inflation Tax, 1980–92
(Percentage of GDP)

Period	Fiscal deficit net of inflation tax	Private surplus net of inflation tax
1980	3.9	0.6
1981	7.4	2.8
1982	9.7	4.3
1983	9.6	5.4
1984	5.5	0.8
1985	1.8	0.0
1986	1.9	-2.0
1987	2.6	-3.6
1988	4.4	0.7
1989	0.1	-4.5
1990	1.8	3.6
1991	0.2	-1.9
1992[a]	1.4	-1.5

Source: Author's calculations based on data from the Secretariat of Finance and the Central Bank of the Republic of Argentina.
[a] Provisional data.

row, the sharp drop in national savings (particularly in the private sector), and the inflation tax are the three factors which best explain the shortage of credit in the Argentine economy throughout the adjustment period of the eighties.

The Domestic Transfer Problem

In order not to weaken the financial system further, the government should have generated a primary surplus equal to the difference between the accrued interest and available external financing. It would thus have avoided having to borrow on the domestic credit market. Assuming, based on the experience of the adjustment period, that the nonrefinanced part of the external interest (i.e., the amount of interest due that is actually repaid) is approximately equal to the trade surplus, then the primary result would necessary be approximately equal to that trade surplus.[4]

In the eighties the trade surplus averaged 2.9 percent of GDP. As the relevant column of Table 2.1 shows, the government was far from attaining a pri-

---

[4] For simplicity's sake we are ignoring the role of domestic interest. Strictly speaking, to avoid domestic borrowing the primary surplus should cover not only nonrefinanced external interest (approximately equal to the trade surplus) but also domestic interest in its entirety.

Table 2.3. Argentina: Fiscal Deficit and the Government's Domestic Financing Requirements with Respect to M1, 1980–92
(Percentages)

Period	Fiscal deficit/M1	(Fiscal deficit - External credit)/M1
1980	95.6	51.6
1981	191.3	118.3
1982	304.9	194.7
1983	380.5	270.0
1984	301.1	177.4
1985	158.9	108.9
1986	76.8	8.4
1987	132.3	13.1
1988	256.4	144.2
1989	171.8	240.7
1990	204.4	108.8
1991	49.3	55.5
1992[a]	28.0	9.3

Source: Author's calculations based on data from the Secretariat of Finance and the Central Bank of the Republic of Argentina.
[a] Provisional data.

mary result on similar magnitude. Between 1980 and 1991 the public sector not only failed to generate a primary surplus, but averaged a primary deficit on the order of 3.5 percent of GDP.

It is worth pointing out, nevertheless, that in the eighties this imbalance was more than one and a half points of GDP below the average figure for the preceding decade. This fact highlights the importance of the financial factors in the fiscal crisis of the past decade: even if the primary deficit went down during that period, when accrued domestic and external interest is added to it (about five points of GDP on average) the total deficit is well above what it was in the seventies.

The impossibility of generating a primary surplus of the required magnitude helped establish a recurrent tendency for instability in the financial system. The figures in Table 2.3 show the size of the financial imbalances in the aftermath of the debt crisis. Those in the first column give the ratio between the fiscal deficit and the stock of M1. If the authorities had decided to finance the entire deficit by printing money between 1980 and 1991, the stock of M1 would have had to rise, on average, more than 200 percent each year.[5] In the 10 years preceding the crisis that average had stood at around 75 percent.

---

[5] Here we are referring to the consolidated nonfinancial public sector deficit. Therefore, the quasi-fiscal deficit of the central bank would have to be added to this imbalance.

Since the public sector has in fact financed part of the deficit abroad, the second column shows the ratio between the net public sector demand for domestic credit and the stock of M1. Clearly, availability of external credit for the stabilization of the domestic financial ratios is crucial inasmuch as it helps to reduce the appropriation of domestic financial resources by the public sector, thus freeing loanable funds for the private sector.

Inflation, Uncertainty and Monetary Size of the Financial System

The drop in demand for domestic assets was as important as the fiscal imbalance in the determination of the financial disequilibrium. It is obvious that, assuming a constant fiscal deficit, the lower the demand for money, the greater the disequilibrium in terms of the ratio deficit/M1. A very small fiscal deficit may actually give rise to a hyperinflationary process if the demand for domestic financial assets approaches zero. An illustration of this is the fact that Argentina underwent hyperinflationary surges in 1989 and 1990 and not in 1983, when the fiscal deficit appeared much more out of control.

The most important factors driving down the demand for domestic assets are the level and variability of the inflation rate. A higher inflation rate raises the cost of maintaining real balances, and consequently the demand for money dwindles. The variability of the rates at which prices rise has a negative impact on the demand for domestic financial assets because it increases the risk of capital loss, to the extent that it becomes very difficult to predict the real interest rate. Table 2.4, which shows the trend of the liquidity factor of the economy and of the inflation tax, is highly instructive in this regard.

As can be inferred from the table, the demonetization process of the Argentine economy in the eighties could be described as structural, because it persisted throughout the decade. Moreover, it will be seen that, in the brief periods of stability during which the liquidity factor rose, the monetization factor, at equal rates of inflation, was smaller than in the past. This phenomenon seems to suggest the presence of hysteresis in the demand for domestic financial assets.[6]

The monetization process and the hysteresis that seemed to accompany it were nothing but the other side of the coin of a growing dollarization of the economy. The substitution of external financial assets for domestic ones in the

---

[6] Strictly speaking, the fact that the monetization factors were smaller than in the past, at equal rates of inflation, is a necessary but not sufficient condition for the presence of hysteresis. This is because, in principle, nothing guarantees that the observed values are the new equilibrium values. However, the plausibility of the hysteresis hypothesis is reinforced by the fact that the adjustment velocity of the financial markets tends to be very high, particularly in economies adapted to high inflation, as is the case of Argentina. For a more detailed discussion of the question, see Ahumada (1989) and Fanelli, Frenkel and Rozenwurcel (1990).

Table 2.4. Monetization and Inflation Tax in Argentina, 1980–92
(Percentage of GDP)

Period	M1	Inflation tax	M3	Total monetary resources (M3+deposits in dollars)
1980	7.5	1.00	28.4	28.4
1981	6.3	4.70	28.2	28.2
1982	4.9	5.20	20.0	20.0
1983	3.8	4.90	13.6	14.6
1984	3.8	5.90	12.8	13.6
1985	3.6	3.90	12.4	13.7
1986	5.7	2.50	17.2	18.4
1987	5.2	4.30	18.2	19.8
1988	3.3	4.10	15.4	17.2
1989	2.8	4.70	13.2	15.6
I	4.1	0.90	19.5	22.9
II	2.6	2.00	12.4	14.8
III	1.3	1.10	8.8	10.6
IV	3.0	0.70	12.2	15.3
1990	2.5	3.30	5.5	7.0
I	2.0	1.70	4.0	5.2
II	2.3	0.60	4.7	6.2
III	2.5	0.70	5.9	7.6
IV	3.0	0.30	7.2	8.9
1991	4.4	2.00	8.5	11.7
I	3.3	1.60	7.3	9.7
II	4.3	0.20	7.9	11.0
III	4.5	0.10	8.8	12.5
IV	5.4	0.00	9.8	14.0
1992	7.5	0.70	12.5	17.9
I	7.4	0.30	12.3	16.9
II	7.5	0.20	13.7	18.9
III	7.6	0.20	16.1	21.8
IVa	7.8	-0.05	17.0	23.0

Source: Author's calculations based on data from the Secretariat of Finance and the Central Bank of the Republic of Argentina.
a Provisional data.

agents' portfolio does not represent a mere change of holdings in response to the recurrent bursts of inflation. It also reflects a structural change in the composition of the holdings of the agents, who decided to permanently invest a part of their financial wealth in financial or monetary instruments issued by external agents.

The consequences of the demonetization and dollarization of the economy on the availability of credit were also persistent and significant. The lowering of the credit/product ratio affects the public as well as the private sector: total bank credit fell sharply, from the equivalent of over 35 percent of GDP in 1983 to a level below 20 percent at the end of the last decade.

The Situation Following the Convertibility Plan

As explained in the opening paragraph of this chapter, the basic financial imbalance of the Argentine economy was no doubt due to the mismatch between the public sector's considerable needs for domestic financing and the private sector's low voluntary supply of loanable funds. That mismatch worsened steadily over the decade until it led to the hyperinflationary episodes of 1989 and 1990 and the BONEX Plan at the beginning of the latter year. The plan compulsorily rescheduled the domestic debt through the forced exchange of most of the financial system's deposits (which basically consisted of short-term lending to the public sector, given the high exchange requirements and immunity of assets imposed by the central bank) and of the short-term public securities for "external bonds" called Bonos Externos (BONEX, 10-year dollar-denominated public securities). As Table 2.4 demonstrates, this measure reduced the degree of monetization of the economy to a bare minimum: in the first half of 1990, M3 (which adds cash and fixed-term savings deposits to M1) represented only 4 percent of GDP.

The elimination of the chronic excess demand for domestic funds generated by the public sector, as well as the strengthening of the domestic financial system, require at least three conditions: achievement of a sustainable fiscal adjustment, reversal of the demonetization process, and the normalization of the country's relations with its external creditors. Since the end of the second hyperinflationary episode the present government has taken significant measures in all those areas.

With respect to public accounts, under the Convertibility Plan launched in March 1991 the government undertook a profound tax reform which, together with the appreciable improvement brought about in tax administration, enabled it to cut the fiscal deficit considerably. The quasi-fiscal deficit had meanwhile practically been eliminated by the BONEX Plan, which did away with remunerated cash reserves. Since 1990, moreover, a bold policy of privatization had been in effect, its revenues helping not only to finance the deficit but also to significantly reduce the public sector's external indebtedness through the mechanism of debt conversion.[7] Despite those successes, the main question on this front concerns the sustainability of the fiscal closure achieved, once the privatization process is completed.

To reverse the trend toward demonetization, the strategy adopted instead of combating dollarization was to encourage the expansion of the dollarized

---

[7] For a more detailed analysis of these matters, see Fanelli, Frenkel, and Rozenwurcel (1992).

segment in the domestic financial system. Law 23.578, enacted in 1989, had granted greater legal security to the regime to attract foreign exchange deposits, since this rule obliges financial institutions to return the deposits in the currency in which they were received, and the central bank is prevented from relying on these funds. There were significant institutional changes which tended to support this strategy in one way or another: the free convertibility of domestic currency with backing in foreign currency of 100 percent of the monetary base present at the start of 1991; the new organizational charter of the central bank established in 1992; the complete freedom of financial institutions to allocate credit in pesos and dollars; and the deregulation of the securities market (in particular allowing financial institutions and businesses to float negotiable obligations in foreign currency). Greater access of Argentine banks to the international capital market was an important factor working in the same direction.

Based on the premise that in the wake of the domestic and external changes of the last decade the free movement of capital is a practically irreversible phenomenon, the strategy seeks to attract a larger share of domestic savings by offering financial assets more closely resembling the dollar, in the form either of pesos backed 100 percent by foreign exchange or of "Argendollars" (foreign currency deposits), in order to enhance the lending capacity of the local financial system. Especially based on the stabilization achieved by the Convertibility Plan, this strategy proved very successful from the standpoint of the growth of deposits and the system's lending capacity. For the moment, however, there are no signs that the strategy is succeeding in reversing the chronic insufficiency of medium- and long-term credit, which is crucial to the recovery of investment and growth.

The effort to normalize external financial relations centered on renegotiation of external commitments with private creditors in the framework of the Brady Plan. Although the "debt problem" which was such a fixture of the past decade may now be abating, it would be a mistake to think that Argentina has finally left behind its classic problem of external restraint. In particular, the use of privatization to reduce the external public debt (the mechanism that the Brady agreement made feasible) will significantly affect the structure and rigidity of the factor services account.

In any event, since the second hyperinflationary episode was brought under control the financial system has begun to show signs of recovery. These began tentatively, following the relief brought by the elimination of the short-term public debt, with a slight improvement of the fiscal situation throughout 1990. They became more marked with the implementation of the Convertibility Plan in March of the following year which, as already noted, promptly brought down inflation and considerably speeded up the fiscal improvement. Remonetization of both the peso and dollar segments of the financial system is now definitely setting in. M1, which in the first quarter of 1990 stood at the equivalent of only

Table 2.5. Trend of Total Deposits in Argentina, 1988–92
(Millions of current dollars)

Period		In national currency	Percentage of total	In foreign currency	Percentage of total	Total
1988		9,334	88.3	1,231	11.7	10,565
1989		5,505	84.0	1,051	16.0	6,556
1990		3,998	70.1	1,705	29.9	5,703
1991	January	6,219	66.4	3,150	33.6	9,369
	February	4,630	58.6	3,274	41.4	7,904
	March	5,156	60.4	3,387	39.6	8,543
	April	5,535	59.7	3,741	40.3	9,276
	May	5,796	57.5	4,278	42.5	10,074
	June	6,036	56.8	4,594	43.2	10,630
	July	5,973	55.2	4,838	44.8	10,811
	August	6,452	55.3	5,209	44.7	11,661
	September	6,789	54.3	5,720	45.7	12,509
	October	7,185	54.1	6,108	45.9	13,293
	November	7,615	54.5	6,363	45.5	13,978
	December	8,096	55.2	6,560	44.8	14,656
1992	January	8,471	54.9	6,970	45.1	15,441
	February	8,692	53.9	7,446	46.1	16,138
	March	9,027	53.3	7,898	46.7	16,925
	April	9,535	53.8	8,200	46.2	17,735
	May	10,566	55.0	8,648	45.0	19,214
	June	11,532	55.8	9,147	44.2	20,679
	July	11,859	55.5	9,522	44.5	21,381
	August	12,726	55.8	10,082	44.2	22,808
	September[1]	13,031	55.5	10,453	44.5	23,484
	October[1]	13,190	55.2	10,706	44.8	23,896
	November[1]	13,342	54.9	10,977	45.1	24,319
	December[1]	13,841	55.2	11,219	44.8	25,060

Source: Author's calculations based on data from the Secretariat of Finance and the Central Bank of the Republic of Argentina.
[1] Provisional data.

2 percent of GDP (and had even dropped to 1.3 percent in the third quarter of 1989), stood at almost 8 percent of GDP in the last quarter of 1992. In the same time frame M3 grew by 4 percent to 17 percent of GDP, thus recovering its 1986 level.

The same period also saw dollar deposits soar. As Table 2.5 shows, while at year-end 1988 foreign currency deposits in the financial system amounted to barely $1.2 billion (less than 12 percent of total deposits), they came to slightly over $11 billion (almost 45 percent of the total) in December 1992.

On the basis of these figures it is obvious that with the Convertibility Plan a bimonetary financial system has taken shape. In this context, a more appropriate measure of the economy's total monetary resources should also include dollar deposits. By this measure, total monetary resources in the last quarter of 1992 already represented 23 percent of GDP (Table 2.4).

It is important to point out, however, that although the remonetization triggered by the Convertibility Plan was swift and very significant, the starting point, thanks to hyperinflation, was exceptionally low. Also, the economy's liquidity coefficients are still well below those observed not only in the industrial countries but also in other economies at a similar level of development, and they are indeed rather below those attained in the country prior to the financial crisis of the early eighties.

Furthermore—and this is one of the central problems of the present Argentine economy—private savings have remained practically stagnant (Table 2.1), so that the practically exclusive source of the remonetization process has been the return flow of capital from abroad.

Obviously, this situation cannot continue indefinitely. In the first place, as was already mentioned, privatizations have been an important autonomous factor attracting capital to the country. But although a few sizable enterprises remain to be privatized (in particular the state-owned oil company, YPF), the end of the process is fairly near.

The other factor determining the inflow of capital has been the progressive adjustment of the private sector's financial portfolios to the new conditions created by the Convertibility Plan. This factor cannot operate indefinitely either.

Initially, in effect, capital inputs caused a strong expansion of credit and a significant reduction of domestic interest rates by fueling swift growth of domestic absorption. That gave rise to a substantial reactivation of productive activity, but it also tended to keep inflation well above international levels, accentuating the exchange lag (which existed from before the Convertibility Plan), the deterioration of the trade balance, and the current account of the balance of payments.

It is important to stress, however, that since the start of convertibility, and even during the period when the capital inflow was at its height, an appreciable differential between domestic and external interest rates persisted. An examination of the difference between the internal rate of return (IRR) of the BONEX and the LIBOR rate as proxy of the country risk, and of the difference between the average borrowing rate of the peso deposits and the IRR of BONEX as proxy of the devaluation expectations (Table 2.6), discloses that these differences were practically nil throughout the period. Therefore, the change in the differential between the domestic and external rates was determined basically by the country-risk premium. Although the premium shows a sharp decline from the February 1990 peak, the culmination of the second hyperinflationary episode, it finds a floor of approximately 5 percent per year in April 1992 and thereupon begins to rise again, albeit moderately.

As a result of borrowing rates above the international level and gross spreads that, though declining, remained very high, interest rates on lending in

Table 2.6. Argentina: Rates of Interest, Country Risk and Projected Devaluation, Jan. 1990–Oct. 1992

(Percentages, annualized)

Period	Domestic interest rate[a]	IRR BONEX 89[b]	LIBOR rate[c]	Estimated rate of country risk	Projected annual devaluation	Projected monthly devaluation	Actual monthly effective devaluation
1990 January	1,555.40	34.46	8.38	24.07	1,131.15	23.27	27.03
February	3,939.22	43.87	8.38	32.75	2,707.55	32.04	108.81
March	9,721.67	36.74	8.69	25.81	7,082.74	42.79	34.67
April	302.31	32.37	9.00	21.44	203.93	9.71	2.82
May	178.19	30.25	8.50	20.05	113.58	6.53	0.94
June	249.85	26.63	8.44	16.78	176.27	8.84	5.53
July	238.67	20.59	8.06	11.59	180.84	8.99	0.98
August	178.19	24.04	8.13	14.72	124.27	6.96	13.33
September	440.63	24.90	8.44	15.18	332.85	12.99	-3.54
October	224.27	26.96	8.06	17.49	155.41	8.13	-4.07
November	108.16	27.44	8.00	18.00	63.34	4.17	-5.47
December	94.49	25.99	7.56	17.14	54.36	3.68	-2.82
1991 January	197.15	21.47	7.06	13.46	144.62	7.74	28.50
February	331.61	21.08	6.88	13.29	256.48	11.17	42.35
March	207.74	19.58	6.50	12.29	157.34	8.20	0.84
April	19.56	17.11	6.31	10.16	2.09	0.17	3.31
May	23.14	16.68	6.25	9.81	5.54	0.45	0.85
June	22.71	16.74	6.56	9.55	5.11	0.42	0.73
July	25.34	18.02	6.31	11.01	6.20	0.50	-0.01
August	22.71	12.41	5.88	6.17	9.16	0.73	-0.01
September	19.00	12.19	5.69	6.15	6.07	0.49	-0.28
October	17.60	11.85	5.38	6.15	5.14	0.42	-0.04
November	17.32	11.64	4.94	6.39	5.09	0.41	-0.04
December	18.44	11.19	4.38	6.53	6.52	0.53	0.10
1992 January	15.25	10.97	4.25	6.45	3.86	0.32	-0.14
February	14.84	11.26	4.38	6.60	3.22	0.26	-0.02
March	16.21	10.12	4.56	5.31	5.53	0.45	0.15
April	17.46	9.66	4.25	5.19	7.11	0.57	-0.15
May	17.74	10.26	4.19	5.83	6.78	0.55	-0.05
June	15.94	10.11	4.06	5.81	5.29	0.43	0.06
July	15.25	10.45	3.63	6.59	4.35	0.36	0.09
August	15.94	10.77	3.63	6.89	4.67	0.38	-0.08
September	16.08	10.49	3.25	7.01	5.06	0.41	-0.03
October	15.39	11.67	3.56	7.83	3.33	0.27	-0.02

Source: Author's calculations.
a Rate of annualized 30-day fixed-term deposits.
b Annualized BONEX 89 internal rate of return.
c LIBOR rate: annualized 180-day LIBOR rate.

Table 2.7. Argentina: Actual Monthly Interest Rates and Financial Spread, July 1990–December 1992
(In national currency)

Period		Nominal rates		Real rates[1]		Financial spread
		Lending	Deposit	Lending	Deposit	
1990	July	14.4	11.10	6.90	3.82	3.30
	August	14.2	9.80	-1.48	-5.28	4.40
	September	20.3	16.70	6.68	3.48	3.60
	October	14.6	10.90	8.75	5.24	3.70
	November	11.0	6.70	6.18	2.07	4.30
	December	9.1	6.70	5.89	3.56	2.40
1991	January	16.1	13.60	6.51	4.21	2.50
	February	21.0	16.70	-8.94	-12.18	4.30
	March	17.1	11.60	10.73	5.53	5.50
	April	4.3	1.40	1.14	-1.67	2.90
	May	4.7	1.60	3.18	0.12	3.10
	June	3.9	1.70	2.02	-0.14	2.20
	July	4.1	1.80	2.74	0.47	2.30
	August	3.5	1.40	3.05	0.96	2.10
	September	3.6	1.10	2.57	0.10	2.50
	October	3.2	1.10	2.18	0.10	2.10
	November	3.1	1.10	3.00	1.00	2.00
	December	3.9	1.30	4.06	1.45	2.60
1992	January	3.1	1.10	1.53	-0.44	2.00
	February	2.9	1.00	1.83	-0.05	1.90
	March	2.7	0.90	0.98	-0.79	1.80
	April	2.7	1.00	1.78	0.10	1.70
	May	2.6	0.90	1.99	0.30	1.70
	June	2.4	0.80	1.39	-0.20	1.60
	July	2.8	1.00	1.68	-0.10	1.80
	August	2.6	0.90	1.84	0.15	1.70
	September	2.5	0.90	1.99	0.40	1.60
	October	2.4	0.95	1.69	0.25	1.45
	November	2.5	1.05	3.33	1.86	1.45
	December	2.6	1.05	3.12	1.56	1.55

Source: Central Bank of the Republic of Argentina.
[1] Deflated by Combined Price Index (IPCOM in Spanish).

the local financial system stayed at excessively high levels, especially in real terms (Table 2.7). Among other things, this highlighted the persistence of high intermediation costs on the part of the financial institutions and clearly hurt the prospects for a recovery of private investment. If it continues over time, it will moreover affect the quality of the institutions' assets. In addition, the high level of lending rates in the domestic financial system, which according to central bank data fluctuated around 2.5 percent a month on average in 1992 but for consumers and small and medium-sized businesses practically doubled that level, especially in the interior of the country, suggests the presence of a marked segmentation from the standpoint of the availability of funds. In fact, major economic groups were much less affected by this factor because of their access to external credit and to the local capital market.

The capital inflow began to show signs of slowing down from roughly mid-1992. The more obvious of these, aside from sharply falling prices on the security exchange, include the relative stagnation of international reserves and the remonetization process, as well as the moderate but systematic rise in the differential between domestic and external interest rates. The first indications of a slackening in productive activity were the direct consequence of that slowdown.

According to the monetary balance of payments approach, a second contractive phase would have to correct the exchange lag through the nominal deflation of domestic prices, as well as the current account deficit, by means of the price effect as well as the effect of income on the trade balance. The increase in domestic interest rates, meanwhile, would make financing the transaction possible.

However, the problem raised with this adjustment mechanism is the possibility of asymmetries between the initial, expansive phase of the plan and the subsequent contractive phase. Without undertaking to discuss the plausibility of the nominal deflation, the magnitude of the recession required to correct the current imbalance, or the time necessary for adjustment to take place, the fragility of the financial system is without a doubt one of the fundamental reasons for this possible asymmetry. That fragile state derives primarily from the potential volatility of the financial system's borrowings, which stems from the scant volume of the current accounts and the short average length of the fixed terms.

In a context of complete liberalization and financial openness, in fact, the perception of the agents with respect to the long-term viability of the external closure of the economy becomes a variable fundamental to the financial system's stability. Obviously, as was illustrated with the collapse of the "exchange guidelines" policy in 1980 and 1981, an unfavorable change in the expectations of devaluation can trigger an abrupt recomposition of portfolios capable of destabilizing the situation of the financial institutions. But even if exchange expectations remain stable (or become irrelevant owing to the total dollarization of the financial system), an increased country-risk can have the same consequences. Specifically, even if no sudden changes in relative prices are expected, a situation of that nature could arise if a deep, long recession were in prospect, inasmuch as it too would adversely affect the expected solvency of the system's debtors.

It ought to be added that the risks of insolvency of the local financial system are accentuated by the high participation in the total indebtedness of the providers of nontradable goods and services, whose incomes are not dollarized and depend entirely on domestic absorption.

The fragility of the Argentine financial system became evident in mid-November of last year. At that time the fear that the government might abandon the convertibility rules and devalue the peso unleashed a run on foreign exchange, an incipient run on the banks, and a sudden rise in interest rates, especially on the interbank market. Although the central bank was able to stem the run by selling $302 million in only three days, the episode touched off a significant increase in country-risk and in domestic interest rates, both in pesos and dollars.

In order to prevent the run on the banks from continuing, the central bank took a number of steps intended to make the use of the dollar even more routine in all economic transactions: the banks were authorized, within certain limits, to maintain their cash reserves in either pesos or dollars without distinction; beginning in January of this year current accounts were allowed to be opened in dollars; and the proportion of resources borrowed in dollars that the banks could lend in pesos was raised.

The central aim of these measures was to avoid capital flight: if the private sector wishes to maintain a higher proportion of its assets in dollars, the new provisions, in principle, increase the incentive to do so within the domestic financial system. The economic authorities furthermore expect the new scheme to permit interest rates in pesos and dollars to converge, underscoring the equivalence of the two currencies.

Despite the financial market's initial reaction, doubts remain concerning the system's viability in more permanent terms. First, the external resources that may enter the banks if they decide to cover possible shortfalls in peso cash reserves with dollars are very short-term. Second, the creation of current accounts in dollars may make domestic credit less instead of more available. In fact, if businesses decided to replace term deposits with current account deposits as a way of preserving their liquid assets, no new deposits would appear and bank credit would actually contract because of the higher reserve requirements on current accounts.

Furthermore, and fundamentally, deepening dollarization makes it harder rather than easier to solve the problem that exists with respect to relative prices. If at some time the private sector expects the external situation to grow worse, it could react by deciding to cover itself against the greater country-risk by reducing its holdings in pesos and "Argendollars" (dollars deposited in the country), increasing instead its dollar holdings "under the mattress" or outside the country. That would cause a strong contraction of domestic credit, higher interest rates, more serious recession, and sharp financial imbalances which could eventually cause a crisis of the system.

Structure and Operation of the Financial System

Size

Despite the small volume of funds it intermediates, the Argentine financial system possesses a relatively high number of institutions and branches. At year-end

Table 2.8. Argentina: Trend of the Number of Institutions and Subsidiaries in the Financial System, 1980–91

Types of institutions	1980		1991	
	No. of institutions	No. of subsidiaries	No. of institutions	No. of subsidiaries
Public national	4	695	5	538
Public provincial	26	1,083	25	1,225
Public municipal	5	62	5	57
Total public banks	35	1,840	35	1,820
Foreign	27	215	31	351
National private	152	1,784	102	1,892
Total private banks	179	1,999	133	2,243
Total banks	214	3,839	168	4,063
Finance companies	135	216	28	49
Credit banks	92	24	19	23
Savings & loans	28	40	3	3
Total Nonbanking institutions	255	280	50	75
Financial System Total	469	4,119	218	4,138

Source: Central Bank of the Republic of Argentina.

1991 it consisted of 218 financial institutions which had 4,138 branches. Of that total, 168 were banks with 4,063 branches, and 50 were nonbanks, which had 75 branches (Table 2.8).

At the end of 1980 the number of institutions in operation was much higher: 469, of which 214 were banks and 255 nonbanks. This gives some idea of the difficult process of mergers and restructuring in which the financial system has been immersed since the crisis of 1980 and 1981.

Most affected by that process were the nonbanks, whose ranks were thinned by more than 80 percent, but national private banks also saw their numbers dwindle, with barely two-thirds as many in August 1992 as there had been at year-end 1980. The number of public and foreign banks, by contrast, remained practically constant.[8]

---

[8] Five new foreign banks opened their doors in the first half of the eighties, but in recent years three other foreign banks ceased operations in the country. In regard to the official banking system, a restructuring process began to which we shall refer later. It has already resulted in the privatization of three provincial banks.

Table 2.9. Argentina: Financial System Productivity Indicators, Dec. 1992
(In thousands of dollars)

Type of institution	Attraction of deposits by banking institution	Total deposits/ total bank employees[1]
Banking institutions		
Public banks		191.09
- National	8,418.5	
- Provincial and municipal	3,777.2	
Private banks		225.42
- National Private (Federal capital)	6,118.0	
- National Private (interior)	3,247.9	
- Foreign	11,747.6	
Nonbanking institutions	5,559.5	134.28
System total	6,056.1	205.28

Source: "Indicadores del sistema financiero," Central Bank of the Republic of Argentina.
[1]Due to the lack of information, the number of employees in December 1991 is used.

The change in the number of branches did not parallel that of the institutions. From end-1980 to end-1985 the number of branches rose from 4,119 to 4,696, and although it fell in the years that followed it still stood at 4,138 at end-1991, slightly above the 1980 figure.

This amounts to a little under 8,000 inhabitants per banking facility, a "banking density" comparable with that of industrial countries but inconsistent with a degree of monetization that, as previously noted, is well below that of those countries. Despite the significant growth of deposits fostered by the Convertibility Plan, at end-1992 the total attracted per branch was only slightly over $6 million (Table 2.9).[9]

These comparisons suggest that hypertrophy, a longstanding phenomenon reinforced by the Financial Reform of 1977, remains a problem in the Argentine financial system.[10]

The number of branches did not grow at the same rate for all types of institutions. Nonbank branches closed along with the institutions themselves. Bank branches, on the other hand, multiplied from 3,839 in 1980 to 4,503 in 1985, and although their number then declined it still stood at 4,063 in 1991, almost 6 percent higher than in 1980. In addition, that expansion encompassed private

---

[9] It is interesting to note that this indicator shows appreciable differences by type of institution, with foreign and national public banks situated well above the average, and domestic private banks of the interior and provincial and municipal public banks well below it.

[10] See Giorgio (1980), where it is shown how the opening of branches by financial institutions is closely linked to the strategy of maximizing their share of receipts from the inflation tax.

Table 2.10. Argentina: Trend of Personnel Employed in the Financial System in Selected Years, 1980–91

Type of institution	1980	1989	1990	1991
Banking institutions	146,140	146,613	133,545	120,587
Public Banks	79,714	82,674	75,718	67,670
- National		48,667	42,112	37,662
- Provincial and municipal		34,007	33,606	30,008
Private banks	66,426	63,939	57,827	52,917
Nonbanking financial institutions	10,833	2,462	1,678	1,493
Financial system total	156,973	148,701	135,223	122,080

Source: Central Bank of the Republic of Argentina.

domestic and foreign banks along with public ones. Expansion in the latter category was due to a burgeoning of provincial bank branches, which outpaced the closing of branches in the national and municipal banking systems.

Figures on the number of persons employed in the system tend to confirm the hypertrophy thesis, although from 1990 on a significant process of adjustment becomes evident (Table 2.10). The end of 1989 saw some 149,000 people working in the financial system, 55 percent of them in the official system, 43 percent in private banks, and 2 percent in nonbanks.

Despite the drastic monetary reduction undergone by the system during the 1980s, as described in the previous section, this figure was barely 5 percent lower than that for the number of employees at year-end 1980. Even more remarkable, that small reduction in the aggregate level of employment was due almost exclusively to cuts in nonbank staff. In the private banking system the reduction was practically imperceptible and in the official banking system payrolls actually increased.

The subsequent dramatic reduction of the system's monetary size resulting from the two hyperinflationary episodes and the BONEX Plan finally set in motion a deeper adjustment to the system's physical size, which manifests itself by, among other things, a much steeper drop in the number of people employed. In this way, total employment in the sector end-1991 stood at around 122,000 persons, for a reduction of 18 percent in relation to the figure posted two years earlier.[11]

This time the adjustment encompassed the public as well as the private banking system: staff was cut in both systems in almost identical proportions (slightly over 15 percent), so that employment distribution remained very simi-

---

[11] Although more recent figures are not available, the circumstantial evidence from various sources suggests that staff cuts continued into 1992.

lar to that of 1989. It should be noted, however, that at the official level the adjustment was greater in the national banks (a 22.5 percent drop) than in the provincial banks (12 percent).

In any event, at the end of 1992 the volume of deposits per employee was estimated at only $205,000, a figure consistent with the low levels of attraction by branch referred to above. Obviously, these very low productivity indicators explain the high cost of loans and other services offered by the domestic financial system.

Operating Characteristics

Argentine financial legislation has traditionally placed commercial banks at the center of financial activity.

Law 21.526, which was enacted in 1977 and, as amended, continues to regulate financial activity, confirmed that tradition by authorizing commercial banks to carry on any activity not expressly prohibited by law.

This rule resulted in the preponderance of this type of institution, now referred to as "universal banks." The law also makes provision for Bancos de Inversión e Hipotecarios, or investment and mortgage banks, but as it also sets forth various restrictions on such institutions there are virtually no investment banks in existence and only one mortgage bank, which is publicly owned. The small amount of investment and mortgage business is therefore also carried out almost entirely by the commercial banks.

The other categories of authorized institutions are investment companies, savings and loan corporations, and credit banks, whose operations are also very restricted under the current rules.

Consequently, the preeminence of the commercial banks in attracting deposits and granting loans is almost absolute: as of June 1992, the banks were handling around 98.5 percent of the loans and deposits, and practically all of this business was in the hands of commercial banks, with nonbanks accounting for the rest (Table 2.11).

Institutional Categorization

The public banks have a significant share in the financial system. In addition to the recently created Bank for Investment and External Trade, there are five other nationally owned banks: two commercial banks, the Bank of the Argentine Nation and the Bank of Tierra del Fuego National Territory, the National Mortgage Bank (in the process of reorganization), the National Development Bank (to cease operations shortly), and the National Savings and Loan Bank (in the course of privatization). The Bank of the Argentine Nation is the country's leader in volume of loans and deposits.

Table 2.11. Argentina: Share of Financial Institutions in Deposits and Loans, June 1992

(Percentages)

Type of institution	Deposits	Loans
Banking institutions	98.5	98.6
- Public banks	43.8	54.7
- National private banks	39.1	29.2
- Foreign banks	15.6	14.7
Nonbanking financial institutions	1.5	1.4
- Finance companies	1.4	1.3
- Credit banks	0.1	0.1
- Savings and loan associations	0.0	0.0
Financial system total	100.0	100.0

Source: Author's calculations based on data from the "Estado de las entidades financieras," Central Bank of the Republic of Argentina.

There are 24 commercial banks belonging to the provinces, five municipally owned banks, and a provincially owned public investment bank. Some of these banks are very important parts of the financial system. The Bank of the Province of Buenos Aires ranks second in volume of deposits, and the Bank of the City of Buenos Aires is seventh.

At the end of 1991 the private domestic banks functioning as corporations numbered 57, and those organized as cooperatives, 45. Most of the cooperatives are the result of mergers of cooperative credit banks. These banks work mainly with small and medium-sized businesses, professionals and employees, and have a significant presence in small localities.

Finally, at the end of 1991 there were 31 foreign banks. These fall into two distinct groups with different strategies. One group specializes in wholesale investment and corporate banking, with few branches or none. Many of these banks have incorporated since 1977, when the Argentine financial market entered the international marketplace. The other group, which includes banks with a long presence in the Argentine market, has a commercial strategy that combines attracting deposits from the public and personal bank services with wholesale banking. To that end they have branch networks of various sizes.

With some ups and downs, the share of the different types of banking institutions in total loans and deposits has remained relatively stable over the last decade. The most important thing in this respect is the weight retained by the official banking system, which in the period 1983–92 accounted for around 50 percent of the deposits and 63 percent of the loans. The domestic private banking system accounted for 35 percent and 25 percent, respectively, and foreign banks handled the rest.

The fact that the public banking system's share of loans is greater than in total deposits highlights the important role the central bank's policy on reserve requirements and rediscounts has had in the financial system's intermediation activity.[12]

Starting with the remonetization process begun in early 1990, and to a considerable extent as a consequence of the structural reform of the national public banking system, the official banking system has tended to lose some of its importance from the standpoint of both deposits and loans, though only to a moderate degree thus far and without erosion of its predominant position in the system. In June 1992 it held 43.8 percent of the deposits and 54.7 percent of the loans. The share of the private banking system, both domestic and foreign, grew accordingly: by that date the former handled 39.1 percent of the deposits and 29.2 percent of the loans, while the latter handled 15.6 percent and 14.7 percent, respectively.

As these data show, there continues to be a significant discrepancy in the distribution of the stock of loans and deposits, attributable to intervention by the central bank. Although the granting of new rediscounts has been very restricted since convertibility and the new flows of loans and deposits have tended to balance one another, the problem of carryover persists: at the start of 1992 central bank lending represented 32 percent of the deposits of the national public banking system and 53 percent of those of the provincial banking system.

Degree of Concentration

An important trait of the Argentine financial system is its relatively high and growing degree of concentration. At the end of 1979 the five major banks accounted for 27.7 percent of total deposits; the corresponding percentage was 40.2 for the top ten banks and 56.6 percent for the top twenty. At the end of 1990 the figures stood at 41.2 percent, 54.1 percent and 67.8 percent, respectively (Table 2.12).

Given the increasingly bimonetary character of the financial system, it would be advisable at this point to see if a significant difference exists between the concentration of peso and dollar deposits.

With respect to the first 20 banks, the figures for March 1992 show no appreciable changes in comparison with year-end 1990: this group's share remained at slightly over 67.5 percent in both domestic and foreign currency deposits. Nor do major changes show in peso deposits for the top five and ten banks: in March 1992 these groups held 39.3 percent and 53 percent, respec-

---

[12] It should be added that this role has entailed substantial costs for the central bank, that these costs have been quite high at times and have been the source of the so-called quasi-fiscal deficit.

Table 2.12. Argentina: Distribution of Deposits by Group of Banks for Selected Years, 1979–92

(Percentage of the banking system total)

Group of banks	End of year			March 1992	
	1979	1985	1990	National currency	Foreign currency
The 5 largest	27.7	42.5	41.2	39.3	28.9
The 10 largest	40.2	54.6	54.1	53.0	47.5
The 20 largest	56.6	66.7	67.8	67.9	67.6
All others	43.5	33.4	32.2	32.1	32.4
Total banks	219.0	198.0	170.0	166.0	166.0

Source: Author's calculations based on data from the "Estado de entidades financieras," Central Bank of the Republic of Argentina.

tively, of total peso deposits. With respect to dollar deposits, however, these two groups posted somewhat lower shares at that date: 28.9 percent and 47.5 percent.

This difference indirectly reveals another important feature of the Argentine financial system, already referred to above: the public banks' predominant representation among major banks. In March 1992, five of the system's ten biggest banks by volume of deposits were public (two national, two provincial, and one municipal), two belonged to the domestic private banking system, and three were foreign banks.[13]

The fact that the foreign banking system is more "specialized" than the domestic (public and private) banking system in handling dollar deposits (Table 2.13) and that its share is larger in the top twenty banks than in the top ten and five explains the smaller relative concentration in regard to the handling of foreign currency deposits.

Table 2.13 also incidentally brings out the extent to which the financial system has recently become "dollarized." For the system as a whole, the share accounted for by foreign currency deposits reached 34 percent at the end of 1990 and exceeded 46 percent in August 1992. As already noted, the foreign banks show the greatest specialization in this type of deposit, with more than 62 percent of their borrowings dollarized by that date.[14] The trend toward dollarization is also very marked in the other institutions, although important differences among them remain.

Concentration is also high in the private banking system. The top five banks handle 31 percent of total private bank deposits, the top ten 49.6 percent and the

---

13 Two public banks, the Nación and the Provincia de Buenos Aires, together account for almost 25 percent of the system's total deposits.

14 Strictly speaking, by that date the nonbanks were even more tilted toward dollar deposits, which represented a little over 70 percent of their total deposits. As we have seen, however, nonbanks are a minor factor in the system as a whole.

Table 2.13. Argentina: Share of Deposits in Foreign Currency, 1990–92
(Percentage of total deposits)

Type of institution	December 90	December 91	August 92
Banking institutions			
- National public	20.58	36.59	33.51
- Prov. and munic.	10.85	24.38	25.20
- National Private (Federal Capital)	46.77	59.36	59.96
- National Private (Interior)	35.24	51.35	48.72
- Foreign	60.40	69.00	62.09
Nonbanking institutions	30.67	74.38	70.22
Financial system total	34.10	48.10	46.40

Source: "Indicadores del sistema financiero," Central Bank of the Republic of Argentina.

top twenty 66.8 percent. There are 133 private banks in all. Concentration is somewhat more pronounced in foreign currency deposits. Of the top twenty banks, moreover, seven are of foreign capital.

After the financial crisis of 1980 and 1981, several of the private banks with domestic capital took over institutions in difficulty or purchased branches of banks liquidated by the central bank.

Similarly, many of the principal local banks form part of economic groups with diversified economic interests. The banks have contributed actively to the financing of the businesses of their economic group, although at present that support is restricted by specific central bank regulations setting a ceiling on support to related enterprises.

Lending is also highly concentrated. The system's "principal debtors" (a central bank category encompassing the first 50 debtors of each institution and all debtors with balances of more than 342,000 pesos) had taken out 60 percent of all loans as of June 30, 1992. This high average proportion receives the impact of the concentration of assets of the public banking system, where the "principal debtors" (a category encompassing the debtors belonging to the public sector) account for 72.9 percent of total credit. In the private sector, meanwhile, the "principal debtors" account for 40.8 percent of the portfolio.

Characteristics of Banking Activity

The commercial banks engage in "universal banking." The largest private (local and foreign) banks offer a wide range of services along with traditional borrowing and lending activities: currency exchange and foreign trade, personal bank products (credit cards, collections), marketing of nonbank products (insurance, travel), real estate (financing and selling through associated companies), corporate banking products (financial engineering, acquisitions and mergers, project evaluation), and capital market products.

The precise definition of the spectrum of services to be offered by commercial banks is not yet complete. Hitherto, the law had barred banks from operating commercial, industrial, agricultural, or other types of businesses. However, in response to the economic deregulation pursued by the present government, the banks have sought ways and means of conducting various kinds of business outside the field of banking.

The central bank regulations facilitated this trend by increasing the authorized ratio between shares held in businesses and equity from 3 percent to 25 percent. In addition, a recent change in the Law on Financial Institutions empowers the central bank, on a case-by-case basis, to waive the prohibition on conducting businesses on a bank's own account. In this sense, the precise definition of what banks may do is delegated to the central bank.

Some banks, however, engage in more specialized activity. One group of commercial banks are clearly wholesalers and do not engage in personal banking services. Cooperative banks, most private banks in the country's interior, and some public provincial and municipal banks are clearly retailers that stress traditional banking services and personal bank products.

In addition, commercial banks recover a high proportion of their costs by charging commissions for their services. That proportion is 59 percent for local private banks, 53 percent for foreign banks, and 37 percent for public provincial and municipal banks. These commissions are charged on services connected with the handling of deposits, lending and other bank and nonbank services. Widening the range of services offered is a basic component of the adjustment which the institutions are carrying out, since it enables them to make profitable use of their facilities and realize the sales potential embodied by their clientele.

The Banks and the Capital Market

The stock market has historically been of marginal significance. Recently, however, it has expanded considerably, particularly since the inflow of external capital was prompted by the Convertibility Plan.

The banks have had a leading role in this incipient development of the capital market. This function has been practically monopolized by the wholesale banks (for the most part foreign) and by large local private banks. The salient features of this participation are:

• Issuance of negotiable obligations and shares of businesses. The banks that traditionally service large enterprises have participated in the design, guarantee, underwriting, and placement abroad of the issues. Some of the issues reflect the refinancing of debts already contracted with those institutions.

• Issuance of the banks' negotiable obligations and commercial papers. To date, 17 banks have issued negotiable obligations. The bulk of these have been issued by the leading private national banks. Five institutions account for 82 percent of bank issues. In the three largest issues, international banks led the operations, all placements were made abroad, and the majority of the funds belong to Argentine investors.

International and local banks complement each other in that the former guarantee placement abroad while the latter can channel these funds to retail credit transactions—particularly mortgage loans—which can support the relatively high cost of attracting the funds.

• Privatization of public enterprises. The major national and foreign private banks have participated actively in the privatization process, performing the following functions: (1) financial advisors to the national government, (2) corporate participation in consortia, (3) financial engineering and financing of grantees, through issuance of negotiable obligations and shares, or the making of loans with local or external resources, and (4) placement of shares of privatized enterprises.

• Active participation in the secondary trading of bonds and shares, both on the open market as agents and on the commercial exchanges. Foreign and local banks have set up brokerage houses in order to participate directly in the securities market. The banks have also set up and are administering investment funds with local and foreign investors.

The Role of the Central Bank

The central bank manages monetary policy and supervises the financial system, which operates on the basis of a fractional reserve requirement system. Under its new charter, its authorities act independently of the executive, are elected by the latter with the consent of the senate, and serve six-year terms of office.

The central bank is autonomous, nevertheless its discretionality in monetary policy management is very carefully delimited by the Law on Convertibility and its own charter. In effect, with very few exceptions the central bank can only issue money that is backed by international reserves. It is barred from lending to the government in domestic funds, and can constitute reserves only with public bonds in foreign exchange up to a limit of 30 percent of total reserves, provided that the new annual issue necessary to reach that limit does not represent more than 10 percent of the bonds already included as reserves (thus far this possibility has only been used with extreme prudence, so that the share of reserves consisting of public securities has not risen above 12 percent).

In addition, the bank is practically unable to act as a lender of last resort under conditions of illiquidity or insolvency of the financial institutions because the new charter prevents it from guaranteeing the deposits of the institutions and imposes strict quantitative and temporal limits on its rediscounting operations.

The key features of the central bank's current regulations are described below.

Reserve Requirements

In the last few years the Argentine financial system has operated with high reserve requirements, owing to monetary policy decisions designed to offset other sources of monetary expansion (in particular, fiscal imbalances and loans made by the central bank to the financial institutions).

In March 1991 the average reserve requirement for deposits in local currency stood at 40.8 percent, while the requirement for foreign currency deposits was 5.9 percent. In December 1992 the reserve requirements were 33.3 percent and 11.4 percent, respectively.

The minimum cash ratios differ greatly based on the type of deposit and the maturity period. In December 1992 the highest reserve requirement was the one for current accounts, with a 71 percent ratio, while at the other end fixed terms left for more than 30 days had a reserve requirement of 3 percent.

The lowering of the average reserve requirement during the convertibility period was due partly to the reduction of the minimum cash ratios, but primarily to a lengthening of the deposit period, which benefited deposits with less stringent reserve requirements.

Public provincial and municipal banks currently have smaller reserve requirements on deposits belonging to the public sector of their jurisdictions, but the central bank intends to gradually reduce this benefit.

Deposit Guarantee

Enactment of the convertibility law prompted the economic authorities to take steps to reduce potential risks of an expansion of the money supply without a counterpart in foreign exchange. One such step was the virtual abolition of the deposit guarantee.

Under its new charter the central bank is not authorized to guarantee the financial system's borrowings. A Limited Special Fund was set up in its stead, by order of the central bank. This fund consists of the equivalent $50 million contributed by the central bank in public securities issued in dollars (Bonos Externos series 89), plus the inputs of the institutions governed by the regime. Joining the fund is optional, but banks that do join must pay into it.

The smallness of the amount in relation to the system's deposits prompted the banks not to join the new regime. In addition, the banks were already heavily engaged in the foreign currency deposits segment, which had no official guarantee. In fact, after some institutions opted not to join, joining the new regime could be interpreted by savers as a sign of weakness, in addition to the differential costs which it entailed in relation to the system. Consequently, the new regime is virtually nonexistent for all practical purposes.

Rediscounts

While convertibility was in effect, a very strict rediscount policy was applied. A line of rediscounts was kept in effect only to address situations of illiquidity on account of reduced amounts and maturities and high cost. Under the new charter, the maturities cannot exceed 30 days, are not automatically renewable, and require guarantees in securities or real assets. All pre-existent lines (support to provincial banks, regional economies and financing or exports) were eliminated.

The nominal rediscount amount, however, grew from April 1991 to June 1992 from 16.917 billion to 19.740 billion pesos, as a result of the accrual of interest on the remaining balances. In any case, the relative stagnation of the rediscounts and the significant growth of the deposits caused the ratio between central bank loans and system deposits to fall from 59.2 percent to 16.2 percent between April 1991 and June 1992.

The sharpest drop occurred in the public banking system, which was receiving the bulk of the central bank's lending. In the national public banks, that ratio fell from 135.6 percent to 28 percent and in provincial and municipal public banks it fell from 95.6 percent to 46.0 percent.

Minimum Capital Requirements

Until 1991 the minimum capital requirements of financial institutions varied by type of institution and their geographic location. This year the Basel criteria gradually began to be introduced.

Under the mixed system currently in place, the capital requirement is established as a summation of a proportion of the frozen assets and a proportion of the assets subject to risk. The assets, in turn, are weighted on the basis of their generic risk and a specific risk indicator for loans, which depends on the lending rates charged. The floor based on the type of institution and the geographic location also remain in effect.

Purpose of Credit

As noted, the remonetization of the first stage of convertibility proved a tonic to the financial system's capacity to lend, as reflected in an increase from less than $6 billion in March 1991 to more than $30 billion at year-end 1992.

The enhanced lending capacity benefited the private sector, while lending to the public sector slid about 25 percent from end-1990 to April 1992.

Table 2.14. Argentina: Financing and Delinquency Indices by Economic Activity, March 1992
(Percentages)

	Share of each activity in total financing	Share of the irregular portfolio in total financing	Share of the sector in GDP[1]
Primary production	11.5	23.7	10.6
Manufacturing industry	20.4	16.9	25.3
Construction	5.8	10.8	5.5
Electricity, gas, water, and sanitation services	2.8	58.6	1.9
Wholesale trade	5.5	12.8	
Retail trade	6.8	20.6	Services total
Services and finances	21.1	22.3	53.9
Households	22.7	7.7	
Miscellaneous	3.4	35.0	
Total financing	100.0	18.2	

Sources: "Financiación por actividades" and "Indicadores económicos," Central Bank of the Republic of Argentina.
[1]Data for 1991.

Despite this easing of pressure from the public sector, it is still receiving a considerable share of the system's available funding. In February 1992 the system as a whole devoted a third of its credits to the public sector (25.5 percent in domestic currency and 8 percent in foreign currency), and somewhat less than two-thirds to the nonfinancial private sector (30 percent in domestic currency and 30 percent in foreign currency), while the rest went to the financial sector itself.

As one would expect, the official banking system directs almost half of its loans to the public sector—slightly over 38 percent in pesos and 11.5 percent in dollars. This trend is more marked in the provincial and municipal than in the national banking systems. The private banks meanwhile steer less than 2 percent of their loans to the public sector and focus their activity on the nonfinancial private sector, which receives almost 90 percent of their credit. Unlike the official banks, moreover, the bulk of private bank lending—more than 65 percent—is denominated in dollars.

The greater part of the public sector's debt is owed by provincial and municipal jurisdictions (treasuries, businesses, and public organizations) to their public banks. The improvement in the fiscal situation and the privatization of public enterprises (which in some cases included the cancellation of debts) reduced the public sector's need to borrow from the financial system.

Table 2.14 breaks down bank lending by sector. Sectoral participation in the total volume of credit approximates the sectoral contribution to gross domestic product. The available data appear to indicate that no significant changes came about in the sectoral breakdown of credit during the convertibility program. Loans to households, meanwhile, reach 22.7 percent of the total.

Table 2.15. Argentina: Average Loan and Deposit Terms, August 1992
(Number of days)

Type of Institution	Loans		Deposits	
	National currency	Foreign currency	National currency	Foreign currency
Banking institutions	316	82	15	39
Public banks	638	197	16	69
- Nationals	534	232	13	93
- Provincial and municipal	750	118	19	27
Private banks	40	51	14	31
- Nationals	41	52	15	31
- Foreign	32	51	16	33
Nonbanking institutions	81	27	17	51
Financial system total	311	80	15	39

Source: "Indicadores financieros," Central Bank of the Republic of Argentina.

The productive sector's use of funds reduces itself almost exclusively to meet transitory needs for cash or to partially finance working capital requirements. This affirmation is supported by more diffuse loan procedures, the short average maturity of loans, and borrowing costs incompatible with any other use of the funds.

The most widespread loan procedure is that of advances on current accounts, and to a lesser extent the discount of third-party documents and direct loans.

Based on the average short term of the deposits, which in August 1992 was 15 days for those in pesos and 39 days for those in dollars (Table 2.15), the average maturity of private bank loans was only 40 days for peso transactions and 51 days for dollar transactions. The official banking system, by contrast, assumed a greater risk of loss by operating with average maturities of 638 days for peso loans and 197 days for dollar loans. However, this fact does not meet the long-term credit needs of the productive sectors, which basically rely on the private banking system, and it is indeed one of the reasons for the greater financial weakness of the official banking system.

The average rate of accrued interest on lending in the time frame from April 1991 to June 1992 was extremely high: 52.6 percent per year. The cost of borrowing furthermore shows wide disparities in terms of the following variables: type of currency, size of enterprise, type of financial institution, and geographic location of institution. Based on these variables, credit in pesos can range from 15 percent annually for a loan from a bank in Buenos Aires to a blue-chip company, to 125 percent for a loan from a small bank in a province to a small local business. The range is narrower for loans in foreign currency, from 11 percent to 22 percent annually.

Although statistics to quantify it are not available, it is safe to say that the volume of credit earmarked for investment is small. Only a limited fraction of the foreign currency lent is devoted to medium-term loans for investment purposes.

With respect to personal loans, the bulk of the funds goes for consumer loans, in the form of personal loans or the financing of credit cards. Some financial institutions are granting loans to finance housing, in dollars and with five- to ten-year terms. Funding is obtained through external lines or placement of negotiable obligations issued by the institutions. In any event the amounts are not significant and the annual cost of credit is not lower than 20 percent per year.

The financial system as a whole is burdened with high rates of delinquent loans. As Table 2.14 shows, in March 1992 nonperforming loans (in arrears and in litigation) accounted for 18.2 percent of all lending. The primary production sectors, electricity, gas and water, retail trade and services, and finance show higher than average delinquency rates. The primary production sector is affected by the substantial delay in the production of industrial crops, which have been associated with heavy borrowing for years. The figures for the electricity, gas, water, services, and finance sectors show the delay incurred by the public sector.

The average arrears index, however, is much affected by the public banking system. In August 1992 the public banking system's delinquency index surpassed 34 percent, while the same index stood at less than 12 percent for the national private banking system of the interior, 5 percent for the domestic private banking system of Buenos Aires, and less than 4 percent for the foreign banking system.

Evaluation of Reforms and Policy Proposals

Chief Problems of the Financial System and Effects on the Economy

Low Levels of Intermediation, High Costs, and Absence of Medium- and Long-term Credit

While the convertibility program was in effect, borrowing and lending by the financial system grew very significantly. But the current levels are still well short of meeting the economy's funding needs and below the cash ratios shown by other developing or industrialized economies.

The two main determinants of the high cost of available credit are, at the sectoral level, the bloated size of the system (given the current level of intermediation) and, at the macroeconomic level, the uncertainty regarding maintenance of the external closure in the context of the current convertibility rules. This latter factor has also been one of the basic factors limiting the length of maturity periods in connection with the system's borrowing and lending.

Weakness of the Financial System

The extremely short terms of the financial institutions' obligations pose a serious latent risk to the system as a whole. The problem is particularly critical for the public banking system, where the average term on loans is considerably longer than on deposits, which would substantially aggravate liquidity problems in an unfavorable context. In addition, the financial system's liquidity risk is accentuated in a context in which deposit guarantees are virtually nonexistent and the central bank offers only limited financial assistance to ease liquidity shortages.

Another important risk concerns the performance of loans, considering the rapid growth in foreign currency borrowings by firms that produce or market nontradable goods and services, and the increasing number of personal loans spent on consumption or to finance housing by users who have fixed incomes in local currency and depend on the level of domestic business activity.

Excessive Concentration of Credit

The excessive concentration of credit granted by the financial system is intensifying the shortage of funds available to many businesses and consumers. Small and medium-sized businesses, deprived of working capital and money for investment in equipment and technology, are especially caught short.

The development of the capital market, and in particular of direct financing by means of negotiable obligations and commercial paper regardless of positive effects, gives further impetus to the concentration of financial resources.

Weaknesses of the Public Banking System

Most of the public banks have been wrestling in the last several years with problems concerning equity and profitability, high rates of nonperforming loans, high costs of intermediation, and high dependence on funding from the central bank. However, it should be noted that individual banks find themselves in widely differing situations, particularly those belonging to provinces and municipalities, where conditions range from bankruptcy to acceptable levels of solvency and profitability.

The weakness of many of the public institutions, both national and provincial, leave them strapped for funds with which to accomplish their original mission of offering financial support to certain activities or regions of the country with insufficient access to the private banking system. Moreover, since the public banking system continues to channel a very significant portion of total resources, the crisis it is experiencing affects the overall financing of economic activity.

Ongoing Reforms and Policy Proposals

The foregoing summary stressed the difficulties facing the Argentine financial system in its efforts to carry out its specific functions and the need for far-reaching change in this area. The most significant ongoing reforms are discussed below, and additional policy recommendations are put forward.

Reforms in the National Public Banking System

In response to the grave crisis faced by the public banks at both the national and provincial levels, a profound restructuring process has been in progress since 1991. Once completed, it will substantially modify the banks' operating procedures and their participation in the financial system.

When the reform of the national banking system has been completed there will be only one first-floor bank of national scope, the Banco Nación, which will primarily serve small and medium-sized businesses in all sectors of economic activity, and two wholesale banks, the Banco de Inversión y Comercio Exterior (BICE) and the Banco Hipotecario Nacional. The National Investment Bank will be liquidated and the National Savings and Insurance Bank privatized.

Achievement of the declared goal of reorienting resources by primarily serving small and medium-sized businesses will be the key to reversing the preexisting situation, in which funds flowed to large enterprises or were granted according to extra-economic considerations involving political or personal ties.

It will also be important to improve the operational efficiency of the public institutions. In this sense, coupling the private banking system to them in a second-floor capacity seems a reasonable approach.

However, the greatest uncertainties relate to the availability of funds from these institutions. In the case of the Banco Nación, its role as depository, though diminished in recent years, assures it a stable and relatively significant foundation. The achievement of its objectives therefore depends largely on the continuation of the asset recovery process (many assets are still frozen) and efficient management.

With respect to the Banco Hipotecario and BICE, access to external lines and placement of securities in the local marketplace are crucial to the availability of funds. In regard to external financing, for the moment the funds of multilateral organizations are already committed in various loans made in recent years. In addition, in recent months a certain saturation of Latin American bonds has begun to make itself felt, along with greater difficulty in obtaining private funds on the part of Argentine firms and banks. The local capital market is still in an incipient state of development, and private papers have been issued at a brisk pace in the most recent period.

In any event, aside from considerations concerning the current state of the international capital market, the phenomenon to underline is the risk inherent in making these institutions' financing capacity dependent upon the availability of funds in the international market.

The limited financial depth of the Argentine economy produces a small supply of credit, at high cost and with excessively short repayment terms. It also causes marked segmentation of the financial markets and inordinate concentration of credit. This suggests that the public sector still has an important function to perform in terms of changing repayment terms, a task unsuited to the private banking system because of the high risks entailed, and in terms of providing credit assistance to sectors whose size or location prevent the private banking system from serving them adequately.

All experience fully justifies the decision not to use central bank discounts to perform this function. In addition to receiving external funds, however, these institutions should capitalize themselves properly with resources included in the national budget. More efficient use of existing funds, such as the National Housing Fund (FONAVI), should also be explored, as should cofinancing of long-term endeavors with the private sector.

Reforms in the Provincial Public Banking System

The provincial public banks are also undergoing a reform process designed to resolve their problems pertaining to equity, lending, overindebtedness to the central bank, and administrative efficiency. Although their situations vary from bank to bank, the majority are making efforts along the following lines: (1) cost-cutting programs, in some cases including voluntary staff retirement schemes, (2) gradual uncoupling from the corresponding public sectors, (3) improved loan recovery, and (4) reduced dependence on central bank financing.

The courses of action are also varied from the institutional point of view. In one case, 51 percent of the institution was privatized (Banco de la Provincia de Corrientes). Another bank is to be privatized shortly (Banco de la Provincia de Misiones), and several other privatizations are in progress (San Luis, Entre Ríos, Formosa, etc.). In some cases (including the two most important banks, Provincia de Buenos Aires and Provincia de Córdoba) it has been decided to retain total provincial ownership. The Banco de la Provincia de Santa Fe, which has been turned into a corporation and whose management has been privatized, will also remain the exclusive property of the province. Several banks have been partially taken over by private capital in various proportions, and have delegated their management to the private sector. In addition there are the provincial banks that came into being with a mixed ownership structure.

The central bank has concluded agreements with certain provincial banks providing for joint rationalization and adjustment of the institutions, including a debt cancellation program with funds from jointly collected taxes, in return for payment facilities and reductions of penalties on arrearages. Provision was also made to earmark 50 percent of the funds from the privatization of the Caja Nacional de Ahorro y Seguro to finance the indemnifications required for personnel cuts.

That the reforms have, however, brought very few significant results thus far is indirectly evidenced by the current performance indicators for this group of institutions, as noted in the preceding section.

The provincial banks have an important function in the Argentine financial system. In addition to their role as financing agents of the provincial treasuries, these institutions are the only ones that offer financial services in the most disadvantaged localities, under conditions which often make losses inevitable. They are furthermore, together with the cooperative banking system in some cases, the only institutions capable of making financial resources available to small and medium-sized businesses throughout the country.

In order to perform this function, the provincial public banking system has some comparative advantages. First, it has a vast network of branches and customers. In addition, it is familiar with the areas it serves, and it has sources of low-cost funds in the public sector.

In order for the system to make use of these advantages and carry out its original role, the ongoing restructuring must proceed in accordance with the following guidelines: (1) advance the rationalization of its structures and costs, (2) step up efforts to recover more loans, (3) establish in its organizational charts precise limits and appropriate guarantees for loans to the public sector, (4) eliminate the implicit guarantee of the provincial states to these institutions, and subject them fully to the authority of the central bank, making the necessary constitutional changes and, whenever possible, reorganizing them as corporations, (5) generalize the agreements with the central bank under conditions that adjust the cancellations of debts to that institution and refine and streamline loan recovery programs, and (6) facilitate the system's access to international funding by earmarking part of the external resources intermediated by BICE for these institutions.

It is also essential to coordinate the activity of the national and provincial public banking systems, which often suffer from an irrational redundancy of branches and functions. Proper coordination will make it possible to optimize the structures and significantly reduce operating costs. A second stage should include considering the merger of small provincial banks into larger regional institutions.

Evolution and Prospects of the Private Banking System

At the level of the private banking system, it seems likely that the concentration process will continue, though assuredly in a gradual manner. The tendency to concentration arises from several factors.

First, large differences exist in access to financing generated through the international marketplace and the marketing of negotiable obligations floated by the institutions.

Second, the absence of an official guarantee will hurt the smaller institutions. The newly launched activities of the Calificadores de Riesgo (Risk Assessors), recently approved by the Comisión Nacional de Valores (National Securities Commission) will strengthen the position in the marketplace of the larger and stronger institutions.

Third, the institutions participating in the privatization award consortiums will derive new business and good profits from their stock participations.

The largest institutions will probably expand their networks of branches so as to ensure coverage of the country's principal localities. This process will be facilitated if progress is made in deregulating the mechanism for opening branches.

From a longer-term perspective, the stronger institutions are evaluating the consequences of the establishment of MERCOSUR. In this context, cooperation agreements between some Argentine and Brazilian banks have been signed. In any event, potential competition in Argentine territory from the major Brazilian banks, which have far larger operating volumes and more branches than the Argentine banks, may have a considerable impact on the local financial system.

It is to be expected that, in response to the ongoing concentration process and the possible effects of MERCOSUR, a process of mergers and takeovers will develop which will mainly affect the medium-sized retail banks, as the expected profit squeeze will leave them unable to cover their operating costs.

In the last few years, foreign banks have invested rather heavily in Argentine banks with sizable branch networks and an established place in the financial market. It is possible that, similar to the increase in concentration, this process will continue based on the new financial and productive businesses that are opening in the country. [15]

Shifts should also be expected in the wholesale banking sector, with active interest on the part of the external investment banking system. To the extent that narrower spreads and the disintermediation process are affecting sectors of the wholesale banking system, banks financed with foreign capital have clear advantages in positioning themselves, thanks to their international links and their experience with the capital market.

---

[15] In this connection it should be noted that recently the central bank significantly expanded the universe of business accessible to the banks by authorizing them to trade Brady bonds, and by permitting them to operate without any restrictions on the securities exchange and as real estate brokers.

Reduction in the Cost of Credit

Despite the existence of macroeconomic and other factors pertaining to the operation of the financial system which allowed lending rates to decline somewhat in the wake of the Convertibility Plan, these rates remain too high.[16]

To bring about a more significant reduction, the central bank adopted two direct regulatory measures at the beginning of the plan: (1) it imposed on the national and provincial banking system a maximum lending rate of 2 percent per month for discounting documents and 3 percent monthly for personal overdrafts and loans, and (2) it introduced into the formula for computing the minimum capitals of the institutions, a risk indicator tied to the level of lending rates which raises capital requirements when rates over a certain level are charged.

The first measure brought down the public banking system's rates, although compliance with it was not uniform in the provincial banking system. The second one had only a minor impact. The measure did not have practical consequences for the banks with high equity accountability levels. In addition, some institutions offset the reduction imposed on their lending rates with concealed increases in the form of commissions.

In early 1993 a new package was introduced to achieve the same objective. The most important measure was the prohibition of fixed terms shorter than 30 days, offset by authorization to open savings banks without limits on amounts received from corporations and individuals. At the same time the structure of reserve requirements was simplified by making them less dispersed and trying to keep their impact on the money stock neutral: the minimum cash requirements for fixed terms were abolished, and the reserve requirement on current accounts and savings banks in pesos and dollars was standardized at 40 percent (it had been 71 percent and 26 percent, respectively). At the same time the restrictions on securities exchange transactions (in pesos and dollars) were lifted, and a minimum term of 30 days was established on such transactions. The minimum term of negotiable obligations was reduced from 90 to 30 days. The package was completed with the easing of restrictions on the granting of credit to small and medium-sized businesses with collateral, and the abolition of the stamp tax on loans and other contracts (at the national level for now, although an effort is underway to extend it to the provincial level as well).

---

[16] The following specific provisions designed to reduce the institutions' costs deserve special mention: the abolition of taxes on bank debits and on the transfer of securities and foreign exchange, the substitution of the VAT for the tax on financial services, and the adoption of certain deregulating measures such as the easing of some aspects of deposit regulations, banking hours and rules on the installation of automatic tellers.

The elimination of miniterms would tend to reduce spreads by lowering the risks of illiquidity and administrative costs. In addition, the costs would be reduced by the abolition of the stamp tax and certain specific deregulation measures that would accompany the package, such as the elimination of filing requirements. Competition from new financing alternatives (swaps, securities, and 30-day commercial papers) should also exert downward pressure on the intermediation spreads of the financial institutions.

In addition, the context of low inflation and a quiet financial market made it possible to renew a large portion of the funds deposited for less than 30 days—which represented 56 percent of the fixed-term total—on longer terms without causing a significant rise in borrowing rates.

Longer loan maturities are essential for purposes of making the financial system less fragile and improving its performance. The central bank resolution demonstrates that, given prudent action in a stable context, an active policy can be adopted in this regard.

For the moment, however, lending rates are not coming down discernibly, although it is still too early to make a final judgment on the effect of the latest measures.

There are other specific measures that could be adopted in order to reduce the institutions' high cost of intermediation. First, without affecting the rules intended to preserve the system's solvency and liquidity, the reduction of operating costs can be furthered by pursuing the process of deregulating financial activity. Some pertinent examples are the simplification and automation of information to the central bank, the easing of the rules governing the composition of cash assets, and the simplification of safety rules.

Second, revision of the specific tax policy affecting the sector can help to reduce this component of the operating cost. The contribution to the Institute of Social Banking Services (2 percent on loan interest rates and commissions earmarked for bank staff benefits, which is added to the normal employers' contributions), and the tax on gross revenue (which is provincial in character and varies by jurisdiction) are obvious candidates for such revision.

Third, the development of an interest rate futures market would make it possible to lengthen the maturities and cut the costs associated with the rate risk.

In any case, the basic determinants of the high internal cost of credit are macroeconomic in nature. Any significant reduction in that area will therefore depend on how those factors evolve.

Financial Assistance to Small and Medium-sized Businesses

The concentration of financial resources and the credit rationing experienced by small and medium-sized businesses are longstanding phenomena in Argentina. The remonetization induced by the Convertibility Plan does not seem to have reversed them. On the contrary, they may be given further impetus by current trends such as the concentration of the banking structure, the heavy demand for financing that will come from privatized enterprises, and the growing importance of external financing and the capital market, which basically channels funds to large businesses.

In December 1992 the government announced the implementation of measures designed to improve credit assistance to this sector.

First, a fund was set up to offer rebates on the interest rate for loans to small and medium-sized businesses. The fund contains $52 million and will allow rebates of four points annually on loans totaling $1.3 billion. The resources are to be contributed by the banks that decide to join the scheme, and the rebates will be granted through bidding to those which offer their customers a lower rate.

A guarantee fund was also set up for loans designed to finance capital goods purchases. The fund will cover 40 percent of the credit guarantee. The insurance will be open to bids for by insurance companies; and the state will contribute $16 million.

Finally, lines of credit were opened for $400 million to finance exports, with funds contributed by the Banco Nación, and by the central bank, which will distribute among the private banks a $60 million loan from the IDB for microenterprise development.

The mechanisms employed are adequate, but the amounts involved are clearly insufficient. This is especially so if one considers that the announcements lagged after the start of the convertibility program by almost two years, a period in which the small and medium-sized business sector was hard hit by the opening-up of the economy and had to contend with very significant reconversion costs.

As previously noted, once rationalized the public banking system can be an important tool with which to channel financial support to small and medium-sized businesses. To that end, the Banco Nación must resume its traditional role of assisting such businesses. The setting of ceilings by firms, such as those adopted by the Banco Nación, appears an appropriate credit policy measure in that direction. However, it is also necessary to increase the resources allocated for that purpose, especially in the case of the provincial banks. A major step in this respect would be to make external funding more accessible to those institutions, through BICE or other mechanisms.

Changes in the Central Bank's Role

As a result of the convertibility regime, the central bank's management of monetary policy is closely regulated. The institution's new charter turns it into an autonomous agency but keeps it under even tighter rein by prohibiting it from making loans to the government in pesos, imposing a ceiling on the public securities in foreign currency that can be included in its reserves, and setting very strict limits on its loans to other financial institutions. With respect to such loans, the new rules provide that all advances, rediscounts, or loans approved by the central bank must have collateral appraised at market value, and that the rates applied to them may not entail a subsidy in any form.

In addition, the central bank may only grant rediscounts to financial institutions for temporary illiquidity. Such rediscounts may not exceed 30 consecutive days, must have a maximum per institution equivalent to the institution's equity and may not be renewed less than 45 days following their payment. The central bank may also address temporary illiquidity situations by granting advances secured by public securities or other collateral, but with the same limitations regarding amount and term as those established for rediscounts. The sum of rediscounts and advances may not exceed the institution's equity.

Obviously this extreme curtailment of the central bank's power to manage monetary policy was strongly influenced by the recent experience with hyperinflation, and its central objective is to buttress the credibility of the current stabilization policy. Nevertheless, the loss of flexibility is excessive from a longer-range perspective.

From the point of view of financing the government, it means definitively renouncing seigniorage, which in a context of growth and moderate inflation is a legitimate method and the cheapest way of financing the public sector. Naturally, this does not mean that no limits should be set to this approach in order to avoid excesses. But the limits could be set periodically through more flexible mechanisms. One alternative would be, for instance, to include them in the budget law which the Congress must approve every year.

From the point of view of financing the financial institutions, the new regime is not far-reaching enough to ensure the system's stability. National and international experience underscores the crucial importance of the central bank's function as lender of last resort so that it can prevent the difficulties of one institution or group of institutions from spreading throughout the system, triggering a banking crisis.

In that sense, although the maximum amount allowed may be fairly adequate under present conditions, given the banking system's low leverage, it will inevitably lose meaning as the institutions' liabilities and assets grow with respect to their equity. The established maximum maturity is even more restrictive, which may not be enough for an institution that has been experiencing liquidity problems for some time, although its solvency may not be undermined.

Deposit Guarantee

The central bank's new charter prohibits it from guaranteeing deposits. As noted, the present guarantee regime is limited to the existence of a Limited Special

Fund, constituted by a central bank contribution of $50 million in external bonds plus the input of the institutions which voluntarily join it.

In addition, to help protect savers' deposits should the institution go out of business, a special privilege is established whereby the depositors can collect against the reserve requirements constituted in the central bank, with an order of priority that favors small savers and long-term deposits. A privilege is also granted to the depositors on all assets.

The savings protection system provided by these two instruments is not enough to protect small savers and ensure the stability of the system as a whole. The special fund has been ineffective because institutions failed to join it. The privilege with respect to reserve requirements depends on the level of reserves in the central bank, and its backing is uncertain in regard to the amounts and availability of the funds to be recovered.

Numerous reasons exist at the theoretical level, especially connected with unequal information and externalities associated with financial imbalances, to argue in favor of the government's adopting explicit mechanisms to ensure the system's stability. As we pointed out above, the monetary authority's role of lender of last resort is one of them.

An adequate deposit guarantee system is another such mechanism. International experience in this field indicates that it should be obligatory for the institutions and charged to them. Because of the externalities involved, the Treasury should also commit resources for its operation. In addition, the guarantee should be partial in order to minimize the moral risk problems that a regime of this type entails. For the same reason, if an institution goes bankrupt appropriate penalties should be provided for its administration and its shareholders. The institution in charge of the guarantee fund, which would preferably have to be autonomous and under mixed ownership, would also be responsible for managing troubled institutions.

At present, under the amendments made to the Law on Financial Institutions when the central bank's new charter was enacted, if an institution encounters solvency problems, cash shortages, or other difficulties that affect its ability to function, it must undergo a regularization and reorganization approved by the central bank. If the institution does not do so it is automatically closed.

The absence of alternative options, consistent with the intention not to commit public funds to save financial institutions, is simply unrealistic. All national and international experience shows that, explicitly or implicitly, governments have always ultimately recognized that bail-out costs are lower than the costs of a full-blown financial crisis.

In this context the intervention of an agency fitted to the task would make it possible to select the best alternative in each case (sale of assets, intervention, termination, etc.), keeping the cost of the bail-out and averting ad hoc solutions, whose monetary effects always prove negative.

A comprehensively deregulated financial system thoroughly integrated into the international markets calls for stringent bank oversight, especially in an economy with a very small capital market and a recent past as volatile as Argentina's. A deposit guarantee system would make that requirement all the more imperative.

At this time the central bank would not be equal to this task. Its new charter provides that financial activity would be supervised by a Superintendency of Financial Institutions reporting directly to the president of the bank. From an institutional standpoint this condition of semi-autonomy appears adequate. But for the superintendency to perform its function effectively, it will have to be given the technical resources, professionalism, and organization which it currently lacks.

Conclusion: Reforms and the Macroeconomic Context

Of the significant inflow of external capital which took place during the initial phase of convertibility, a certain amount came through the capital market but a large proportion was channeled through the domestic financial system. This sparked a sharp increase in the monetization of the economy and an appreciable improvement in the system's overall performance. In addition, unlike what had been routinely happening since the debt crisis, the newly available funds made their way mainly to the private sector.

It is not clear, however, whether this new state of affairs will last. It is true that the continuity of the fiscal closure, once the revenues generated by privatizations are used up, is far from assured. But over and beyond this question, the central issue in strictly financial terms remains the system's marked fragility.

First, despite the remonetization that has been brought about, the financial development of the economy is still very limited. Second, the average maturity of deposits, in domestic as well as foreign currency, continues to be extremely short. Third, the spreads between domestic interest rates (for peso and dollar deposits) and international interest rates remain very high. Fourth, the intermediation spreads between the system's lending and borrowing rates are still too high. Finally, the financial institutions' lending is highly concentrated in non-tradable sectors.

For these reasons, although the financial system recovered a considerable part of its function as administrator of the community's mediums of exchange, its other central task is still not being accomplished. That is to provide financing for investment on the scale, at the cost and on the terms required for the reconversion of procedural structures and the resumption of growth in the country.[17]

---

[17] Even though the local capital market has expanded by a fair amount, it cannot be expected to perform this task by itself in the near future.

Another continuing problem is the market's segmentation, which imposes severe credit rationing on small and medium-sized businesses and the less developed regions of the country's interior.

Two years after the launching of the Convertibility Plan, there are no signs that these problems are diminishing. This provides new evidence for the hypothesis that in financially immature economies such as that of Argentina, liberalization as well as financial openness by themselves do not automatically solve such problems. The need for state intervention to overcome this "market failure" appears inevitable. In that light the dilemma of whether to intervene or not to intervene would not arise; the question is how to intervene efficiently. Some of the reforms underway, and several of the proposals discussed earlier in this section, especially in regard to the operation of the national and provincial public banking systems, point in that direction.

In addition, the risks of illiquidity and insolvency of the system remain very high. Given that the Convertibility Plan seems to have entered upon a second phase, characterized by a slowing of capital flows, uncertainty regarding the maintenance of the external closure is, in our estimation, the chief factor to explain this situation at the macroeconomic level. In that context, there remains latent the possibility that any unfavorable development may trigger a sudden change in outlook and touch off a run capable of unleashing a financial crisis and derailing the Convertibility Plan.

This problem cannot be solved by an across-the-board reversal of the reforms underway in the financial system. In the first place, as our assessment makes clear, several of them are on the right course. Furthermore, institutionalized to a greater or lesser degree, the openness of the domestic financial markets is a longstanding phenomenon in the Argentine economy. It is probably irreversible and it greatly circumscribes the nature of any possible regulations.

In this sense any discussion concerning the sequence of the structural reforms, which may be important for financially repressed economies, is irrelevant in the Argentine case. On the other hand, two central issues arise with respect to the relationship between the macroeconomic context and the financial markets.

One is that the marked fragility of the financial system requires well-coordinated and consistent macroeconomic policies. In this sense, the main question facing the Convertibility Plan is how to resolve the existing relative price problems without exerting destabilizing pressures on the financial system. The unfavorable impact of the announcements of a commercial policy intended to improve the effective exchange rate on private sector expectations, which in November of last year unleashed the plan's first run, is a clear indication of how complex this question is.

Finally, within the limited choices of regulation available, the best alternatives need to be found in order to cushion the negative effects of the macroeconomic turmoil on the financial system. As was discussed above, efficient bank supervision, the proper performance of the functions of lender of last resort on the part of the central bank, and an adequate deposit guarantee system are three vital elements for keeping the financial system's instability to a minimum.

BIBLIOGRAPHY

Ahumada, H. 1989. "Saldos monetarios reales e inflación: test de efectos asimétricos empleando técnicas de co-integración. Argentina: 1971–88." Paper presented at the Ninth Latin American Meeting of the Econometric Society, Santiago, Chile.

Baliño, T. 1990. "La crisis bancaria argentina de 1980." *Ensayos Económicos* 44. Buenos Aires: Central Bank of Argentina.

Blejer, M. I. and B. Sagari. 1988. "El orden en la liberalización de los mercados financieros." *Finanzas y Desarrollo* 25 (1): 18–21.

Damill, M. and R. Frenkel. 1987. "De la apertura a la crisis financiera. Un análisis de la experiencia argentina de 1977 a 1982." *Ensayos Económicos* 37. Buenos Aires: Central Bank of Argentina.

Dreizzen, J. 1985. *Fragilidad financiera e inflación*. Buenos Aires: Centro de Estudios de Estado y Sociedad (CEDES).

Fanelli, J. M., R. Frenkel and G. Rozenwurcel. 1990. *Growth and Structural Reform in Latin America. Where We Stand.* Document CEDES/57. Buenos Aires: United Nations Conference on Trade and Development.

———. 1992. *Transformación estructural, estabilización y reforma del Estado en Argentina.* Document CEDES/82. Buenos Aires.

Feldman, E. and J. F. Sommer. 1984. "Crisis Financiera y Endeudamiento Externo." Buenos Aires: Centro de Estudios Transnacionales.

Fernández, R. 1983. "La Crisis Financiera Argentina, 1980–82." *Desarrollo Económico* 23 (89): 79–97.

Frenkel, R. 1983. "La apertura financiera externa: el caso argentino." In *Relaciones financieras externas y su impacto en las economías latinoamericanas,* ed. Ricardo Ffrench-Davis. Mexico City: Fondo de Cultura Económica.

Giorgio, L. 1980. "El sistema financiero argentino y la financiación del crecimiento." Buenos Aires. Mimeo.

———. 1988. "El sistema financiero argentino. Evolución y estructura actual." *Monetaria* 11 (1): 15–47.

Machinea, J. L. 1990. "Reformas estructurales en el sector financiero." Buenos Aires. Mimeo.

McKinnon, R. I. 1989. "Financial Liberalization and Economic Development: A Reassessment of Interest-Rate Policies in Asia and Latin America." *Oxford Review of Economic Policy* 6 (4): 29–54.

———. 1991. *The Order of Economic Liberalization. Financial Control in the Transition to a Market Economy.* Baltimore and London: The Johns Hopkins University Press.

The World Bank. 1989. *Informe sobre el desarrollo mundial 1989. Los sistemas financieros y el desarrollo.* Washington, D.C.: The World Bank.

Zahler, R. 1988. *Estrategias financieras latinoamericanas: la experiencia del Cono Sur.* Colección Estudios CIEPLAN No. 23. Santiago.

CHAPTER THREE

BRAZIL

Dionísio Dias Carneiro, Rogério L. Furquim Werneck,
Márcio Gomes Pinto Garcia, and Marco Antônio Bonomo[1]

Structure of the Brazilian Financial System

Principal Characteristics

The debate over the possibilities of rational macroeconomic stabilization in Brazil is taking place in the context of a traditional tolerance toward inflation. This tolerance stems from a tendency to accommodate contradictory and incompatible national demands. It also derives from the relative success of several institutional mechanisms designed to minimize the potential harm that inflation could cause the economy. In the long run, those anti-inflation mechanisms have enabled a surprisingly diversified and structurally interconnected industrial economy to function in spite of megainflation that would have otherwise been ruinous.

A highly sophisticated financial system helps to keep the economy running by satisfying the monetary needs of companies and individuals through the floating of securities which function as quasi-substitutes for money and represent the system's main borrowing. The financial system also, through a very wide spread between its lending and borrowing rates, carries out its traditional task of reviewing and selecting risks among the potential borrowers and channeling short-term savings toward those borrowers so that they can satisfy their financial needs.

The financial sector reform policy was designed and implemented as part of the earlier stabilization efforts in the mid-seventies. Its main objectives were to find noninflationary means of financing the government's shortfall and to spur private saving, even in a context of chronic inflation. One important element of this reform policy was a package of laws including Law 4.595/64, which created

[1] The coordinators of this project would like to thank Pedro Bodin de Moraes for the valuable discussions and comments about a draft of this study, and to Marcelo de Albuquerque e Mello, Monica Tavares Pinto Baumgarten, Ana Christina Adrião Rodrigues, Gustavo Monteiro de Athayde, Cristiano Ribeiro Moura, Ruy Monteiro Ribeiro, Delano Octávio Jorge Franco, and Guilherme Ribenboim for their fine work as research assistants.

the central bank, and the Banking Law 4.728/65, known as the Capital Markets Law.

Institutional Structure

The financial reforms of 1964 and 1965 adopted a system based on specialized financial institutions. The recently created central bank (BACEN) took over most of the functions of a monetary authority performed theretofore by SUMOC (the former Superintendency of Money and Credit) and the Banco do Brasil. The regulatory role of the SUMOC board was taken over by the National Monetary Council, while the Banco do Brasil became a commercial bank, thus withdrawing from its previous functions of financing government expenditure, managing international reserves, and discounting bank loans in cases of illiquidity.

Under the law, the commercial banks would be limited from that time forward to short-term credit transactions backed by sight deposits. The financing companies (*financeiras*) would turn their attention primarily to consumer and personal credit, at a time when expanding output and the sale of durable consumer goods were the driving force of industrialization. Until the reform, the financing companies had been actively lending to consumers; they had become the chief source of these funds while successfully eluding the usury law, which set a legal ceiling of 12 percent per year on the (nominal) interest rate of bank loans. For their part, the investment banks would be the basic institutions charged with (1) creating a long-term capital market capable of handling term deposits and receiving loans from abroad; (2) establishing and administering financial packages in support of long-term projects; and (3) underwriting operations with guarantees. The mutuals and similar institutions overseen by the National Housing Bank (BNH) could offer mortgages and issue indexed savings passbooks. (BNH could act as second-line provider of funds for the system by making use of the obligatory savings fund, FGTS, constituted by the 8 percent monthly payroll tax on each employer and originally designed to finance temporary unemployment and to administer additional retirement funds).

The Capital Markets Law established a rather segmented financial market. In practice, however, the system that finally emerged from that reform was much less segmented than what might have been expected from such a diversity of financial institutions. Several institutions belonging to the same conglomerate were able to operate boards, making use of the same physical and logistical structures, but each with its own individual accounting, in order to comply with the legal requirements.

Another result of the financial reform of the mid-seventies was the emergence of a large number of nonmonetary credit institutions, that is to say, institutions whose borrowings did not consist of traditional forms of payment. The total borrowing of those institutions grew 170 percent in real terms between

1973 and 1978 alone, i.e., 22 percent per annum. This rise in the number of non-monetary intermediaries could be interpreted as an effect of the substitution of nonmonetary assets for monetary assets in the private sector portfolio. The non-monetary institutions' growing share in the total supply of credit since the seventies shows that the financial reforms succeeded in transforming a system based principally on commercial banks into one based on a range of specialized institutions.

Figure 3.1 shows the course of monetary aggregates since the early seventies. The effect of rising inflation is clearly discernible until March 1986. M1 falls constantly in real terms (it falls even more in per capita terms or per unit of GDP). Meanwhile, the other monetary aggregates, which include nonmonetary assets,[2] rose with inflation (the substitution of nonmonetary assets for monetary assets is examined below, in the monetary policy management discussion). In 1986 low inflation following the first Cruzado Plan brought a temporary remonetization of the economy. Several plans followed but did not succeed in remonetizing the economy as had the first Cruzado Plan (probably because few thought that those plans would lower inflation permanently). On March 15, 1990, the recently inaugurated President Collor froze most monetary and nonmonetary assets. Figure 3.1 shows that demand has been fairly firm since then.

In June 1988 the central bank introduced a unified accounting plan for all financial institutions—COSIF—by means of which all the different financial institutions of that conglomerate were unified. In September of that same year, the Accounting Plan of the Institutions of the National Financial System (Plano Contábil das Instituições do Sistema Financeiro Nacional) approved resolution 1.524, which created the so-called "multiple" bank, the most important change in banking law since the mid-seventies. With this measure the failure of the previous reforms' attempt to create a segmented financial system was finally admitted. Under the new regulations, a "multiple" bank is defined as a financial institution that operates with at least two and no more than four departments corresponding to the basic function of two to four of the previous segmented financial institutions: commercial bank, investment bank, finance company, mutual company, and development bank. The other important step in deregulating resolution 1.524 was to stop restricting the number of licenses available for the establishment of financial institutions (this license was called *carta patente* or patent letter). Those patent letters had been the object of a lucrative trade between financial interests. At present, any legally qualified group (i.e., possessing a minimum amount of capital, honest and competent management, etc.) may establish a financial institution.

---

2 M2 is M1 plus federal bonds and notes; M3 is M2 plus savings deposits and M4 is M3 plus term deposits.

Figure 3.1. Monetary Aggregates in Brazil, 1971-93
(Billions of March 1986 dollars)

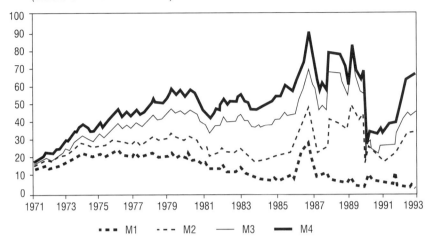

There are currently 171 multiple banks with commercial portfolios. Of another 41 commercial banks, six have already applied for multiple bank status.

Table 3.1 shows the development of the Brazilian financial sector in the wake of the reform from 1988 until June 1992. The conversion of several financial institutions into multiple banks is reflected in the first part of the table. However, it should also be noted that the multiple banks are listed more than once, as they appear in the various categories of financial institutions. The last line shows the number of multiple banks corrected for duplicate listing.

Size and Concentration

At year-end 1991, total assets of independent commercial and investment banks stood at around $200 billion, a figure slightly below 50 percent of GDP. Loans dependent on amortization accounted for about half that amount. According to the last official results of the 1980 census, there were 638,000 workers in the banking industry. It is estimated that at the beginning of the eighties the "output" of the financial sector grew at a rate of seven percent a year, rising from eight percent of GDP in 1980 to 14 percent in 1987. In that period, employment in the financial system almost doubled.[3]

Banco do Brasil is the largest bank, with a total of $57 billion in assets. Table 3.2 shows the market share of the 17 largest commercial banks and of the

---

[3] Bodin de Moraes (1993)

Table 3.1. Evolution of the Brazilian Financial Sector, 1988 until June 1992
(Number of institutions)

	1988	1989	1990	1991	1992
Banks with commercial departments					
— Commercial banks	106	66	50	45	42
— Multiple banks	0	99	148	159	165
Total	106	165	198	204	207
Banks with an investment department					
— Investment banks	56	36	23	21	21
— Multiple banks	0	62	89	94	95
Total	56	98	112	115	116
Banks with a finance department					
— Finance companies	107	70	51	45	45
— Multiple banks	0	89	132	144	147
Total	107	159	183	189	192
Banks with a savings and loan department					
— Savings and loan	57	42	29	25	25
— Multiple banks	0	54	71	74	77
Total	57	96	100	99	102
Banks with a development department					
— Development banks	13	12	10	9	9
— Multiple banks	0	2	5	5	9
Total	13	14	15	14	18
Others					
— Credit cooperatives	661	767	806	831	831
— Savings banks	5	5	3	2	2
— Distribuidoras[1]	447	419	395	386	376
— Brokerage houses	273	282	258	273	274
— Total Multiple banks (493 portfolios)	0	113	166	180	188

Source: Central Bank.
[1] A distribuidora is a brokerage house that does not have a seat on an official exchange.

multiple banking system, based on the total value of its lending in 1991. The two largest banks—Banco do Brasil and Caixa Econômica Federal (CEF), both owned by the federal government—account for 55.9 percent of total loans. The volume of their combined loans is approximately 13 times larger than those of the largest private bank (BRADESCO). Even so, the sum of their deposits is only 4.3 times that of BRADESCO's. In any case, CEF has about $30 billion in total assets and focuses its activities on mortgage loans backed by savings account passbooks. It also administers the FGTS (the workers' retirement fund) and finances the outlays of local governments.

Table 3.2. Brazil: 17 Commercial and Multiple Banks: Market Share, 1991

Bank	Market share (%) Loans	Loans (Millions of US$)	Market share (%) Deposits	Total deposits (Millions of US$)	Ownership	Bank Type
CEF	34.5	20,096.3	25.90	12,861.10	State	Commercial
BRASIL	21.4	12,475.4	13.40	6,655.90	State	Commercial
BANESPA	10.4	6,082.0	6.70	3,339.50	State	Multiple
BRADESCO	4.3	2,506.9	9.10	4,517.40	Brazilian	Multiple
ITAU	3.6	2,070.7	5.70	2,826.40	Brazilian	Multiple
UNIBANCO	2.4	1,390.4	2.60	1,274.50	Brazilian	Multiple
ECONOMICO	2.2	1,269.5	2.40	1,184.40	Brazilian	Multiple
NACIONAL	2.2	1,269.3	2.70	1,333.30	Brazilian	Multiple
BAMERINDUS	1.8	1,055.3	4.10	2,038.80	Brazilian	Multiple
BFB	1.3	747.3	1.20	578.20	French	Multiple
BANFSTADO	1.0	593.8	0.60	304.20	State	Multiple
SAFRA	0.7	424.0	1.80	874.00	Brazilian	Multiple
LLOYDS	0.7	396.5	1.10	536.30	British	Commercial
MERIDIONAL	0.7	394.0	0.60	306.10	State	Multiple
SUDAMERIS	0.7	391.6	1.00	477.90	French	Multiple
CITIBANK	0.6	375.0	0.90	443.20	U.S.	Commercial
REAL	0.6	366.7	1.40	703.10	Brazilian	Commercial
Total	89.1		81.20			
Average		3,053.2		2,367.90		

Sources: Fonseca (1992) and Boletín do Banco Central (September 1992).

A sizable part of the private banking system's deposits is currently channeled into financing the public financial debt and not into loans. For example, BRADESCO, the main provider of credit to consumers, needs only half of its deposits to back its loans; the other half corresponds approximately to state bonds or to other securities guaranteed by the government.

For a more complete understanding of the structure of market shares, at least two additional factors must be taken into account. The first concerns the impact of inflation on the concentration of the banking industry. The results of a recent study (Silva, 1989) point to a positive correlation between inflation and concentration. The study suggests the existence of economies of scale that can be important in the provision of retail credit services, which normally arise from the competition to profit from the inflation tax. When they provide appropriate banking services at "cheap" nominal rates, the banking networks can appropriate a substantial part of the inflation tax. In the first half of the eighties, with three-digit inflation and reasonably stable ground rules, the number of banking offices grew by over 35 percent. However, some of this increase in the number of offices was not productive, since branches are often overstaffed and incur excessive costs.[4]

_____

4 See Bodin de Moraes (1993) and Vasconcelos and Ogasawara (1992).

Although the econometric evidence of Silva (1989) corroborates the importance of inflation and economies of scale in the process of concentration of the Brazilian bank system,[5] a second important consideration has been the federal policy of promoting bank mergers and acquisitions. After the traumatic closing of the third largest private bank, as soon as the central bank noticed that a bank was in danger of going bankrupt, it would approach a solvent institution so that the latter could bail out the troubled bank under the supervision—and often with the financial support of—the issuing institution.

How important is the size of banks for the profitability of the banking system in the Brazilian economy? As is suggested below, the relationship between size and profitability depends on other factors.

Ownership Structure

In October 1992, 30 of a total of 215 banks were public (4 federally owned and 26 state-owned); the remaining 185 were private property. Table A.1 of the annex lists 174 banks and Table A.2 lists the remaining 41 commercial banks.

The existence of a large public segment within an essentially private banking system is an important feature of the Brazilian financial system. Further on we shall see how this feature affects the sector's performance.

Borrowing and Lending Rates: Average Spread

Bank credit in Brazil has traditionally been highly regulated, with several different rates based on the purposes of the loan. Many of those rates are subsidized, either directly by government funds—for example, through the credit provided by the National Bank for Economic and Social Development (BNDES)—or through regulations requiring the banks to supply a given amount of credit for specific activities (such as farm credit). Long-term credit for fixed investments is granted almost exclusively through BNDES, whose funds come from an obligatory savings fund for Brazilian workers (FAT, formerly PIS/PASEP). The tables of the annex show the history of loans dependent on amortization since the seventies, by type of financial institution.

Figure 3.2 shows the series of rates for deposits (rates for unindexed certificates of deposit) and rates for loans (commercial discount rates), as well as the spread between the two. Both interest rates have followed the inflationary path, and the spread, though highly volatile, has tended to be high, with both the mean and the variance rising with inflation. Table 3.3 shows the standard averages and

---

5 The Herfindahl index for sight deposits in private commercial banks, for example, rose from 0.0219 in 1971 to 0.1414 in 1986.

**Figure 3.2. Lending Rates (Commercial Discount Rates) versus Deposit Rates
(Nonindexed Certificate of Deposit Rates) in Brazil, 1973-92**
(Monthly percentages)

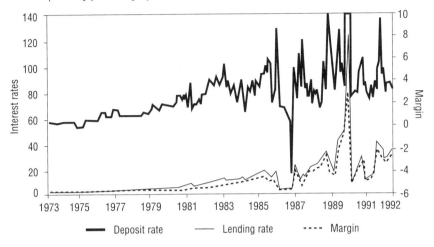

deviations of the series analyzed during three periods: the "low inflation" period
(1973–79), the period of high inflation without economic shocks (1980–85), and
the period of high inflation with economic shocks (after 1985; the Cruzado Plan
was launched in February 1986). The numbers in Table 3.3 corroborate the interpretation of Figure 3.2, showing clearly that in the post-Cruzado era not only did
the average spread grow but its variability became much greater. This result is
consistent with the well-known analysis of the mean and the variance: the economic shocks placed the Brazilian economy in a much riskier yet potentially
more profitable context.

These results are independent of the various lending rates examined and of
whether or not the deposit rate was price indexed. Unfortunately there are no
data that relate volumes and rates; our efforts to reconstruct that set of data have
not been successful.

Behavior of the Financial System

Since Bresciani-Turroni's study (1937) of German hyperinflation, it has been
known that banks are a profitable business in a high inflation environment. The
growth of the Brazilian financial industry in the eighties underscores this fact.
(The peculiarity of the Brazilian experience resides in the fact that inflation may
have proved a bit too good even for the banks. Thus, as suggested by the
increased risk due to spread variance, examined in the previous section, although

Table 3.3. Mean and Variance of Interest Rates (Monthly Percentages) in Brazil in the Seventies and Eighties

	Rates of certificates of deposit	Discount rates	Spread[1]
Mean pre-1980	2.62	3.54	1.00
Mean 1980–85	7.53	11.06	3.27
Mean post-1985	18.51	24.60	4.76
Standard deviation pre-1980	0.64	1.12	0.52
Standard deviation 1980–85	2.78	3.44	1.00
Standard deviation post-1985	14.06	20.59	5.07

[1] The spread was calculated with the correct use of the arithmetic of compound interest. This is the reason why the mean of the spread does not equal the difference between the mean discount rate and the mean certificate of deposit.

the demand for banking services increased with inflation, not only did the demand for loans fall but loan quality declined at many moments of high volatility in the inflation rate during the eighties.)

As lending dwindled from the mid-seventies to the eighties, financial mediation came more and more from the sale of indexed financial assets backed by government bonds. Through formal or informal buyback accords (the same which had existed since the early seventies as part of the central bank's effort to "create a market for the government's debt"), the financial institutions created short-term deposits with almost immediate overnight liquidity and bought long-term state bonds. That change of maturities carried out by several institutions (not necessarily banks) proved to be a source of profits that are only partially reflected in the banking system's balance sheets. The next section analyzes the factors on which the banks' overall profitability depends.

Profitability and Efficiency

As previously indicated, the competition to provide bank services could be a source of inefficiency (for instance, by causing too many offices to open). Vasconcelos and Ogasawara (1992) find that staff costs as a percentage of total assets in the commercial banking sector were very high compared to international standards. They were fluctuating between three and seven percent for the larger banks, although pay scales are most likely lower and automation is certainly high, compared with the same international standards. This fact illustrates the difficulties of making an overall evaluation of how efficient the banking industry is in Brazil, for the net result of banking companies in such a complex financial setting depends on the specific mix of services provided by the bank and on various strategies that determine its leverage, its profit margins, and the turnover of its loans.

Breaking down the net profits of the financial system's core yields useful insight into the factors that determine them. Using the data analyzed by Fonseca (1992), the net profit of the 16 largest commercial and multiple banks (excluding CEF) were separated, based on the following equation:

$$UN/P = (UN/IIF) (IIF/AT) (AT/P)$$

where

UN	=	net profit
P	=	net worth
IIF	=	revenues through financial intermediation
AT	=	total assets
and		
UN/P	=	net profit rate
UN/IIF	=	net margin
IIF/AT	=	turnover ratio
AT/P	=	leverage ratio

The net profit rate is determined jointly by the net margin, the turnover ratio, and the leverage ratio. The results of this breakdown, based on 1991 data, are presented in Table 3.4, which also gives the UN/AT ratio.

The great leverage capacity of the Banco do Brasil and BANESPA may be overvalued by virtue of an underestimation of the value of their assets. This is especially true for the Banco do Brasil because of its role in financing agriculture. This is due to its typical pattern of guarantees, which traditionally entails a higher level of sunk cost than is shown on its balance sheet. The Banco do Brasil also shows a rather low (3.2 percent) turnover ratio compared with other major commercial banks (10 to 20 percent), which is partly offset by a higher leverage ratio. The largest commercial banks, in the same table, also have lower leverage ratios but high spreads, reflecting the low costs of their deposits, due to gains from the inflation tax paid by their depositors. The latter are typically retail banks. For those banks, which operate with similar turnover ratios, the profitability rate depends directly on their net operating margins and hence on their specific market strategy to reap benefits from inflation. An obvious exception in this sample of major banks is SAFRA, which shows the highest net margin with very high turnover, about twice the average for the sample.

Credit Supply and Anti-inflation Mechanisms

In Brazil, public financial institutions have for many years been providers of long-term credit. The most important one in this respect is the National

Table 3.4. Breakdown of the Profitability Rate, 1991, for the 16 Largest Multiple and Commercial Banks in Brazil
(Ratios)

Bank	UN/IIF	IIF/TA	TA/P	UN/P	UN/TA
BRASIL	0.1395	0.0324	11.9477	0.0540	0.0045
BANESPA	0.0588	0.1607	9.4017	0.0889	0.0095
BRADESCO	0.1407	0.1237	4.6047	0.0802	0.0174
ITAU	0.1762	0.1097	4.7889	0.0926	0.0193
UNIBANCO	0.1120	0.1123	7.0976	0.0892	0.0126
ECONOMICO	0.0568	0.1750	7.8215	0.0778	0.0099
NACIONAL	0.0539	0.1690	10.6250	0.0967	0.0091
BAMERINDUS	0.0338	0.1862	8.4283	0.0531	0.0063
BFB	0.0087	0.1624	10.4248	0.0147	0.0014
BANESTADO	0.0928	0.2470	7.3501	0.1684	0.0229
SAFRA	0.0610	0.4978	7.7651	0.2359	0.0304
LLOYDS	0.0005	0.6306	14.8871	0.0043	0.0003
MERIDIONAL	0.0249	0.5585	4.1668	0.0579	0.0139
SUDAMERIS	0.0176	0.1877	9.0167	0.0298	0.0033
CITIBANK	0.0002	0.4386	14.1773	0.0014	0.0001
REAL	0.0664	0.1486	8.1779	0.0807	0.0099
Average	0.0652	0.2463	8.7926	0.0766	0.0107

Source: Fonseca (1992).

Development Bank, with assets totaling about $20.8 billion as of December 1991 and about $13 billion in outstanding loans, creating an annual flow of about $4.5 billion. Its funds are generated basically by forced saving contributions (FAT, formerly PIS-PASEP) derived from the 0.65 percent of the federal sales tax, 40 percent of which must be used to back BNDES loans.

Mortgage credit has been severely limited since the closing of BNH (National Housing Bank) in 1986. Its chief source is the FGTS (derived from the 8 percent payroll tax). Loans funded by the FGTS in 1991 totaled about $24.6 billion. The insurance companies constitute a lesser long-term funding source, since high inflation and instability have caused a low insurance premium ratio with respect to GDP (about 3 percent), with life insurance premiums even lower.

Pension funds are a relatively new segment of the financial industry and their assets have been estimated at $18.2 billion (barely 4 percent of GDP compared with 50 percent in the United States). New stock issues have played a very small part in funding investment: the total value of shares traded on the Rio and São Paulo stock exchanges represent less than 10 percent of GDP. Table A.18 of the annex presents estimated figures on the flow of funds for certain years, so that both the chief funding sources and their performance in the eighties can be evaluated.

Figure 3.3. Total Financial Sector Lending to the Private Sector in Brazil, 1974-92 *(Percentage of GDP)*

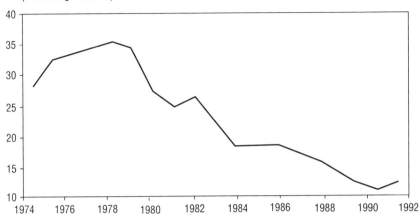

The banking sector, both private and state, has been the chief provider of short-term loans in the economy. Figure 3.3 shows the total value movement of the financial system's loans to the nonfinancial private sector since the mid-seventies, as a percentage of GDP. An increase sustained until 1978 as a consequence of the first wave of financial innovations generated by the reforms of the mid-sixties was followed by a long cyclical decline reflecting a drop in the number of loans. This number fell from its peak, 35 percent of GDP, to 11 percent in 1991. The phenomenon illustrates how the shrinking of credit activity in the financial sector across the board affected banks and nonbanks both public and private, as shown in Table A.16.

The two main reasons for this phenomenon are, of course, linked to rising inflation, which increases risk to both borrowers and lenders. The conversion of the banking system from credit provider to issuer of money-substitute instruments has therefore been an essential part of the surge in financial activity during the eighties, when the economy was traveling the road of high inflation. Controlling such a system—and its contribution to the mechanisms, apparently rooted in the Brazilian economy, whereby inflation perpetuates itself—is a controversial concept, hard for nonspecialists in that field to understand. Nevertheless, the next subsection will attempt a brief description of the principal difficulties. The same topic will be revisited in the section examining the role of the financial system within the country's macroeconomic relationships.

Regulation and Supervision of the Financial System

The central bank is the Brazilian financial system's main regulatory authority. It acts under the rules established by the CMN. It regulates all types of financial institutions, even ROSCAs (mutuals or savings and revolving credit societies) established for the purchase of durable consumer goods.

The securities exchange market is regulated by the CVM (Securities Commission), an agency designed to be the Brazilian equivalent of the U.S. Securities and Exchange Commission (SEC). The insurance institutions are supervised and regulated by SUSEP (Superintendency of Private Insurance) and by the IRBs (Reinsurance Institutes of Brazil).

Monetary Policy: Open Market Operations, Rediscounts and Legal Reserve Requirements

In Brazil, monetary policy is carried out mainly through open market operations. Rediscounts (discounted loans) are very costly and are used only as a last resort. Reserve requirements are kept fixed, except in special circumstances.

Trading in state securities on the open market is carried out through the central bank's transactions board. The bank also holds formal auctions of public debt papers every Tuesday. Central bank bonds (BBCs) are the most liquid instruments and the principal market instrument for reserves. These are discount bonds with a maturity of four to six weeks. Existing bonds are worth around $25 billion, of which about $4 billion's worth belong to state companies, about $5 billion to funds managed by the banking system, and $16 billion to financial institutions, backed by their own capital or by term deposits, or financed by very short-term deposits, including interfinancial deposits with almost immediate liquidity (overnight).

A very controversial aspect of the Brazilian monetary system is the inflationary role of the buyback agreements signed by the central bank in relation to the sale of government securities. Many economists feel that these buyback agreements are the leading cause of persistent inflation and ascribe little importance to the country's fiscal imbalance. This question is still moot in Brazil, and the various points of view concerning it could have profound consequences in the next attempt at stabilization, which will necessarily take place in an uncertain future.

The impact of daily fluctuations of supply and demand for money on bank reserves in the Brazilian economy is enormous compared to what it would be in a country with low inflation. This phenomenon is due to Brazil's small money supply caused by very high inflation. To make these fluctuations acceptable to the banks, the central bank holds daily informal auctions, called go-arounds, to soak up the excess demand or supply of bank reserves. When the central bank draws excess reserves out of the market, it does so by selling state securities under buyback agreements. The buyback agreements are necessary because the existence of available reserves is very costly to the banks. If the banks had to hold state securities to maturity and the central bank did not introduce (cheap) liquidity into the system, the banks would have to maintain a much higher volume of available reserves or go to the discount windows more often. However, both alternatives would be too costly for them. In the end, cash management has become the Brazilian banking system's main activity. The actual consequences of the buyback agreement scheme will be discussed in the section on macrofinancial relations.

It is open to discussion whether an alternative monetary regime without the extensive use of buyback agreements would be viable. If such an alternative system became very costly for the banks, a possible effect of the disappearance of this "indexed money" (the holding of securities overnight with a buyback guarantee) is that the banking system would cease to provide money substitutes, thus paving the way for capital flight. In other words, indexed money might be a necessary condition for the economy to be able to meet the demand for national financial assets in the context of very high and volatile inflation.

With respect to the use of discount windows as a monetary policy instrument, Brazil has experimented with two different systems. Until 1985 the banks used to resort to the discount windows very often. Prior to this period, the discount rates were set by underestimating market interest rates in a period of escalating inflation. In 1985, the discount rates began to follow the daily interest rate in the marketplace, with a penalty margin. Since then, because of the substantial increase in the cost of loans, the discount window has been used only in extreme situations. The banks' reluctance to use it also derives from the fact that the central bank applies the "Rieffler Doctrine," automatically sending a supervisory team to all the banks that use the window. At present, the banks have an active interbank market which provides cash to most of the solvent institutions.

All the sight deposits, including the "floating" bank deposit (checks that are being processed) are subject to a reserve requirement. Currently there is no legal reserve requirement for term deposits. The rates vary by region of the country and in accordance with the size of bank loan transactions. Recently (February 1993) the differences between them have diminished and the average rate has increased. The highest reserve requirement is 50 percent.

The Brazilian central bank practices a deferred reserve requirement system, which also has recently been modified. The current deferred reserve requirement system undermines the effectiveness of monetary control. Market conditions prevailing at the time the banks have to maintain their mandatory reserves are often different from those prevailing when the reserve requirement was fixed. This lag tends to make interest rates more volatile. A simultaneous reserve system like the one in the United States would improve the central bank's control over the money supply.

Composition of Commercial Bank Assets

Most of the recent problems in the banking sector occurred in the state banks or in the state savings banks, because the central bank lacks *effective* authority to close down (technically) bankrupt state institutions. Both the last president of the central bank, in his farewell speech in October 1992, and his successor stressed the lack of authority over state institutions as the most important problem the new government had to face.

Table A.17 illustrates the problem. This list contains all the central bank's official interventions in the banking sector since 1986. Of the 23 actions taken since 1986, 19 were in state banks.

The problems in the state banks began in 1982, when the banks were used irresponsibly to finance the election costs of the state governments. Since then, those institutions have been routinely used as sources of funds for the respective states and municipalities. This practice is possible thanks to a convenient vacuum in banking law.

National Monetary Council Resolution 1.088 limits the leverage of most of the banks. The regular banks (i.e., the nonstate banks) may not keep more than 10 times their net worth in state and municipal bonds. The central bank is currently attempting to fill that vacuum.

When government and municipal securities look less attractive, the central bank is called upon to bail out the state banks. The usual way in which this has been done is by swapping the state banks' state and municipal debt for federal debt of equal nominal value (and much greater real value). In this way the state banks, by avoiding the rules governing all the other banks, have virtually become local central banks, able to act as quasi-banks of issue.

The state banks have greatly exceeded the limit, through risk diversification, set by the central bank, which established a ceiling of 30 percent of the bank's net worth on the amount granted to any one customer, whether as a loan or as collateral. The same ceiling applies to underwriting. In order to prevent manipulation of accounts, the rules prohibit the refinancing of bad loans. But, as previously noted, the state banks need not comply with those rules when purchasing local state or municipal bonds. It is therefore not surprising that nowadays the banking sector's biggest problems are found in the state banks.

Table 3.5 shows the level of the state banks' loans to state companies and governments. In the years mentioned in the table, the state banks earmarked two-thirds of their lending to finance state enterprises and state governments. As a result, those banks are highly exposed to risk from all points of view. The best estimate of the state banks' total adjusted net worth is approximately $2 billion.

Without effective control over the state banks, any attempt at stabilization is doomed to failure. Recent experiences have demonstrated that those

Table 3.5. Brazil: State Bank Loans to the State Governments, June 1988–Dec. 1990
(Millions of Cr$)

	(1)	(2)	(3)	(4)	(1)/(2) %	(3)/(1) %	(4)/(1) %	(4)/(2) %
June 88	2,565.5	3,745	1,443.4	1,634	68.5	56.3	63.7	43.6
Dec. 88	9,031.5	13,224	5,771.2	6,517	68.3	63.9	72.2	49.3
June 89	23,148.0	37,245	14,764.2	16,728	62.2	63.8	72.3	44.9
Dec. 89	162,279.0	267,767	102,161.0	115,728	60.6	63.0	71.3	43.2
June 90	1,205,868.0	2,268,484	639,853.0	721,582	53.2	53.1	59.8	31.8
Dec. 90	2,573,922.0	4,459,669	1,497,973.0	1,663,328	57.7	58.2	64.6	37.3

(1) Total state bank loans.
(2) Total state bank assets.
(3) Total state bank loans to state governments.
(4) Total state bank loans to state enterprises and state governments.
Source: Andrade (1992).

banks can act as central mini-banks, with actual power to cover state and municipal deficits. We shall return to this point in the section on policy recommendations.

No serious bad loan problem exists in the private banking system as a whole. Most of the loan problems are primarily with mortgage loans in the hands of the private banks, and have resulted from government subsidies, not from nonperformance on the part of debtors. The total value of these credits is guaranteed by the federal government. A reasonably reliable estimate of government obligations under this heading would be roughly $20 billion.

Deposit Insurance and Monetary Controls

Brazil does not have an official deposit insurance system. The central bank is obligated by law to guarantee all savings passbooks. It has also been the case in practice that when the central bank intervenes or closes down a bank, all sight deposits are also guaranteed. This guarantee does not apply to term deposits, which are paid with the remaining assets, after the sight deposits are reimbursed.

As mentioned previously, the central bank intervenes every day to provide the banks with liquidity. Several monetary regimes have been tried, but one feature common to all has been that the central bank always supplies the liquidity necessary for the system. A natural consequence of this type of behavior is a lack of control over the economic aggregates.

In the past there was a great deal of debate in Brazil about the pros and cons of setting up a deposit insurance scheme. The Constitution of 1988 called for the creation of such a system and resolution CMN 1.524, which created the multiple bank system, conditions the creation of a multiple bank on the bank's obligation to adhere to the deposit insurance system when that system is set up.

The debate about the desirability of insuring deposits revolves around the same points already discussed in other countries. This debate measures the benefits of providing the financial sector with stability against the costs on account of moral risks entailed.

The idiosyncrasy of the Brazilian case is that the state banks do not wish to pay any insurance premium on the deposits, because they believe that simply by virtue of being public institutions they cannot go under. Naturally, the private banks do not want to take on the comparative disadvantage of having to support all the costs of the deposit insurance fund. Consequently, the fund has yet to materialize.

The Financial Sector and Macrofinancial Relations

The development of the Brazilian financial system in the last 20 years has, in many respects, followed the evolution of the Brazilian economy's inflationary process. The institutional reforms of the early seventies, and the more recent trends in bank regulations and the choice of monetary policy instruments, all occurred against the background of a political reaction to what seemed to be the chief causes of inflation. The rise and fall of institutions, the development of financial instruments, and the organizational principles of the financial industry (bank size, number of institutions, concentration, and operating strategies) constitute, in different degrees, responses to the inflationary context and the stabilization policies.

This section examines the consequences of the current institutional agreement, with special emphasis on the impact that thwarted attempts at stabilization have had on the development of the financial system. Also presented are some conclusions concerning certain topics that are important from the political economy standpoint, in the context of a new kind of financial repression that seems to have grown out of the singular Brazilian response to the country's high and persistent inflation.

High Inflation and the Financial System

High inflation is attractive but potentially destructive to the financial market. High and unstable rates make it impossible to determine an interest rate capable of matching the supply and demand for loans, because the risk premium required to offset future interest rates becomes prohibitive. The combination of aversion to risk with growing and unpredictable inflation has the effect of shortening the terms of contracts and thus makes some of them irrelevant. The monetary correction introduced in the sixties—initially used to adjust the nominal values of tax debts and thus curb the incentive to postpone tax payments, and then to revise the nominal values of mortgage loans and the main funds backing them, namely savings passbooks—gradually turned into an apparent panacea, when a widespread trend promoting contract indexation emerged. This movement was certainly useful for letting the economy continue functioning in the presence of high inflation. A large number of financial innovations, contracts, and practices developed around the idea that "appropriate" indexation would fulfill the function of compensating risk-averse investors and debtors for the high risks associated with high inflation.

As noted earlier, the index-based approach gained on practically all fronts and led to a fantastic growth in all aspects of financial intermediation services (number of institutions and offices, employment in the financial sector, etc.). It also led to far more sophisticated transactions, as manifested in a wave of financial innovations in the credit and money markets.

As we will see further on, a clear line of demarcation exists between the basic survival and adaptation of financial institutions under conditions of chronic inflation and the role of those survival mechanisms in the transition period to what might be called "mega-inflation:" a high and unstable inflationary environment in which the potential volatility of the monthly rate leads to the conviction that the ground rules can be changed, in the context of attempts to put an end to the high rate of inflation, through price freezes by other mechanisms of coordination.

Public Debt and Money Substitutes

The current financial system was shaped in a context of strong and disruptive inflation, together with no less unsettling stabilization policies. An interest rate which in 20 years rose from 20 percent per year to more than 20 percent per month wrought profound changes in the country's financial institutions. Rules and methods were developed through which the financial system made a permanent evolutionary adaptation to the environment.

One prominent feature of this change must already be obvious: the association that developed between the government and the financial system to provide money substitutes, thus averting the degeneration of megainflation into outright hyperinflation and preventing capital flight, which has occurred in most countries with a similar inflationary experience.

This association began with the strategic decision, following the financial reforms of 1964 and 1965, to establish a market for state securities. That commitment was an attempt by economic policymakers to avoid the need to "resort to inflationary financing," in the words of the PAEG macroeconomic assessment (the economic plan of the 1964 military government)—that is, to resort to issuing "money" in order to finance the government shortfall.

In those years the central bank accomplished its task of furnishing money substitutes. At first it provided those substitutes directly to the "nonfinancial" public, and then indirectly, by supplying liquidity for the assets maintained as backing for private deposits in private institutions. In some cases these institutions issued indexed substitutes for sight deposits based on loans with maturities of up to 20 years. Growing economic integration took place, first between banks and nonbanks and then through the "financialization" (the growing prevalence of financial transactions) of nonbanks. In the former case, that integration gradually led to the organization of the multiple banking system. The integration of different institutions in the same financial group inevitably brought the rise of "treasury operations," or mechanisms for managing the liquidity of bank assets. Those efforts eventually became more essential to keeping the system going than the traditional provision of credit, in which the review and selection of borrowers on the basis of the creditworthiness and the borrowing of funds with similar maturities constitute the main focus.

There was a second level of integration between bank and nonbank activities through takeovers of nonbanks or through the acquisitions of partial control, with participation in holdings established to diversify the activities of the financial group.

In the financial sector, the magnitude of treasury operations led to a concentration on daily transactions involving public securities with all types of maturities. While these could be used as bank reserves they were subject to frequent transactions among banks and between the banking sector and the central bank. The central bank acted as a dealer in government bonds, thus guaranteeing their liquidity. In the seventies this became an acceptable practice of the bank, as such guarantees helped to increase the public's demand for public debt. Banks and nonbanks, as well as brokerage houses and *distribuidoras*, were interested in the opportunities they could pursue as dealers and brokers in public securities: the higher the inflation rate, the greater the spread and therefore the greater the profits to be made by arbitrage.

In the nonfinancial sector, daily cash management offered a way of eluding or at least minimizing the inflation tax. For some institutions—including the financial supermarkets, which are typically generators of cash because they sell cash and have deferred payments as part of their routine business practice—this development turned financial activity into an important source of income. With high inflation, a retailer with deferred payments can operate with a nominal negative profit margin so long as the nominal interest received on short-term deposits is enough to pay the retailer's current costs plus capital costs. The nonbanks' mix of financial and nonfinancial activities constitutes the essence of this "financialization" of various activities, a process that became widespread in the Brazilian experience with high inflation.

What this process accomplished, in macroeconomic terms, is that it prevented the phenomenon of money substitution (see Dornbusch and Giovannini, 1991) so typical of the experiences of high inflation (Argentina, Bolivia, and even Mexico, whose inflation rate was much lower), thanks to its success in furnishing "domestic substitutes" through the central bank with the help of the financial system. But the costs of this experience still have to be evaluated. It is difficult to provide a full accounting of the consequences of the economic distortions and the inefficiencies generated by the predominance of financial activity over practically any other type of activity in the economy—a predominance created by the profits to be made eluding the inflation tax.

High Inflation and Mega-inflation

The successful adaptation of the financial system to conditions of high inflation may have created significant distortions in the economy, most of them related to the manner in which activities involving cash management expanded into nonfinancial sectors. The macroeconomic interpretation of this phenomenon is as follows: to the extent that high inflation reduces the demand for money, and money substitutes are found, the inflation rate inevitably becomes more resistant to demand policies, owing to the inertia of formal contracts and the tendency of informal contracts to rely on past trends. In addition, the tendency of the monthly rate is to turn upward, driven by supply side shocks. While indexation spreads, the counterpart of these different effects (known as Fisher-Gray results) depends on the strict performance of contracts.

In other words, currency substitution, which could lead to outright hyperinflation, can be prevented, as the Brazilian experience shows, if indexed contracts—the new basis for the "anchoring of nominal values"—are respected and disseminated. Obviously, minimizing the distortions based on inflation does not mean that they could be totally eliminated. Some dangerously high levels of inflation existed in Brazil in the first half of the eighties, while annual rates rose by 40 percent in the late seventies, 100 percent from 1980–82 and 200 percent from 1983–85.

The higher the inflation rate, the more difficult it is for political as well as economic reasons to respect universal indexation rules. There are three reasons for this: (1) an atmosphere of financial fragility develops because small differences in the relative price of some debtors can cause large inconsistencies between revenue and loan repayment commitments; (2) small differences in relative incomes can be amplified excessively by different adjustment regimes (either through the frequency of adjustments in compensation and other revenues or through the degree to which the reestablishment of former peaks of real value is sought); and (3) since not all debts or credits are corrected on the basis of retroactively based indexation measures (typical indexation), the expected differences in rates can generate wide differences between the real values of indexed debts and those of discounted debts (which tend to diminish but do not disappear, for example, in the case of commercial credit between companies).

Efforts to curb inertial inflation through a sudden break with past rules, as was done in the second half of the eighties (see following section), gave rise to another element in the behavior of the economic agents, which has had a significant effect on the workings of the financial system: uncertainty as to the rules.

In the case of the Brazilian economy, this new regime further shortened the duration of financial contracts and increased the cash premium charged by the owners of wealth to stay with domestic assets instead of switching to dollars.

Transactions have not yet been dollarized in Brazil. The demand for Brazilian currency is due to the high transaction costs of maintaining dollars. It is evident that there has been some currency substitution whenever uncertainty rises with respect to the rules of the financial market. Yet the holding of foreign currency by individuals as a "means of maintaining purchasing power"—which, according to Milton Friedman, is the definition of "money"—has never replaced the holding of domestic assets, despite the dramatic changes in indexation rules over the years.

Nevertheless, as we shall see shortly in greater detail, this mega-inflation regime has other important consequences, both for the management of the financial system once its stabilization is achieved and for the demand for state bonds.

The need for buyback agreements to sustain the demand for bonds is greater when the risk that the rules may change increases. This need for buyback agreements has been recognized as a potential source of greater instability. If the central bank issues reserves in return for government bonds, deeming them perfect substitutes, the intermediaries are encouraged to behave like banks by increasing their leverage, and thus their exposure to the risk of nonperformance or illiquidity. In the mid-eighties, the mounting need for inflationary financing may have led the central bank to permit and respect the increasing leverage of nonbanks, thus complying with the mandate received in the mid-sixties to create a market for government debt. In addition, when those institutions underestimated the cost of their inactive capital, pressure was exerted for the central bank to bail out its members in the state bond market. As noted earlier, the conflicts stemming from the central bank's dual role as federal bond dealer and monetary authority have been at the center of the debate on the possibilities of an active monetary policy in Brazil. Only in the last two years has a serious attempt been made to separate the central bank completely from treasury operations, in compliance with the 1988 Constitution, which prohibits the central bank from financing the treasury.

Financial Innovations

The long experience with high inflation has left Brazil with a very sophisticated financial system. Obviously the wide-ranging activities involving cash management require expertise in arbitrage operations, since the securities (public and private) have to be traded daily on the open market as well as on the exchanges. The chance to gain capital attracts talented analysts and dealers specialized in making use of arbitrage opportunities and knowledgeable about the latest financial management techniques. Under conditions of high inflation, the opportunities for capital gains often have more weight than the profitability rate. This phenomenon is even more marked when inflation is high. And when there is a great variance in the "signal" sent by the real rates, the changes are distorted by the "interference" (i.e., by inflation's erratic, unimportant movements).

Experience in securities trading in a high inflation environment brings familiarity with sophisticated financial techniques which in one way or another become part of the know-how of managers and analysts. The techniques generated by the spillover of speculative activity into other areas are bound to generate some kind of permanent financial culture. Futures trading is an example.

According to Pacias (1990), futures trading was introduced to the market in commodities (especially coffee and livestock), which for many years was the only market in which it was used. In 1960, for example, 92 percent of the futures contracts were in grains and livestock. However, in 1983 financial contracts represented 38 percent of the contracts; apparently the outlook had already changed owing to high inflation.

The Futures and Commodities Exchange (BMF) was founded in 1986 and is today the world's sixth-largest exchange specializing in futures trading in terms of the number of contracts negotiated. In the first half of 1992 the BMF handled an average of 140,000 contracts daily, of which 50 percent covered futures of interbank deposits, these being a means of protection against interest rate fluctuations.

The sudden growth of the derivatives (options and futures) market is a product of high inflation, but the availability of those derivatives constitutes a financial innovation in the technical sense that they change the demand for securities and the way in which risk is shared in the economy. The long-term repercussions of those innovations are difficult to determine, but they will probably continue to be useful in a more financially open economy. They make it possible to offer holders of assets a broader range of risks and thus, in a more stable economy, they could help lower the costs of intermediation.

The Financial System and Unorthodox Stabilization

The Brazilian experience in the second half of the eighties shows that the relationship between high inflation and the financial system differs from the familiar norm. The difference is clearly discernible in the effects of the Brazilian attempts to bring about an unorthodox stabilization.

From the point of view of macrofinancial relations and their relevance to the design of stabilization policies, the three Cruzado plans and the two Collor Plans can be described as seeking to bring about a drastic deceleration of the inflation rate. In so doing they intruded into private contracts by changing clauses referring to the correction of monetary securities.

However, these unorthodox experiments were not the only frustrated attempts at stabilization that had significant effects on the financial system. From 1979 to 1981, the stabilization policies went from ceilings on interest rates, plus a devaluation (which resulted in a loss of credibility, as well as $3 billion in external reserves), to a liberalization of interest rates, with a ceiling on bank credit supported by domestic funds, as a desperate attempt to reverse the external flows.

The impact of these policies on the financial sector was again to further the process of concentration through the merger of a number of institutions. From 1979 to 1982 the number of brokerage houses (*corretoras* and *distribuidoras*) declined from 733 to 689. The inflation rate's jump to a new plateau—after the second oil shock and the change in the wage readjustment law—had an appreciable impact on financial activity in Brazil. By taking over a number of brokerage houses and distribuidoras, the banks became more important intermediaries. The number of bank employees rose from 269,618 in 1979 to 384,966 in 1983 and the number of offices rose from 17,000 to 24,400 in the same period, while the annual inflation rate soared from 40 percent to 200 percent and real income per capita fell about 7 percent. This expansion of the financial sector was not followed by a significant increase in the number of loans to the public. The new institutions owed their establishment not to the market but to the expansion of those already in existence. Meanwhile, the number of head offices of banks remained practically flat over 1979–85, but the number of employees of the largest private domestic bank (BRADESCO) grew by more than 50 percent from 1981 to 1984. However, after 1985 the unorthodox experiments changed the outlook for the financial industry, making explicit its exposure to the changes in the basic rules of the game.

The Cruzado Plans

It was expected that financial intermediation would play an important part in the mechanism for transmitting the inertial inflation. This mechanism could be outlined as follows: the inertial component, thanks to the widespread indexation, became the most important element for determining inflation, ensuring that the sum of the previous inflation limit plus the effect of the shocks on supply and demand determined the lower limit for the actual inflation. When a shock to supply, such as a devaluation or a poor harvest, made prices rise faster, real illiquidity resulted and interest rates tended to move up, while the banks fought over the scarce reserves. If the central bank refused to finance it, the liquidity of marginal enterprises appeared under the form of larger requests for reserves, which stepped up the pressure on the central bank. The rescue operations finished by increasing the system's liquidity and thus allowing the larger index.

Because of the long inflationary tradition, the financial savings tended to flow into short-term lending, with a continuous process of rate renegotiation. In this way, a large portion of the economy's human and technical resources—both in the financial system and in the productive sectors—was devoted to making forecasts about inflation and monitoring resources in the financial markets. When the government decided in 1986 to mount a monetary reform designed to stop inflation in its tracks, based on the elimination of short-term indexation, an immediate concern was how that would affect the financial system or, in other words, how harsh the adjustment of the existing system would be in order to bring it into line with the low inflationary rates.

No sooner had the Cruzado Plan been announced than the government, in an effort to wipe inflationary expectations from the memory of the economic agents, set "zero" inflation as the target. At this juncture there were two phenomena critical to the financial sector's future development: (1) the high level of uncertainty as to the rules, given the policy shift reflected by the program, which was accompanied by announcements concerning an important financial reform being considered by the government, and (2) marked changes in the structure of assets toward a greater demand for money to replace the quasi-money that was yielding interest. For the financial system in general, this meant that the market for banking activities was narrowing.

This state of affairs was expected to produce the following effects: (1) bankruptcy of marginal enterprises in the financial sector; (2) redefinition of banking operations, including the introduction of rates for banking services that had been implicitly included in idle deposits; and (3) major adjustments in the surviving enterprises, including cuts in payrolls and in the number of branches. The speed and cost of the adjustments would depend, obviously, on the type of monetary policy followed by the central bank after March. With lower inflation, the economic agents opted to demand greater liquidity, though it is difficult to demand how much greater. In such situations, if the central bank follows a tight policy or underestimates the increase in the demand for money, interest rates rise and the banks lose more, both through the smaller deposits and through the higher costs of bank reserves. However, if the central bank is too "accommodating" (i.e., expands liquidity in order to match the higher prices) or underestimates the demand for money, it runs the risk of injecting excess demand into the system.

A point to consider is that the first Cruzado Plan was announced as a nonrecessionary approach to ending inflation. Although the government relied on the total support of the population, the program had hardly been launched when a large part of the opposition pointed to the possible recessive effect of the price freezes. The government opted to reduce the nominal interest rate immediately with three aims in mind: (1) to make downward corrections in nominal prices less likely in view of the falling financial costs; (2) to boost the expectations of "zero" inflation, so that the economic agents would see the nominal interest rates as the probable real ones; and (3) to spur economic activity to counter the fear that the high degree of uncertainty caused by the drastic rules change might shrivel investment. It is therefore understandable that monetary policy in the wake of the Cruzado Plan was biased toward excessive monetization. Toward the end of 1986 high inflation returned and expectations began to look explosive.

The second Cruzado shock, better known as the Bresser Plan in reference to Minister Bresser Pereira, came as a blessing to the banking system, which had expanded the credit supply following the optimistic upturn in economic activity and the swift shrinkage in the market of the cash management services in the wake of the falling inflation rate. With the return of monthly two-digit inflation in early 1987, there was a serious deterioration in the quality of the bank assets, while hopes of a business recovery to low inflation levels dwindled.

In addition to the short-lived freeze, the plan brought a new conversion index for fixed-yield assets. The exceptions thus introduced gave rise to a series of legal disputes because revenues were being transferred from creditors to debtors without any monetary reform.

The third Cruzado shock—officially named the "Summer Plan," in obvious reference to the Argentine Spring Plan, which preceded that country's hyperinflation of early 1989—was announced in January 1989, when the expected inflation surpassed Cagan's magic hyperinflation limit of 50 percent per month. A monetary reform was introduced prohibiting short-term (less than three months) indexation and containing nominal post-price-freeze high interest rates (14.8 percent in February and 13.1 percent in March for inflation rates of 3 to 7 percent), as an attempt to further the return of short-term financial transactions with fixed interest rates and to restrict transactions with indexed floating rates to longer contracts. In April 1989, with the return of two-digit inflation, short-term indexation returned, again paving the way for numerous court actions, most of which have yet to be settled.

The Collor Plans

The process of repressing hyperinflation was to be pursued by two other plans, which are characterized by significant interventions in financial contracts and in indexation rules. The first Collor Plan, which began by barring the economic agents from access to their financial assets at a level equivalent to approximately 10 percent of GDP (thus reducing M4 from 15.7 percent of GDP on March 13,

1990 to 5.2 percent on March 19, the date on which the financial market was reopened), was the most serious intervention in private contracts ever carried out in Brazil. Once again, the exceptions to the rule of access to liquid assets brought an early return of liquidity—with the inability of the government to administer the interest indexation law which it succeeded in getting passed by the Congress—possibly the return of high inflation rates as well (Carneiro and Goldfajn, 1990).

The experiment with active monetary policy of the second half of 1990 put an end to the central bank's automatic purchases of government bonds. Indexed bonds, which had remained the government's chief financing tool in the years following the first Collor Plan, were replaced by traditional treasury bonds (LTNs) sold at a discount, which to some extent restored the central bank's control over the money supply. Fluctuations in interest rates rose as the banks had to finance their occasional reserve shortages among themselves, until the short-term high rate prompted them to resort to the central bank. The experiment came to an abrupt end when in December 1990 the political intention to permit some heavily indebted state banks to go under became evident.

The second Collor Plan radically changed the indexation rules in February 1991 by prohibiting retroactive short-term indexation and introducing a forward benchmark interest rate (TR), determined each month by the central bank on the basis of the 30-day certificates of deposit rate. This rule allows the central bank greater flexibility to vary short-term interest rates without creating large discrepancies between similar assets, such as savings passbooks and 30-day deposits. The new legislation also introduced the so-called FAF (Financial Application Fund), managed by the banks, which could be the final holders of public bonds.[6] Overnight their shares in the fund replaced the indexed accounts of individuals, which were banned. Issuance was authorized of several alternative short-term financial assets, with great flexibility for the specialized closed funds.

The recomposition of liquidity after the initial restoration of short-term liquidity required a very conservative monetary policy with the highest recorded interest rates, although the restoration of basic confidence in domestic assets was also achieved with surprising success, even in the middle of a very severe political crisis which led to the impeachment of the president. Nevertheless, the Collor Plan ushered in a new kind of risk which is the nightmare of holders of financial assets, who see the end approaching whenever the newspapers involve themselves in financial reform.

---

6 The banks currently hold an estimated 20 percent to 30 percent of unpaid public bonds.

The degree of financial liberalization attained after the second Collor Plan is the highest in Brazilian financial history. Interest rates are still very high, while the government continues to talk about the need for a new stabilization plan. Financial reform is always among the political measures that will accompany the next stabilization plan.

After Stabilization

It is difficult to assess the outcome of Brazil's mega-inflationary experience because it will depend on the nature of the stabilization policies that are adopted. Needless to say, the possibility of some form of hyperinflation resulting from a flight of domestic capital cannot be ruled out. In this case the result could be the end of the private banking system, because a default on the public debt could spill over into private assets and drain away the shares in the funds, which would undermine public confidence in the private banks. Existing proposals for the dollarization of financial assets are based on the belief that such a failure of confidence could be limited to assets denominated in cruzeiros, which may well be the case. Similar thinking underlies proposals to create dollar-denominated public bonds supported by a guarantee based on the central bank's reserves, possibly in the safekeeping of a neutral agency.

The fact is that all the proposals share the belief that the present private core of the financial system will only survive a flight of domestic assets if the government permits financial dollarization. It is legitimate, then, to speculate on the characteristics that one might expect a post-stabilization Brazilian financial system to exhibit.

The first observation, obviously, is that on the supply side of financial intermediation the financial system is more than ever a strong potential provider of credit, for reasons previously mentioned and for reasons relating to the country's unique financial experience: hard-won technical experience in financial analysis and risk assessment, and with the model of technical and financial innovations that are today part and parcel of the country's daily financial activity. Treasury and brokerage activities should certainly decrease, but matching their level to the tasks necessary for expanded lending does not seem difficult to achieve.

On the demand side, as Table A.16 of the annex shows, an extraordinary contraction of credit as a proportion of GDP has taken place, from approximately 35 percent in the mid-seventies to less than 12 percent in the nineties. This drop has led to a situation in which an economy is functioning virtually without credit, in large measure similar to what McKinnon called a repressed economy, because the official financial system cannot fulfill its regular function of providing loans to the private sector.

A sizable part of this reduction in total private sector debt affects household debt, because consumer loans have to be completed through informal credit activities such as financing through presigned checks that are discounted by retailers in nonfinancial institutions. Factoring through independent agents is also comparable with informal market activities such as those performed in financially repressed traditional economies. The current financial repression grew out of the long period in which the Brazilian financial system adapted to high inflation. As will be seen in the following section, there now seems to be plenty of room for growth driven by credit expanded through consumer loans (personal and mortgage) and to a large number of businesses which in a more stable environment will be willing to take out medium- and long-term credit.

Policy Proposals and Reforms

As part of broader economic reforms and the stabilization effort itself, in the next few years the Brazilian financial system will undergo inevitable changes in several areas. The Constitution of 1988 laid down guidelines that are too general to be applied operationally, and they still need to be regulated by legislation currently being discussed in the Congress. On the other hand, it is probable that the Constitution itself will be considerably amended in the near future. This section looks at some of the policy issues that inform the debate on the directions to be followed by financial reforms in Brazil.

As noted in previous chapters, the recent history of the financial system was strongly influenced by the behavior of inflation and by the whims of a series of anti-inflationary shock treatments. The system has also been distorted, particularly since the mid-eighties, by the public sector's burdensome financing needs. That effort diminished the more traditional roles of the financial institutions and made them more vulnerable to a default on the domestic public debt, as took place partially in March 1990.

The necessary reform of the financial sector should be based on two objectives: first, improvement of the possibilities of stabilization policy, and second, strengthening the financial sector that will emerge from the current crisis following stabilization. The first two of the three following sections will discuss the reforms inspired mainly, though not completely, by the need to improve the possibility of a successful stabilization policy by making the central bank more independent and rebuilding the state's financial institutions. The third section speculates on the form the financial sector will take following a successful stabilization effort and on policies that might strengthen the sector and further its development.

Toward a More Independent Central Bank

Brazil was recently the scene of an extensive debate on the ideal degree of the central bank's independence. This debate was spurred by a critical view of the implications of the current financial institutional framework for the effectiveness of stabilization policies.

The well-known argument in favor of an independent central bank was succinctly formulated as follows by Cukierman (1992, p. 350):

> The transfer of authority of the political authorities to the central bank can be understood as an act of partial obligation. By delegating part of their authority to a relatively apolitical institution, politicians accept certain restrictions on their future freedom of action. The main reason for such delegation is usually to preserve price stability. This aim competes with several others, such as achieving a high level of economic activity, financing the budget, etc. By delegating part of their authority to the central bank, the political authorities try to reduce the range of circumstances under which price stability would be sacrificed at the expense of other objectives. The greater the central bank's independence, the greater the obligation.

Recent comparative studies have produced interesting data on the varying degrees of autonomy enjoyed by the central banks of different countries. In some of the studies an index has been devised by which the independence of the monetary authorities can be measured. The simplest such index is based on the sum of the various indirect indicators of the degree of autonomy granted to the central bank by each country's laws. According to the overall legal independence devised by Cukierman (1992), on which zero represents the least possible independence, Switzerland has the most autonomous (formal) central bank with a score of 0.68, closely followed by Germany with 0.66. On the same scale, Brazil's central bank scores 0.26. Curiously, Japan, with 0.16, is classified as one of the six countries with the least independent central banks of the 68 countries in the sample, yet in 1980 it had, together with Switzerland and Germany, the lowest average annual geometric inflation rate (3 percent), in contrast to Brazil's 230 percent.[7] Table 3.6 allows comparison of the various legal independence indicators—which form the overall legal independence indicator—between West Germany and Brazil.

The list of variables in Table 3.6 and the low score given Brazilian legislation in some of them serve to indicate the paths to follow to a reform designed to grant the central bank greater independence. In fact, since 1992 the Congress has been discussing, within a more comprehensive reform of the financial system,

---

[7] France, with 0.28 on the same scale, is another important "anomaly," but as Swinburne and Castelo-Branco (1992) point out, it could be argued that French monetary policy is thoroughly regulated by agreements with the EMS.

Table 3.6. Brazil: Indices of the Central Bank's Legal Independence in the Eighties

Definition of the variable	West Germany	Brazil
Term of office of the general manager	1.00	0.00
Who appoints the general manager?	1.00	0.50
Provision for dismissing the general manager	1.00	0.00
Is the general manager allowed to hold another position?	0.00	0.00
Who establishes monetary policy?	0.67	0.33
Provisions of government and settlement of disputes	1.00	n.a.
Does the central bank participate actively in the drawing up of the national budget?	0.00	0.00
Objectives of the central bank	1.00	0.00
Ceiling for advances	0.67	0.67
Ceilings for guaranteed loans	0.67	0.00
Who decides loan conditions?	0.67	0.00
How wide is the circle of potential borrowers from the central bank?	0.33	1.00
Type of limit (if any)	1.00	n.a.
Maturity of the loans	1.00	0.00
Restrictions on interest rates	0.25	0.25
Prohibitions on loans in primary markets	0.00	0.00
General legal independence[1]	0.66	0.26

Source: Cukierman's data (1992).
n. a. Not available.
[1] Scale from zero (least independence) to 1.00.

ways and means of granting that institution greater autonomy. An already long experience with annual three-digit inflation has tended to spread the belief in Brazil that giving the central bank autonomy might be the only necessary step toward a successful stabilization policy. The discussion of how to grant that autonomy has perhaps put too much emphasis on the first four items noted in Table 3.6, which refer to the appointment and removal of the bank's board of directors. However, even defenders of independence for the central bank acknowledge that such independence "is more effective as a preventive measure than as a remedy," and that "when inflation reaches hyperinflationary dimensions, the guarantee of the formal independence of the central bank is generally insufficient to restore price stability, if it is not accompanied by additional measures." Stabilization policy requires the "active participation of the central government and of other institutions and the simultaneous development of policy measures in various areas" (Cukierman, 1992, p. 449).[8]

The debate in the Congress on the degree of independence to give the central bank has given rise to two opposing proposals, both formulated by members of Congress.[9] The first, the Maia Proposal,[10] involves bolder changes. The central bank would be managed by a five-member executive board supervised by an eleven-member consultative committee, four of whose members would also sit on the board of directors. The members of both bodies would be elected by the president and subject to approval by the senate for staggered six-year terms. Removal would have to be approved by a 60 percent majority of the senate.

The other proposal, known as the Serra Proposal,[11] reflects the fear that the degree of independence for the central bank under the Maia Proposal might make it difficult to conduct a consistent macroeconomic policy. Accordingly, the Serra proposal provides for a Financial Policy Board, composed of four members of the government (the Minister of Economic Affairs, the National Secretary of Finance, the Manager of the Exchange and Securities Commission, and the Manager of the Supervisory Body of Insurance Companies) and four members of the board of directors of the central bank.[12] This financial policy board would "formulate monetary, credit, and exchange policies."

The Congress will likely approve a reform soon granting more autonomy to the central bank. But it is certainly difficult to believe that such a reform will be the only one necessary to deliver the Brazilian economy from megainflation. As long as the country does not develop and firmly adopt a public policy designed for low inflation, and as long as the prevailing propensity to resolve conflicting

[8] The same author also cites a well-known historical lesson on the abuse of central bank independence. "A dramatic illustration is the privatization of the Reichsbanks during the post-World War I German hyperinflation. In May 1922, at the allies' insistence, the president of the Reichsbank had to report to an independent board of directors and not to the German chancellor. The hope was that this procedural change would reduce the discount of treasury bonds in the central bank. But the central bank continued to discount treasury bonds at an accelerating pace and furthermore began to discount bonds of private industrialists and bankers who, after the change, were better represented on the Reichsbank's board of directors. Instead of using its recently instituted independence to stabilize monetary growth, the new board of directors continued to accommodate the budget shortfall while simultaneously allowing private interests to access part of the revenues through seigniorage" (p. 449).

[9] See Rigolon (1992) for an in-depth discussion of both proposals. See also Dias, Afonso, Patury, and Parente (1992).

[10] In reference to deputy Cesar Maia of Rio de Janeiro.

[11] In reference to Deputy José Serra from São Paulo.

[12] The proposal concerning this board of directors would have to be amended to account for the fact that the Ministry of Economic Affairs was split into two ministries in October 1992.

claims at the expense of the fiscal budget is not ended, granting greater independence to the central bank will not be sufficient in itself to ensure a successful stabilization effort. There is reason to believe that only when such a public policy is established and rooted in low inflation will the central bank be able to be actually and not only legally independent.[13]

However, in the short run the creation of an independent central bank can be an essential step toward finally allowing the monetary authorities to deal appropriately with long-deferred problems rooted in the operation of public financial institutions. This possibility will be looked at in the next subsection.

Reform of Public Financial Institutions

Traditionally, public financial institutions have played a crucial role in the process of savings allocation in Brazil. In recent years, however, much of the criticism of the performance of the Brazilian financial markets has concentrated on important segments of the public banks. That criticism includes the following points: allocation of forced savings through the administration rather than the market, abusive political use of workers' pension funds, and abuse of the public commercial banks by the federal and state governments.

The behavior of commercial banks in state hands has been one of the principal obstacles to a successful stabilization policy, since their excesses enabled state governments to operate unimpeded by firm fiscal restraints. The events of 1990 illustrate some of those difficulties. The central government's efforts at fiscal austerity were partly thwarted by the excessive spending of local governments, which was driven by tough electoral competition at the state level. This situation also affected the management of monetary policy, because part of the major loan requirements of local and state governments were met by the state banks, which were finally bailed out by the central bank acting under political pressure from state governors.

From mid-1991 to mid-1992, the central bank obtained enough political support to maintain reasonable control over the state banks. But with the political crisis that led to Collor's impeachment in late September 1992, the central bank encountered mounting difficulties in maintaining such control. These difficulties appear to be continuing under the Itamar Franco administration, owing to its attempts to obtain political support from the state governors.[14] The most trou-

---

[13] See Swinburne and Castelo-Branco (1992).

[14] The difficulties imposed on the stabilization policy by local and state governments are analyzed by Werneck (1992).

bled banks are those that are in the hands of the economically most important and therefore most powerful states, because their governors are a potential threat to the new administration, particularly through their strong influence on their states' deputies and senators.

Most of the state banks are obviously overstaffed and a large proportion of their assets become nonperforming. A situation of this sort generally arises from excessive lending, either to the state government itself or to its public enterprises and agencies. Although the financial institutions are legally barred from lending to their principal stockholders, this prohibition is plainly ignored by the state banks. Another part of their assets, often nonperforming, consists of loans made to favored private sector customers on the basis of political considerations.[15]

As previously mentioned, control over the state banks is a political matter in which a more independent central bank would immediately make a crucial difference. To deal with a serious conflict between the monetary authorities and the states, the political support of the president would also be needed, the obvious example being the choice between letting one of the banks of the most powerful states go under or letting the central bank intervene. However, an independent central bank can tip the scale in favor of the monetary authorities in such a way as to influence the state banks' behavior to the point of making such measures unnecessary. Ideally, with a more independent central bank dissuasion could prevail over sanctions, which would be conducive to a more credible monetary policy.

The federal financial institutions usually echo the behavior of the state banks at the national level. They operate under strong pressures from the state governors, mayors, and private lobbyists, and typically from the most difficult area for the finance minister to control. The directors are often appointed by the president of the republic, which makes them feel sufficiently secure to oppose the finance minister's directives. Another common procedure is the selection of directors by the governors and other politicians. The performance of these institutions is also adversely affected by overstaffing. Salary levels are often below market. Nonperforming assets are very significant, particularly in the Federal Savings Bank, many of whose loans were made to state and local governments and their agencies.

A more independent central bank would certainly help control the federal financial institutions. A more structured solution could entail privatizations, an idea that will inevitably trigger strong opposition from the well-organized unions and the powerful network of executives of public financial institutions, who have

---

[15] Werlang and Fraga (1992) attribute the poor allocation of funds in the state banks to the high turnover of directors elected out of political considerations. For a more detailed examination of the state banks, review Andrade (1992).

become members of congress. Beginning with the less troubled commercial banks, the federal government could launch similar efforts at the state level.

After Inflation: Reconstruction of the Financial System

The several decades-old crisis of the Brazilian economy and the unresolved problem of chronic high inflation should not discourage us from looking beyond the present juncture as we try to envision the type of financial system that may grow out of a successful stabilization program and identify the policies that might strengthen the development of this new financial system.[16]

Obviously much will depend on the design of the stabilization program itself. An important reference point will be the manner in which the program deals with the domestic public debt. Although the domestic debt stands at barely over 10 percent of GDP, debt service represented a significant share of the public budget in 1992. The risk of default—particularly since the first Collor Plan in March 1990—forced a high premium to be added to interest rates.[17] In addition, when the public debt is perceived as exceptionally risky, the debt's very short-term structure leaves the economy exposed to a sudden loss of confidence in public bonds, which could be the first step to full-blown hyperinflation because of investors quickly trying to convert their bonds to foreign currency or to real assets.[18]

That possibility has received a great deal of attention in the economic debate in Brazil over possible approaches to "resolving" the domestic debt problem, in order to improve the chances of a successful stabilization program.[19] Obviously, the holders of public bonds correctly see this public discussion of the domestic public debt as a signal indicating a growing risk of default. This forces up interest rates, which further stimulates the discussion of a possible "solution" to the debt problem.[20] Naturally, the perverse effect of this vicious cycle may increase if the administration seems to sympathize with this type of "solution"

---

[16] There has already been a debate on this topic, led by Bodin de Moraes (1993).

[17] According to preliminary estimates, the primary public sector surplus reached 1.9 percent of GDP in 1992, generating 2.3 percent of the GDP's operational deficit, after including the interest of the public debt. Of the 4.2 percent of GDP paid in interest, 1.2 percent corresponds to interest on the external public sector debt and the remaining 3.0 percent to interest on the domestic public sector debt.

[18] The decision taken on the first day of the Collor administration to freeze for 18 months a sizable mass of financial assets was prompted by the fear of the difficulties that might arise from a sudden change in the composition of portfolios caused by the high degree of uncertainty about the way the authorities would tackle the public debt. See Carneiro and Goldfajn (1990) and Werneck (1991a).

[19] See, for instance, Giambiagi and Zini (1993).

[20] Marques and Werlang (1988, 1989).

instead of being emphatic and convincing about its decision to prevent a new default on the domestic debt. Another especially feared type of default is the compulsory conversion of very short-term liquid bonds into far less liquid long-term bonds. In any case, this type of conversion may be completely avoidable if the government is restored to solvency through a plan consisting of stabilization that would in a natural manner increase the demand for long-term bonds and lead to a longer-term public debt structure. The difficulties of this debate have their origin in a question of what should come first. Should a credible stabilization come before or after the creation of a longer-term debt structure?

A default would have decisive effects on the type of financial system that would emerge from the crisis. There is no margin for attempting a "surgical" operation that might restrain and control the effects of the default, as was demonstrated with the first Collor Plan. It is true that approximately 20 percent of the public debt is being financed with short-term funds (financial application funds, or FAFs), in which the risk is borne by the investors and not by the financial institution administering them.[21] But the possibility of combining protection against inflation with a high degree of liquidity has drawn a significant share of the economy's total financial wealth into bonds, including a substantial part of the working capital of businesses. Banks too have financed part of the domestic debt through certificates of deposit and even savings passbooks. Consequently a default on the debt may touch off a chain reaction of bankruptcies that could profoundly change the current landscape of the financial system.

As was seen in the eighties, financing the public debt became perhaps the main function of Brazil's financial system. If that function were to disappear suddenly because of a default, the surviving system would be substantially different from what would come out of a stabilization program that had not resorted to a default on the domestic debt. The debt would in any event be financed in the stabilized economy, but making a default on the domestic public debt a part of the stabilization program might mean having to renounce borrowing for a number of years. (In fact, it is the fear of not having access to future financing of the debt that often keeps governments from defaulting.)

A large part of the debate on the domestic public debt has centered on the stock of public bonds payable. However, there are many other types of public sector obligations that could be redeemed only partially, most notably the FCVs, a government obligation to financial institutions resulting from compensation through past subsidies to mortgage contracts on housing.[22] Another such public sector obligation is the FGTS—the retirement fund described in the first sec-

---

[21] The 20 percent of the shares includes DERs, indexed deposits resulting from the unfreezing of Cruzado deposits.

[22] Estimates of the value of FCVs range from $20 to $30 billion, or 5 to 7 percent of GDP.

tion—a large part of which was used to finance states and municipalities through long-term loans that have been mostly unproductive.[23] As is natural, the degree of nonperformance in those other forms of public sector debt would also substantially affect the financial system.

Even without a default, intermediation of the public debt is bound to lose in importance in comparison with other more traditional functions of the financial system, for cash management activities will inevitably become less profitable. Consequently, stabilization could revive private credit operations that have been eclipsed by high inflation and the fiscal crisis. As previously mentioned, after stabilization there should be much more room for economic growth abetted by credit. In a less uncertain climate, the demand for consumer loans, both personal and mortgage, must decline sharply and businesses will be much more inclined to take out medium- and long-term loans. Insurance companies and pension funds seem to be the natural candidates to take over as funding sources, replacing forced savings of high inflation economies.

Stabilization will also entail dismantling the enormous structure erected during the long period of high inflation to collect the inflation tax. During the short earlier phases of swiftly falling inflation some forerunners of this kind of adjustment were witnessed, particularly in 1986 after the Cruzado plan. The financial sector showed a surprising power to adapt to the changed climate, swiftly closing hundreds of branches and carrying out massive layoffs.[24] Indeed, that adaptability served as a warning to many financial groups. When inflation accelerated again, reaching much higher levels than those seen during the Cruzado plan, those groups did not restore the structures they had previously maintained to collect the inflation tax. Not all the branches were reopened, nor were all the employees rehired. Computerization gained ground, offering the public new ways to combine protection from inflation with a high degree of liquidity. In addition, charges for services, introduced during the Cruzado plan, were not eliminated.

However, if annual inflation declines to a two-digit rate, a new round of adjustment will be necessary. Some of the large government-owned commercial banks may have difficulty adapting to the changed circumstances. It has been estimated that not more than five or six of the major banks will be able to maintain large nationwide systems of branches, for it is estimated that almost three-quarters of the agencies receive deposits as their basic function.[25] The medium-sized banks will probably be subjected to severe pressures and find themselves obliged to cut their costs and seek new opportunities; this sector

---

[23] The last available estimate, of April 1992, placed the value of the FGTs at $24 billion, approximately 6 percent of GDP.

[24] See Carneiro and Bodin de Moraes (1988).

[25] See Barros, Pinotti and Bairros (1991).

will probably resort to mergers or takeovers as a response to the new conditions. Many small banks, which have proliferated since the deregulation of 1989—most of them well-capitalized institutions—could close with little difficulty or turn themselves into investment banks. Small and medium-sized banks can find some market niches that the larger banks will probably find it hard to move into.[26]

The foregoing suggests a simple economic policy consideration. It is clear that the stabilization program will affect the shape of the financial system, although considerations regarding the financial system can also affect the design of the stabilization program. The concern of economic policymakers about the possible impact of stabilization on the financial sector will affect both the direction and the pace of the stabilization program itself. It is probable that the stabilization program will be designed with much emphasis on the need not to overburden the financial sector nor to subject it to an overly rapid adjustment.

Having less segmented financial markets would facilitate the adjustment to a certain extent. Although the degree of segmentation in Brazil today is certainly much less than the analysts of the mid-sixties foresaw, the financial markets remain highly segmented. In most cases this segmentation is the result of over-regulation, which simply places obstacles in the way of efficient allocation of funds on the part of the financial system.

Another point to consider is what will be the participation of foreign banks in the domestic market after stabilization. It has been maintained that only those that already have an established system of agencies will remain in the market, having ensured their competitiveness through better access to external financing. The rest will have to leave the country or simply maintain a local office.[27] Other more likely possibilities are not difficult to imagine. The liberalization of trade and successful renegotiation of the external debt will certainly attract foreign banks to Brazil, particularly in an environment of sustained growth. Much will depend on the nature of the restrictions governing the foreign banks' operations and the deregulation of external flows of funds.[28]

Such deregulation is a topic that has received growing attention in Brazil. Much of the present debate centers on the timing and pace of deregulation rather than on its essential merit. The idea as such commands a surprising consensus, due to the country's long tradition of controlling capital flows.[29] The principal

---

[26] Elaborate financial engineering and specialized credit operations, for example, have typically proved difficult to carry out in a large multiple bank.

[27] See Barros, Pinotti and Bairros (1991).

[28] Bodin de Moraes (1990).

[29] Controls on capital flows were imposed in 1930 and have been kept in place throughout the last six decades (Abreu, 1990).

question here, which relates to the risks and benefits of liberalizing those flows before successful stabilization takes place, ought to be properly examined.

In 1991, and especially in 1992, the inflow of foreign capital was considerable. This inflow has heretofore been explained largely by the direct or indirect repatriation of funds by Brazilians abroad. The repatriation was due to the combination of very low international interest rates and extremely high real interest rates in Brazil, a result of the tight money policy.[30] That inflow could grow even more in the near future, once the renegotiation of the debt had led to a reestablishment of normal relations with the international financial markets. Addressing the direct effects of the inflow of foreign capital in the financial sector—as well as its indirect effects through pressures exerted on monetary policy—constitutes a relatively new challenge for economic policy in the country.

A final stimulus for financial reform has been the establishment of a long-term capital market, a goal on the country's political agenda for several decades. The very modest results in the past were mostly neutralized by high inflation. Even after a successful stabilization experience, no one knows for certain how long the country's very short-term capital markets will take to become normal markets, especially if annual two-digit inflation persists.

Carneiro and Bodin de Moraes (1988) and Carneiro and Werneck (1992) have pointed out some of the hurdles that complicate setting up a long-term capital market in the Brazilian economy. The interest in that market, which partly inspired the reforms of the mid-sixties,[31] evaporated when runaway inflation set in. At the present juncture very little can be achieved in the way of establishing a vigorous long-term capital market as the necessary channel for transforming the public's savings into private investment. Even when indexed loans exist, high inflation makes them too risky.[32] Discussion of this topic therefore assumes a post-stabilization scenario.

Even if much optimism exists about the possibility of stemming inflation and creating a long-term capital market, it will probably take time for the state to give up its historical role as an important purveyor of long-term financing for private investments. The National Bank for Economic and Social Development (BNDES) is one of the few financial institutions in Latin America with a relatively clear history, having warded off political abuse reasonably well thanks to a stable and professional staff.[33] However, the time may soon come to start

---

[30] See Calvo, Leiderman and Reinhart (1992).

[31] See Behrens (1978)

[32] See Dreizzen (1985).

[33] A major exception was the policy followed in the mid-seventies, when BNDES was forced by the government to establish an annual interest ceiling of 20 percent in the indexation of its long-term loans. This led to enormous subsidies for the industrial sector, as a result of which inflation rose to more than 200 percent in the early eighties. See Najberg (1989).

developing the private side of a long-term capital market. One possible approach would be to allow BNDES to cofinance long-term loans, injecting cash into financial institutions when they have to refinance their loans because of rising interest rates. This would reduce the risk for the private sector that long-term financing entails and could ensure a volume of long-term loans well above what BNDES could have brought about by itself. The agreement would furthermore reduce BNDES' administrative costs, since the evaluation of investment projects would be performed in part by private institutions.[34]

---

[34] For a more detailed discussion of this issue, see Carneiro (1992).

BIBLIOGRAPHY

Abreu, M. de P., ed. 1990. *A Ordem do Progresso: Cem Anos de Política Econômica Repúblicana, 1889–1989*. Rio de Janeiro: Campus.

Andrade, E. 1992. "Os Bancos Estaduais no Brasil: Do Final dos Sessenta a Crise dos Anos Oitenta." Master's thesis, Department of Economics, PUC-Rio.

Barros, J. R. M., M.C. Pinotti and M. Bairros. 1991. "O Mercado Financeiro em um Cenário de Estabilização." São Paulo: MBE Associados.

Behrens, Alfredo. 1978. "O Papel dos Bancos de Investimento como Instituições de Crédito a Longo Prazo." *Revista Brasileira de Mercado de Capitais* 4 (10).

Bodin de Moraes, P. 1986. "Essays on Stabilization Policies." Ph.D. dissertation, Massachusetts Institute of Technology.

———. 1990. *Foreign Banks in the Brazilian Economy in the Eighties*. Working Paper 241. Department of Economics, PUC-Rio.

———. 1993. "Financial Sector in a Highly Inflationary Economy: How to Finance Growth after Stabilization?" Department of Economics, PUC-Rio. Mimeo.

Bresciani-Turroni, C. 1937. *The Economics of Inflation. A Study in Currency Depreciation in Post-War Germany.* London: George Allen and Unwin, Ltd.

Calvo, G. A., L. Leiderman and C. M. Reinhart. 1992. *Capital Inflows and Real Exchange Rate Appreciation in Latin America: the Role of External Factors.* IMF Working Paper, Research Department. International Monetary Fund, Washington, D.C.

Carneiro, D. D. 1992. "O Mercado de Capitais de Longo Prazo e o Papel do BNDES." Department of Economics, PUC-Rio. Mimeo.

Carneiro, D. D. and P. Bodin de Moraes. 1988. "La Inflación y la Evolución del Sistema Financiero Brasileño." In *Deuda Interna y Estabilidad Financiera*, eds. C. Massad and R. Zahler. Buenos Aires: Grupo Editor Latinoamericano.

Carneiro, D. D. and I. Goldfajn. 1990. "Reforma Monetária: Pros e Cons do Mercado Secundário." In *Plano Collor: Avaliações e Perspectivas*, ed. C. Faro. Rio de Janeiro: LTC—Livros Técnicos e Científicos.

Carneiro, D. D. and R. L. F. Werneck. 1992. *Public Savings and Private Investment: Requirements for Growth Resumption in the Brazilian Economy.* Working Paper 283. Department of Economics, PUC-Rio.

Cukierman, A. 1992. *Central Bank Strategy, Credibility, and Independence: Theory and Evidence.* Cambridge, MA.: The MIT Press.

Cukierman, A., S. B. Webb and B. Neyapaty. 1992. "Measuring the Independence of Central Banks and Its Effects on Policy Outcomes." *The World Bank Economic Review* 6 (3).

Dias, G. J., R. R. Afonso, L. C. R. Patury and P. P. Parente. 1992. "A Lei Complementar do Sistema Financeiro Nacional: Subsídios e Sugestões para a Sua Elaboração." *Cuadernos de Economia* 07. Brasilia: Programa Nacional de Pesquisa Econômica.

Dornbusch, R. and Giovannini, A. 1991. "Monetary Policy in the Open Economy." In *Handbook of Monetary Economics*, eds. Benjamin Friedman and Frank Hahn. Amsterdam: North-Holland.

Dreizzen, J. 1985. *O Conceito de Fragilidade Financeira num Contexto Inflacionário.* Rio de Janeiro: BNDES.

Fonseca, D. S. 1992. "Rentabilidade dos Bancos Comerciais: Um Exercício de Descomposição." Graduation Monograph. Department of Economics, PUC-Rio.

Giambiagi, F. and A. A. Zini Jr. 1993. "Renegociação da Dívida Interna Imobiliária: Uma Proposta." *Economía Política*, 13, 2 (50), April-June.

Goldsmith, R. W. 1986. *Brasil 1850–1984: Desenvolvimento Financeiro sob um Século de Inflação.* São Paulo: Harper & Row do Brasil, Ltd.

Lohman, S. 1992. "Optimal Commitment in Monetary Policy: Credibility versus Flexibility." *American Economic Review* 82.

Marques, M. S. B. and S. R. C. Werlang. 1988. "Moratória Interna, Dívida Pública e Juros Reais." Brazilian Institute of Economics, Getúlio Vargas Foundation. Mimeo.

———. 1989. "Désagio das LFTs e a Probabilidade de Moratória." Graduate School in Economics, Getúlio Vargas Foundation. Mimeo.

Najberg, S. 1989. "Privatização de Recursos Públicos: Os Empréstimos do Sistema BNDES ao Setor Privado Nacional com Correção Monetária Parcial." Master's thesis, Department of Economics, PUC-Rio.

Persson, T. and G. Tabellini. 1990. "Macroeconomic Policy, Credibility and Politics." In *Fundamentals of Pure and Applied Economics* 18. Switzerland, London, New York and Melbourne: Harwood Academic.

Rigolon, F. J. Z. 1992. "A Independência do Banco Central: o Caso do Brasil." Department of Economics, PUC-Rio. Mimeo.

Rogoff, K. 1985. "The Optimal Degree of Commitment to an Intermediate Target." *Quarterly Journal of Economics* 100.

Silva, M. R. 1989. "Estructura de Mercado: Determinantes e Implicações sobre a Política Monetária." Department of Economics, PUC-Rio.

Swinburne, M. and M. Castello-Branco. 1992. *Central Bank Independence: Issues and Experience.* IMF Working Paper. International Monetary Fund. Washington, D.C.

Vasconcelos, J. R. and R. S. Ogasawara. 1992. *Análise Econômico-Financeira dos Bancos Estaduais.* Policy Document 7. Institute of Applied Economic Research (IPEA).

Werlang, S. R. C. and A. Fraga. 1992. "Os Bancos Estaduais e o Descontrole Fiscal: Alguns Aspectos." *Ensaio Econômico* 203.

Werneck, R. L. F. 1991a. "Oportunidades Perdidas na Política de Estabilização de 1990." In *A Economia Pós Plano Collor II*, ed. C. Faro. Rio de Janeiro: Livros Técnicos.

————. 1991b. "A Crise Financeira dos Estados." In *A Carta Econômica.* Rio de Janeiro: Associação Nacional dos Bancos de Investimento e Desenvolvimento (ANBID).

————. 1992. "Fiscal Federalism and Stabilization Policy in Brazil." Paper presented at the Seminar on State Reform and Stabilization Policy in Latin America, Latin American Macroeconomic Research Network, Washington, D.C.

ANNEX

The tables that follow provide various data on Brazilian banks and related macroeconomic and financial statistics.

Table A.1. Brazil: Multiple Banks with Commercial Portfolios
Table A.2. Brazil: Remaining Commercial Banks
Table A.3. National Accounts, Brazil: Gross Domestic Product, 1970–91
Table A.4. National Accounts, Brazil: Gross National Available Income, 1970–91
Table A.5. National Accounts, Brazil: Capital Account, 1970–91
Table A.6. Brazil: Gross Domestic Product. Total and Per Capita, 1970–91
Table A.7. Brazil: Gross Domestic Product (GDP) and Gross Fixed Investment (GFI), 1970–91
Table A.8. Brazil: Public and Private Gross Fixed Investment, 1970–91
Table A.9. Inflation in Brazil: General Price Index, Wholesale Price Index and National Consumer Price Index, 1991–93
Table A.10. Inflation in Brazil: General Price Index, Wholesale Price Index and National Consumer Price Index, 1980–92
Table A.11. Brazil: Monetary Base and Money Supply, 1980–92
Table A.12. Brazil: Monetary Base and Money Supply, 1980–92
Table A.13. Brazil: Monetary Base and Money Supply, 1980–92
Table A.14. Brazil: Monetary Base and Money Supply, 1980–92
Table A.15. Brazil: Public Sector Financing Needs, 1980–92
Table A.16. Brazil: Loans to the Financial System by Final Lenders, 1974–92
Table A.17. Central Bank Interventions in the Brazilian Banking System (between January 1, 1986 and January 10, 1992)
Table A.18. Brazil: Estimated Composition of Available Income, 1980–90
Table A.19. Brazil: Estimates of the Composition of Goods and Services, 1980–90

Table A.1. Brazil: Multiple Banks with Commercial Portfolios

	Opening date	Ownership
ABC ROMA	04.08.90	Private
ADOLPHO OLIVEIRA	22.01.90	Private
AGRIMISA[1]		Private
AGROINVEST	01.11.89	Private
AMERICA DO SUL[1]		Private
ANTONIO DE QUEIROZ[1]		Private
APLICAP	01.08.90	Private
ARAUCARIA	12.02.90	Private
ARBI	01.06.89	Private
AUGUSTA	27.09.89	Private
B B C[1]		Private
B C N[1]		Private
B E C[1]		Public (state)
B E M[1]		Private
B F C	02.10.90	Private
B H M	01.08.89	Private
B I G	01.08.90	Private
B M C[1]		Private
B N B[1]		Public (federal)
B N L	21.10.91	Private
B P A		Private
B R B[1]		Private
BAHIA[1]		Private
BAMERINDUS[1]		Private
BANCESA[1]		Private
BANCORP	01.08.90	Private
BANCRED	13.09.89	Private
BANDEIRANTES[1]		Private
BANDEPE[1]		Public (state)
BANESPA[1]		Public (state)
BANESTADO[1]		Public (state)
BANESTES[1]		Public (state)
BANORTE[1]		Private
BANPARA[1]		Public (state)
BANRISUL[1]		Public (state)
BBA-CREDIT	19.07.89	Private
BEMGE[1]		Public (state)
BOAVISTA[1]		Private
BOREAL	22.01.90	Private
BOZANO[1]		Private
BRADESCO[1]		Private
BRASBANCO (THECA)	10.06.91	Private
BRASEG	01.08.89	Private
CACIQUE	01.11.89	Private
CAMBIAL	02.10.89	Private
CAPITALTEC	12.07.89	Private

Table A.1. Brazil: Multiple Banks with Commercial Portfolios (cont.)

	Opening date	Ownership
CASH	15.03.91	Private
CEDULA	01.02.90	Private
CHASE MANHATTAN[1]		Private
CIDADE[1]		Private
CLASSICO	11.09.89	Private
CONTINENTAL	26.03.90	Private
CREDIBANCO	01.08.89	Private
CREDIREAL MG[1]		Public (state)
CREDIREAL RS[1]		Private
CREDIT COML FR	10.07.89	Private
CREDITO SP	10.08.89	Private
CREFISA		Private
CREFISUL	18.08.89	Private
CRUZEIRO	15.08.89	Private
DAYCOVAL		Private
DESTAK	01.08.90	Private
DIBENS	03.07.89	Private
DIGIBANCO[1]		Private
DIME		Private
DIMENSAO	01.08.90	Private
DRACMA	05.03.90	Private
ECONOMICO[1]		Private
EMPRESARIAL	16.11.89	Private
ESTADO DE ALAGOAS[1]		Public (state)
ESTADO DO AMAPA	19.02.92	Public (state)
ESTADO DO AMAZONAS[1]		Public (state)
ESTADO DA BAHIA		Public (state)
ESTADO DE GOIAS		Public (state)
ESTADO RORAIMA[2]	30.04.90	Public (state)
ESTADO RONDONIA		Public (state)
ESTADO SERGIPE[1]		Public (state)
EUROINVEST	25.08.89	Private
EXCEL	01.06.90	Private
FATOR	01.08.89	Private
FENICIA[1]		Private
FIBRA	01.09.89	Private
FICRISA	03.07.89	Private
FICSA	01.07.91	Private
FINANCIAL INT.S.A.	21.06.90	Private
FINIVEST	15.12.89	Private
FR. BRASILEIRO[1]		Private
GARAVELO	01.03.90	Private
GENERAL MOTORS	03.09.90	Private
GERAL COMERCIO[1]		Private
GOLDMINE	01.11.91	Private

Table A.1. Brazil: Multiple Banks with Commercial Portfolios (cont.)

	Opening date	Ownership
GRAPHUS	17.07.89	Private
GUANABARA	01.03.90	Private
GULFINVEST	23.11.89	Private
HERCULES	24.11.89	Private
ICATU	14.07.89	Private
IND.COMERCIAL[1]		Private
INDUSCRED[1]		Private
INDUSVAL	02.05.91	Private
INTER-ATLANTICO	11.09.89	Private
INTERCAP	02.07.90	Private
INTERPACIFICO	31.07.90	Private
INTERPART	01.10.89	Private
INTERUNION	26.07.89	Private
INVESTCORP	01.06.92	Private
INVESTCRED	02.10.89	Private
INVESTOR	01.10.90	Private
IOCHPE[1]		Private
ITAMARATI[1]		Private
ITAU[1]		Private
LAVRA	24.11.89	Private
LIBERAL	21.08.89	Private
LUSO BRASILEIRO	01.11.89	Private
MANTRUST	30.06.89	Private
MAPPIN	20.11.89	Private
MARTINELLI	13.07.89	Private
MATONE	03.07.89	Private
MERCANTIL BRASIL[1]		Private
MERCANTIL S.A.[1]		Private
MERCANTIL SAO PAULO[1]		Private
MERIDIONAL[1]		Private
MIL BANCO	10.07.89	Private
MITSUBISHI BRAS.[1]		Private
MONTREAL	14.04.89	Private
MULTIBANCO	01.10.89	Private
MULTIPLIC[1]		Private
NACIONAL[1]		Private
NORCHEM	20.10.89	Private
NOROESTE[1]		Private
NOSSA CAIXA/N.BANCO[1]		Public (state)
OMEGA	14.07.89	Private
OPEN	15.01.90	Private
OPERADOR	01.07.92	Private
PACTUAL	09.06.89	Private
PANAMERICANO	02.05.91	Private
PARANA BANCO	01.08.89	Private

Table A.1. Brazil: Multiple Banks with Commercial Portfolios (cont.)

	Opening date	Ownership
PATENTE	01.11.89	Private
PAULISTA	01.02.90	Private
PEBB	24.09.90	Private
PECUNIA	13.02.90	Private
PERFORMANCE	01.09.89	Private
PIRELLI FINTEC	03.02.92	Private
PONTUAL[1]		Private
PORTO REAL S.A.[2]	04.05.92	Private
PRIMUS	01.07.91	Private
PROGRESSO[1]		Private
PROSPER	16.07.90	Private
REGIONAL MALCON	04.09.89	Private
RENNER	02.01.91	Private
ROSA	15.08.89	Private
ROYAL BANK CANADA[1]		Private
RURAL[1]		Private
SAFRA[1]		Private
SANTISTA	15.03.90	Private
SANTOS NEVES	07.10.91	Private
SCHAHIN CURY	02.10.89	Private
SEGMENTO	17.09.91	Private
SISTEMA	03.07.89	Private
SOFISA	01.06.90	Private
SOGERAL[1]		Private
SRL		Private
STOCK	24.07.89	Private
STOTLER DIME	02.07.90	Private
SUDAMERIS[1]		Private
SUL AMERICA SCAND	08.06.89	Private
SUMITOMO[1]		Private
TECNICORP	17.03.92	Private
TENDENCIA	03.09.90	Private
TOKYO[1]		Private
TRIANGULO	19.03.90	Private
UNIBANCO[1]		Private
VARIG	01.11.89	Private
VOTORANTIM	12.08.91	Private
VR	13.03.90	Private

Source: Central Bank of Brazil.
[1] These multiple banks were originally commercial banks.
[2] These banks have already requested conversion into multiple banks.

Table A.2. Brazil: Remaining Commercial Banks

	Ownership
B M G (BCO.COMERC)	Private
BANCO DA AMAZONIA	Public (Federal)
BANFORT	Private
BOSTON	Private
BRAS.IRAQUIANO	Private
BRASIL	Public (Federal)
C E F[1]	Public (Federal)
CAIXA RS	Public (state)
CENTROBANCO	Private
CITIBANK	Private
CREDIPLAN	Private
DEUTSCH SUDAM.AG	Private
DEUTSCHE BANK	Private
EST. DE GOIAS[1]	Public (state)
EST.RONDONIA[1]	Public (state)
EST.BAHIA[1]	Public (state)
EST.MATO GROS[1]	Public (state)
EST.RIO DE JANEIRO	Public (state)
EST.SANTA CATARIN	Public (state)
ESTADO DO AC[1]	Public (state)
EUROPEU	Private
EXT.ESPANA	Private
FINANC.PORTUGUES	Private
GARANTIA	Private
HISP.AMERICANO	Private
HOLANDES UNIDO	Private
LLOYDS BANK PLC	Private
MERCANT.DESCONT	Private
MORGAN	Private
MOSSORO	Private
N M B (NEDERL)	Private
NACION ARGENTINA	Private
NACIONAL BAHIA	Private
PLANIBANC	Private
PROV.B.AIRES	Private
REAL	Private
REP.OR.URUGUAY	Private
SANTANDER	Private
SAO JORGE	Private
UNION C.A.	Private
UNION URUGUAY	Private

Source: Central Bank of Brazil.
[1] These banks have already requested conversion into multiple banks.

Table A.3. National Accounts, Brazil: Gross Domestic Product, 1970–91
(Percentage of GDP)

Year	Final consump. of households	Final consump. of the public administration	Gross fixed investment	Investment in inventory	Exports	Less imports	Expenditures = GDP
1970	68.6	11.3	18.8	1.7	7.0	7.4	100.0
1971	69.4	11.1	19.9	1.4	6.5	8.2	100.0
1972	69.6	10.8	20.3	0.9	7.3	8.9	100.0
1973	69.2	9.9	20.4	1.7	7.8	9.0	100.0
1974	72.0	9.3	21.8	2.5	7.7	13.3	100.0
1975	67.9	10.2	23.3	2.4	7.2	11.0	100.0
1976	68.9	10.5	22.4	0.6	7.0	9.4	100.0
1977	69.2	9.4	21.3	0.7	7.2	7.9	100.0
1978	68.5	9.7	22.3	0.8	6.7	7.9	100.0
1979	69.1	9.9	23.4	-0.2	7.2	9.3	100.0
1980	69.9	9.1	22.8	0.4	9.0	11.2	100.0
1981	67.8	9.4	23.1	0.1	9.5	9.8	100.0
1982	69.0	10.2	21.8	-0.3	7.7	8.4	100.0
1983	70.4	9.9	18.6	-1.5	11.7	9.3	100.0
1984	69.0	8.7	17.7	-1.2	14.2	8.3	100.0
1985	65.9	9.8	16.9	2.2	12.2	7.1	100.0
1986	67.8	10.6	19.0	-	8.8	6.3	100.0
1987	62.4	12.1	22.2	-	9.4	6.2	100.0
1988	59.6	12.6	22.7	-	10.9	5.7	100.0
1989	57.8	14.3	24.8	-	8.2	5.0	100.0
1990	61.4	15.5	21.5	-	7.2	5.5	100.0
1991	64.7	14.4	18.9	-	8.5	6.5	100.0

Note: Since 1985. Inventory investments have been included in final household consumption.
Source: IGBE - National Accounts Department.

Table A.4. National Accounts, Brazil: Gross National Available Income, 1970–91
(Percentage of GDP)

Year	Final consumption	Final consumption by households	Final consumption by the public administration	Gross savings
1970	80.6	69.2	11.4	19.4
1971	81.2	70.0	11.2	18.8
1972	81.1	70.3	10.9	18.9
1973	79.8	69.8	10.0	20.2
1974	82.0	72.6	9.4	18.0
1975	79.2	68.9	10.3	20.8
1976	80.6	69.9	10.6	19.4
1977	79.9	70.4	9.6	20.1
1978	80.0	70.1	9.9	20.0
1979	81.2	71.0	10.2	18.8
1980	81.6	72.2	9.4	18.4
1981	80.5	70.7	9.8	19.5
1982	83.6	72.8	10.7	16.4
1983	85.4	74.9	10.6	14.6
1984	82.5	73.3	9.2	17.5
1985	79.9	69.5	10.4	20.1
1986	82.1	71.0	11.1	17.9
1987	77.4	64.8	12.6	22.6
1988	75.0	62.0	13.1	25.0
1989	74.3	59.6	14.7	25.7
1990	78.7	62.9	15.8	21.3
1991	80.9	66.1	14.8	19.1

Source: IGBE - National Accounts Department.

Table A.5. National Accounts, Brazil: Capital Account, 1970–91

Year	Gross savings	Less current account surplus	Financing of gross investment
1970	19.26	(1.32)	20.58
1971	18.62	(2.66)	21.29
1972	18.65	(2.53)	21.18
1973	20.03	(2.01)	22.04
1974	17.86	(6.45)	24.32
1975	20.53	(5.16)	25.69
1976	19.12	(3.91)	23.03
1977	19.75	(2.28)	22.02
1978	19.55	(3.47)	23.03
1979	18.32	(4.80)	23.13
1980	17.80	(5.42)	23.22
1981	18.74	(4.47)	23.20
1982	15.57	(5.89)	21.46
1983	13.69	(3.46)	17.16
1984	16.49	0.02	16.46
1985	19.04	(0.11)	19.14
1986	17.10	(1.96)	19.06
1987	21.74	(0.49)	22.23
1988	24.00	1.27	22.72
1989	24.99	0.23	24.76
1990	20.75	(0.73)	21.49
1991	18.70	(0.19)	18.90

Source: INGE - National Accounts Department.

Table A.6. Brazil: Gross Domestic Product. Total and Per Capita, 1970–91

Year	Gross Domestic Product Prices¹ Current prices	Prices¹ 1980 prices	Real product indexes 1980 base	Real product indexes Annual fluctuation (%)	Population (thousands)	GDP per capita Prices¹ Current prices	Prices¹ 1980 prices	Real product indexes 1980 base	Real product indexes Annual fluctuation (%)	GDP Deflator Index 1980 base	GDP Deflator Index Annual fluctuation (%)
1970	194	5,419	43.5	-	95,847	0.002	0.057	53.9	-	3.6	-
1971	258	6,037	48.5	11.4	98,226	0.003	0.061	58.6	8.7	4.3	19.2
1972	347	6,758	54.3	11.9	100,624	0.003	0.067	64.0	9.3	5.1	19.9
1973	512	7,700	61.8	13.9	103,050	0.005	0.075	71.2	11.3	6.7	29.6
1974	745	8,336	67.0	8.3	105,516	0.007	0.079	75.3	5.7	8.9	34.4
1975	1,050	8,763	70.4	5.1	108,032	0.010	0.081	77.3	2.7	12.0	34.0
1976	1,635	9,654	77.5	10.2	110,598	0.015	0.087	83.2	7.6	16.9	41.3
1977	2,496	10,130	81.4	4.9	113,207	0.022	0.089	85.3	2.5	24.6	45.5
1978	3,618	10,629	85.4	4.9	115,859	0.031	0.092	87.4	2.5	34.0	38.1
1979	5,964	11,348	91.2	6.8	118,553	0.050	0.096	91.2	4.3	52.6	54.4
1980	12,450	12,450	100.0	9.7	118,623	0.105	0.105	100.0	6.3	100.0	90.3
1981	24,408	11,895	95.5	-4.5	122,918	0.202	0.098	93.7	-6.3	205.0	105.0
1982	49,676	11,959	96.1	0.5	123,256	0.403	0.097	92.4	-1.3	415.0	102.4
1983	114,010	11,546	92.7	-3.5	125,640	0.907	0.092	87.6	-5.3	982.0	138.0
1984	369,149	12,153	97.6	5.3	128,070	2.882	0.095	90.4	3.3	3,037	209.3
1985	1,386,535	13,117	105.4	7.9	130,547	10.621	0.100	95.7	5.9	10,571	248.1
1986	3,673,071	14,114	113.4	7.6	133,072	27.602	0.106	101.1	5.6	26,025	146.2
1987	11,573,643	14,621	117.4	3.6	135,646	85.322	0.108	102.7	1.6	79,155	204.1
1988	86,551,111	14,606	117.3	-0.1	138,270	625.957	0.106	100.7	-2.0	532,585	572.8
1989	1,271,755,529	15,085	121.2	3.3	140,944	9,023.126	0.107	102.0	1.4	8,430,370	1,482.9
1990	32,780,993,700	14,423	115.8	-4.4	143,670	227,980.656	0.100	95.7	-6.2	226,940,493	2,591.9
1991	164,990,697,900	14,559	116.9	0.9	146,449	1,126,655.566	0.099	94.7	-1.0	1,133,281,474	399.4

Source: IBGE - National Accounts Department.
¹In thousands of Cruzados.

Table A.7. Brazil: Gross Domestic Product (GDP) and Gross Fixed Investment (GFI), 1970–91
(Thousands of $CR)

Year	GDP at current prices	GFI at current prices	GFI/GDP (%)	GDP at 1980 prices	GFI at 1980 prices	GFI/GDP (%)
1970	194	37	18.83	5.419	1.115	20.57
1971	258	51	19.91	6.037	1.286	21.30
1972	347	70	20.33	6.758	1.501	22.20
1973	512	104	20.37	7.700	1.816	23.58
1974	745	163	21.84	8.336	2.056	24.67
1975	1,050	245	23.33	8.763	2.256	25.75
1976	1,635	366	22.41	9.654	2.415	25.01
1977	2,496	532	21.32	10.130	2.387	23.56
1978	3,618	805	22.26	10.629	2.500	23.52
1979	5,964	1,393	23.36	11.348	2.597	22.89
1980	12,450	2,835	22.77	12.450	2.835	22.77
1981	24,408	5,627	23.05	11.895	2.484	20.88
1982	49,676	10,834	21.81	11.959	2.317	19.37
1983	114,010	21,257	18.64	11.546	1.944	16.84
1984	369,149	65,197	17.66	12.153	1.968	16.19
1985	1,386,535	234,311	16.90	13.117	2.141	16.32
1986	3,673,071	699,147	19.03	14.114	2.633	18.66
1987	11,573,648	2,573,152	22.23	14.621	2.603	17.80
1988	86,551,111	19,665,260	22.72	14.606	2.477	16.96
1989	1,271,755,529	314,863,526	24.76	15.085	2.507	16.62
1990	32,730,993,700	7,032,458,599	21.49	14.423	2.304	15.97
1991	164,990,697,900	31,175,543,897	18.90	14.559	2.209	15.17

Source: IBGE - National Accounts Department.

Table A.8. Brazil: Public and Private Gross Fixed Investment, 1970–91
(Percentage of gross fixed investment)

Year	Public administration	Households and firms	Others
1970	23.5	75.4	1.1
1971	21.5	77.4	1.0
1972	19.1	79.8	1.1
1973	18.2	80.7	1.1
1974	17.6	81.1	1.3
1975	16.9	81.7	1.3
1976	18.0	80.3	1.8
1977	15.4	82.5	2.0
1978	14.1	82.3	3.5
1979	10.6	86.4	3.0
1980	10.3	85.8	3.9
1981	11.3	85.3	3.4
1982	11.0	86.5	2.6
1983	10.1	86.8	3.1
1984	11.2	87.3	1.4
1985	13.7	84.1	2.2
1986	16.1	80.5	3.3
1987	14.4	83.0	2.6
1988	13.9	83.5	2.6
1989	11.8	85.6	2.6
1990	16.1	80.7	3.2
1991	16.9	82.5	3.7

Source: IBGE - National Accounts Department.

Table A.9. Inflation in Brazil: General Price Index, Wholesale Price Index and National Consumer Price Index, 1991–93
(Percentage of monthly fluctuation)

		General price index[1]	Wholesale price index[2]	National consumer price index[3]
1991	January	19.93	20.32	20.95
	February	21.11	21.57	20.20
	March	7.25	7.48	11.79
	April	8.74	9.04	5.01
	May	6.52	5.45	6.68
	June	9.86	8.77	10.83
	July	12.83	12.45	12.14
	August	15.49	15.60	15.62
	September	16.19	15.17	15.62
	October	25.85	27.34	21.08
	November	25.76	25.52	26.48
	December	22.14	21.50	24.15
1992	January	26.84	27.11	25.92
	February	24.79	25.48	24.48
	March	20.70	19.67	21.62
	April	18.54	17.80	20.84
	May	22.45	21.23	24.50
	June	21.42	20.90	20.85
	July	21.69	22.19	22.08
	August	25.54	27.40	22.38
	September	27.37	27.17	23.98
	October	24.94	24.83	26.07
	November	24.22	24.43	22.89
	December	23.70	23.78	25.58
1993	January	28.73	26.69	28.77
	February	26.51	26.23	24.79
	March	27.81	28.08	27.58

Sources: Getúlio Vargas Foundation (for 1 and 2) and IBGE (for 3).

Table A.10. Inflation in Brazil: General Price Index, Wholesale Price Index and National Consumer Price Index, 1980–92
(Percentage of annual fluctuation)

Year	General price index[1]	Wholesale price index[2]	National consumer price index[3]
1980	110.24	121.33	99.70
1981	95.19	94.30	93.51
1982	99.72	97.72	100.31
1983	211.00	234.04	177.97
1984	223.81	230.30	209.12
1985	214.75	209.51	239.05
1986	65.03	62.56	58.60
1987	415.83	407.19	395.46
1988	1,037.57	1,050.22	993.29
1989	1,782.85	1,748.91	1,863.56
1990	1,476.85	1,449.45	1,585.18
1991	480.23	471.67	475.11
1992	1,157.84	948.98	1,149.05

Sources: Getúlio Vargas Foundation (for 1 and 2) and IBGE (for 3).

Table A.11. Brazil: Monetary Base and Money Supply, 1980–92
(Percentage of annual fluctuation)

End of period	Monetary base	Sight deposits	Money supply	M1	M4
1980	56.88	69.78	73.74	70.57	72.93
1981	69.86	74.11	79.96	75.30	140.33
1982	86.79	84.95	88.47	85.69	110.43
1983	57.48	100.22	86.82	97.38	150.43
1984	264.09	194.08	232.79	201.85	292.49
1985	257.31	310.17	283.54	304.27	304.14
1986	293.45	319.86	257.48	306.76	94.79
1987	181.47	112.15	195.08	127.45	352.61
1988	622.33	515.99	742.74	570.27	959.00
1989	1,754.06	1,191.68	1,831.20	1,384.16	1,643.06
1990	2,304.20	2,341.11	2,327.34	2,335.71	622.97
1991	291.18	367.74	266.49	328.22	763.58
1992	991.27	858.31	1,038.67	918.56	1,574.03

Source: Central Bank Bulletin.

Table A.12. Brazil: Monetary Base and Money Supply, 1980–92
(In billions of US$)

End of period	Monetary base	Sight deposits	Money supply	M1	M4	Difference M4 - M1
1980	10.95	17.81	4.55	22.36	57.46	35.10
1981	9.52	15.87	4.19	20.06	70.66	50.60
1982	9.04	14.92	4.02	18.94	75.62	56.68
1983	3.69	7.75	1.95	9.70	49.13	39.43
1984	4.23	7.17	2.04	9.21	60.64	51.43
1985	4.59	8.93	2.37	11.30	74.38	63.08
1986	12.30	25.53	5.78	31.31	98.73	67.42
1987	7.46	11.68	3.68	15.35	96.32	80.97
1988	5.42	7.23	3.11	10.35	102.58	92.23
1989	7.28	6.77	4.36	11.13	129.19	118.46
1990	10.49	9.90	6.34	16.24	56.11	39.88
1991	6.61	7.47	3.75	11.22	93.20	81.98
1992	6.21	6.15	3.67	9.82	112.46	102.64

Source: Central Bank Bulletin.
Note: Included are federal bonds and bills, savings deposits, and fixed term deposits and M1. Also included in 1991 are investment funds and special yield deposits.

Table A.13. Brazil: Monetary Base and Money Supply, 1980–92
(Percentage of M4)

End of period	Monetary base	Sight deposits	Money supply	M1
1980	19.06	31.00	7.92	38.92
1981	13.47	22.45	5.93	28.39
1982	11.96	19.74	5.31	25.05
1983	7.52	15.78	3.96	19.74
1984	6.98	11.82	3.36	15.18
1985	6.17	12.00	3.19	15.19
1986	12.46	25.86	5.85	31.72
1987	7.75	12.12	3.82	15.94
1988	5.28	7.05	3.04	10.09
1989	5.62	5.23	3.36	8.59
1990	18.69	17.64	11.29	28.94
1991	7.09	8.02	4.02	12.04
1992	5.52	5.47	3.26	8.73

Source: Central Bank Bulletin.

Table A.14. Brazil: Monetary Base and Money Supply, 1980–92
(Percentage of GDP)

End of period	Monetary base	Sight deposits	Money supply	M1	M4	Difference M4 - M1
1980	4.24	6.89	1.76	8.65	22.23	13.58
1981	3.50	5.83	1.54	7.36	25.94	18.58
1982	3.34	5.51	1.48	6.99	27.90	20.91
1983	1.81	3.80	0.95	4.75	24.06	19.31
1984	1.99	3.38	0.96	4.34	28.56	24.22
1985	1.95	3.79	1.01	4.79	31.55	26.75
1986	4.45	9.24	2.09	11.33	35.71	24.38
1987	2.38	3.72	1.17	4.90	30.73	25.83
1988	1.46	1.94	0.84	2.78	27.55	24.77
1989	1.32	1.23	0.79	2.02	23.51	21.49
1990	1.99	1.88	1.20	3.08	10.65	7.57
1991	1.46	1.65	0.83	2.48	17.27	14.79
1992	1.40	1.39	0.83	2.22	25.37	23.16

Source: Central Bank Bulletin.

Table A.15. Brazil: Public Sector Financing Needs, 1980–92
(Percentage of GDP)

Year	Total operations	Nominal total
1980	n.a.	n.a.
1981	6.54	13.73
1982	7.11	16.88
1983	3.18	20.96
1984	2.86	22.86
1985	4.19	28.52
1986	3.63	11.23
1987	5.67	32.21
1988	4.58	52.15
1989	6.85	82.71
1990	-1.30	29.26
1991[a]	-1.32	25.77
1992[b]	1.87	35.27

Source: Central Bank Bulletin.
[a] Preliminary data based on a methodology in process of revision.
[b] January-September estimate.
n.a Not available.

Table A.16.   Brazil: Loans to the Financial System by Final Lenders, 1974–92
(Percentage of GDP)

Year	Total	Monetary system	Banco do Brasil	Commercial banks[1]	Nonmonetary system
1974	28.20	13.94	5.55	8.39	14.26
1975	32.54	16.53	7.37	9.10	16.01
1976	33.64	16.87	7.71	9.23	16.48
1977	34.58	17.21	7.89	9.33	17.37
1978	35.25	17.37	7.62	9.74	17.88
1979	34.20	16.65	6.89	9.76	17.55
1980	27.37	13.54	5.58	7.97	13.83
1981	24.86	11.70	4.33	7.37	13.16
1982	26.25	11.13	3.64	7.49	15.13
1983	22.43	8.27	2.91	5.37	14.16
1984	18.20	6.07	1.70	4.37	12.14
1985	18.45	6.26	1.55	4.70	12.19
1986	18.40	8.25	2.50	5.75	10.15
1987	17.47	7.61	2.49	5.12	9.86
1988	16.14	6.51	2.67	3.84	9.50
1989	14.39	3.88	2.07	4.63	7.70
1990	12.20	1.98	1.29	5.33	5.58
1991	11.03	2.28	1.44	5.74	3.86
1992	12.34	2.71	1.82	6.46	4.06

Source: Central Bank Bulletin.
[1] Includes multiple banks after 1988.

Table A.17. Central Bank Interventions in the Brazilian Banking System (between January 1, 1986 and January 10, 1992)

Bank	Type	Intervention regime	Starting date	Completion date
Agrobanco	Private national commercial bank	Closed	29.07.88	22.02.90
Columbia	Private multiple national bank	Closing	13.11.90	
Credireal	Public multiple state bank	Special (terminated)	15.05.87	15.05.89
State of Bahia	Public commercial state bank	Special (terminated)	18.05.87	17.03.89
State of Alagoas	Public commercial state bank	Special (terminated)	16.11.88	05.09.89
State of Alagoas	Public commercial state bank	Special	05.09.89	
State of Pernambuco	Public commercial state bank	Special (terminated)	27.09.91	17.03.92
State of Acre	Public commercial state bank	Special	07.06.89	
State of Piauí	Public commercial state bank	Closed[1]	07.06.89	20.09.90
State of Piauí	Public commercial state bank	Closing	09.04.91	
State of Rio de Janeiro	Public commercial state bank	Special (terminated)	26.02.87	27.02.89
State of Rio Grande do Norte	Public commercial state bank	Closing	20.09.90	
State of Santa Catarina	Public commercial state bank	Special (terminated)	26.02.87	27.02.89
State of Ceará	Public commercial state bank	Special (terminated)	26.02.87	30.12.88
State of Maranhâo	Public commercial state bank	Special (terminated)	26.02.87	22.09.88
State of Mato Groso	Public commercial state bank	Special (terminated)	26.02.87	27.02.89
State of Paraíba	Public commercial state bank	Closing	20.09.90	
State of Pará	Public commercial state bank	Special (terminated)	29.05.87	29.05.89
Grande Rio	Private multiple national bank	Closing	21.01.91	
Sibisa	Private multiple national bank	Bankrupt	14.09.90	27.03.92
CaixeGo	State savings bank	Closing	20.09.90	
MinasCaixa	State savings bank	Special (terminated)	15.05.87	15.05.90
MinasCaixa	State savings bank	Closing	15.03.91	

Source: Central Bank of Brazil.
[1] Closed. Pending legal appeal.
NB: The dates are expressed in terms of day, month and year.
Observation: The special regime is applicable only to state banks.

Table A.18. Brazil: Estimated Composition of Available Income, 1980–90
(Percentage of GDP)

	Private sector	Public sector	Rest of world
1980			
Gross domestic product (revenues of nonfinancial enterprises)	100.00		
Profits of state enterprises	-2.96	2.96	
Interest on the public debt	0.76	-0.76	
Net profits and dividend payments	-1.40		1.40
Net interest payments		-1.79	1.79
Social security transfers	7.77	-7.77	
Private sector transfers	4.44	-4.44	
Income tax	-11.18	11.18	
Indirect tax	-13.52	13.52	
Available income	83.91	12.89	3.20
1985			
Gross domestic product (revenues of nonfinancial enterprises)	100.00		
Profits of state enterprises	-0.63	0.63	
Interest on the public debt	2.30	-2.30	
Net profits and dividend payments	-1.18		1.18
Net interest payments		-4.08	4.08
Social security transfers	7.24	-7.24	
Private sector transfers	1.28	-1.28	
Income tax	-11.96	11.96	
Indirect tax	-10.57	10.57	
Available income	86.49	8.25	5.26
1989			
Gross domestic product (revenues of nonfinancial enterprises)	100.00		
Profits of state enterprises	0.19	-0.19	
Interest on the public debt	1.44	-1.44	
Net profits and dividend payments	-1.04		1.04
Net interest payments		-1.94	1.94
Social security transfers	7.50	-7.50	
Private sector transfers	-3.13	3.13	
Income tax	-11.17	11.17	
Indirect tax	-10.77	10.77	
Available income	83.02	14.00	2.98
1990			
Gross domestic product (revenues of nonfinancial enterprises)	100.00		
Profits of state enterprises	0.47	-0.47	
Interest on the public debt	1.22	-1.22	
Net profits and dividend payments	-0.83		0.83
Net interest payment		-1.44	1.44
Social security transfers	8.29	-8.29	
Private sector transfers	-2.18	2.18	
Income tax	-13.12	13.12	
Indirect tax	-14.31	14.31	
Available income	79.55	18.18	2.27

Table A.19. Brazil: Estimates of the Composition of the Demand for Goods and Services, 1980–90
(Percentage of GDP)

	Available income	Savings	Revenue of firms	Sum = savings	Sum = surplus
1980					
Private sector	83.91		-69.71	14.20	
		14.20	-16.66		-2.46
Public sector	12.89		-9.20	3.69	
		3.69	-6.67		-2.98
Rest of world	3.20		2.25	5.45	
Total			-100.00	23.34	
1985					
Private sector	86.49		-65.78	20.71	
		20.71	-14.34		6.37
Public sector	8.25		-9.87	-1.62	
		-1.62	-4.85		-6.47
Rest of world	5.26		-5.15	0.11	
Total			-100.00	19.19	
1989					
Private sector	83.02		-57.61	25.41	
		25.41	-19.52		5.89
Public sector	14.00		-14.32	-0.32	
		-0.32	-5.33		-5.65
Rest of world	2.98		-3.21	-0.23	
Total			-100.00	24.87	
1990					
Private sector	79.55		-60.92	18.63	
		18.63	-16.72		1.91
Public sector	18.18		-15.63	2.55	
		2.55	-4.95		-2.40
Rest of world	2.27		-1.77	0.50	
Total			-100.00	21.69	

CHAPTER FOUR

COLOMBIA

Eduardo Lora, Luis Alberto Zuleta, and Sandra Zuluaga[1]

Description of the System

The Colombian financial system has traditionally been based on a specialization of lending operations, with a certain diversification of borrowing activities.

Structure

Types of Intermediaries and Ownership Structure

The system comprises the central bank, commercial banks (hereinafter banks), savings and housing corporations (CAVs), finance corporations (CFs), commercial financing companies (CFCs), other finance service companies (leasing companies, bonded warehouses, and trust companies), some special institutions (the Social Savings Bank, the Agrarian Bank, and the Central Mortgage Bank), the Financial Institutions Guarantees Fund, and other official second-floor official entities (the National Energy Finance Company, the Area Development Finance Company, Finagro, and the Bank of External Commerce).

Pursuant to the Constitution of 1991, the Bank of the Republic functions as an autonomous central bank independent of the government and responsible for monetary, exchange, and credit policy. It operates under the authority of a board of directors composed of five members (appointed for fixed terms), the bank's general manager, and the Minister of Finance. The bank traditionally used to handle a variety of rediscount funds that have been discontinued or transferred to other institutions. The Constitution bars it from lending to the private sector but permits it to rediscount lines of external credit for development purposes. The

[1] The authors are grateful for the comments and suggestions of the IDB's anonymous referees, as well as those received from Roberto Frenkel, Oliver Bernal, Roberto Steiner, and Javier Fernández.

government's primary lending is also severely limited, as it requires the unanimous approval of the board of directors.

The nucleus of the financial system is the commercial banking system, organized around the central bank in 1923. Since then the banks have operated as short-term financial intermediaries and as a banking system for current accounts, basically attending to the needs of working capital for industry and trade. In the sixties they also became intermediaries of rediscount funds and lines of credit for development established in the central bank in support of investment and specific sectors (Ocampo, 1987; Avella and Lora, 1991). Twenty-four banks are currently in existence: eleven national private, five private with foreign capital (mixed), three foreign and five official, including two that were nationalized during the crisis of the eighties and are now slated for reprivatization. The capital and reserves of the banks amount to 1.2 percent of GDP and their loans represent 22.4 percent (Table 4.1). Mixed and foreign banks are smaller on average, although some of the private banks are also small.[2]

Attempts to establish an investment bank go back to the twenties and thirties. The Central Mortgage Bank, an official bank created in 1931 to take over the assets of the bankrupt private mortgage banks, still exists. The Agrarian Bank, an official bank intended for agricultural development, also goes back to that period. The investment banking system received new impetus with the development during the seventies of the finance corporations (CFs), created to further the capital market and the financing of long-term investment. There are 22 CFs (six official and the rest private), with capital and reserves equivalent to 0.5 percent of GDP and assets worth 4.8 percent of GDP.[3] CFs are generally owned by banks, as part of financial conglomerates. In these cases they have concentrated their investment portfolios in enterprises of the conglomerate, and the objective of capitalizing new enterprises has been limited.

The savings and housing corporations (CAVs) were created in 1972 for the dual purpose of spurring private saving and supporting the production of, and demand for, housing. They have had the unique ability to effect all their transactions in "constant purchasing power units" (UPACs). There are nine CAVs (six private and three official), with capital equivalent to 0.2 percent of GDP and

---

[2] Herfindhal's concentration indexes for the banks' loans, assets, liabilities, and net worth are, according to 1991 figures, 0.085, 0.083 and 0.074, respectively. These indexes have not varied appreciably, at least since 1980. These levels of concentration do not significantly exceed those of other countries of the region (0.076 for assets in Bolivia, 0.072 in Ecuador, 0.064 in Venezuela, and 0.173 in Peru). See Zuleta and Maurer (1992).

[3] The Herfindhal indexes for the loans, assets, liabilities, and net worth of the CFs are 0.129, 0.135, 0.132, and 0.116, respectively, according to 1991 statistics, with a slight rise since 1980, when they stood at 0.117, 0.111, 0.113, and 0.09.

Table 4.1. Structure of the Colombian Financial System, 1991
(Millions of pesos)

Institutions	No. of firms	No. of branches	Capital and reserves		Assets		Cap/ assets ratio
			Amount	% of GDP	Amount	% of GDP	
Banco de la República	-	28	37,494	0.14	6,148,191	22.36	0.61
Commercial Banks	24	1990	329,674	1.20	6,155,469	22.39	5.35
Private	11	905	136,443	0.50	2,882,416	10.49	4.73
Mixed[1]	5	105	21,498	0.08	289,461	1.05	7.43
Foreign	3	60	22,634	0.08	257,427	0.94	8.79
Official[2]	5	920	149,099	0.54	2,726,165	0.91	5.47
Savings & loan associations	9	782	59,755	0.22	2,294,725	8.35	2.60
Private	6	536	41,817	0.15	1,543,100	5.61	2.71
Official	3	246	17,938	0.07	751,625	2.73	2.39
Financial corporations	22	197	148,382	0.54	1,332,635	4.84	11.14
Private	16	148	66,310	0.24	1,022,010	3.72	6.49
Official[3]	6	49	82,072	0.30	310,625	1.13	26.46
Commercial financial companies	31	163	69,020	0.25	671,035	2.44	10.29
Private	29	138	59,852	0.22	609,265	2.22	9.82
Official	2	25	9,168	0.03	61,770	0.22	14.84
Other financial institutions			42,313	0.15	255,538	0.93	16.56
Leasing companies	43	-	20,589	0.07	160,262	0.58	12.85
Private	42	-	20,289	0.07	155,837	0.57	13.02
Official	1	-	300	0.00	4,425	0.02	6.78
General bonded warehouses	12	-	14,875	0.05	82,206	0.30	18.09
Private	10	-	12,248	0.04	58,126	0.21	21.07
Official	2	-	2,627	0.01	24,080	0.09	10.91
Trust companies	15	-	6,850	0.02	13,069	0.05	52.41
Private	14	-	5,872	0.02	11,040	0.04	53.19
Official	1	-	977	0.00	2,029	0.01	48.16
Special institutions:			152,573	0.55	2,980,415	10.84	5.12
Corporate Savings Banks (private)	1	123	7,098	0.03	136,985	0.50	5.18
Agricultural Banks (official)	1	926	63,966	0.23	902,498	3.28	7.09
Central Mortgage Bank (official)	1	145	6,203	0.02	641,336	2.33	0.97
National Energy Financing (official)	1	1	75,306	0.27	1,299,596	4.73	5.79
Total private institutions[4]	137		394,062	1.43	6,966,667	25.34	5.66
Total official institutions[2]	23		407,656	1.48	6,723,711	24.45	6.06
Total	160		839,211	3.05	19,838,569	72.15	4.23

Source: Asociación Bancaria de Colombia (Banking Association of Colombia) and Revista del Banco de la República. FEDESARROLLO calculations.

[1] Refers to banks with some percentage of foreign capital.
[2] Refers in all cases to official institutions as well as those that have been nationalized.
[3] Does not include FEN since it is considered a special institution.
[4] For banks, this total includes mixed and foreign banks. Does not include Banco de la República.

amounting to 8.3 percent of GDP.[4] The low capital/assets ratio (2.6 per-
is due to the mortgage backing of all credits. Their network of offices is
extensive, and they boast almost 5 million accounts. All CAVs are owned
by groups of financiers or conglomerates with well-defined economic interests,
in particular the construction and insurance industries.

The commercial financing companies (CFCs) were established in 1979 on
the basis of the financial intermediaries of the nonbank market which had been
overseen by the Banking Superintendency since 1973 and which had been set up
as a result of the severe financial repression of the period. They were then
required to put up minimum capital, and compulsory investments and interest
rate ceilings were imposed on them, as was done with the rest of the regulated
financial system. The CFCs have specialized in financing durable consumer
goods and the business sector. There are currently 31 CFCs (two official, the rest
private), with a capital of 0.25 percent of GDP and assets worth 2.4 percent of
GDP. Although their capital is comparable with that of the CAVs, they represent
a very small segment of the financial system because of their high capital/assets
ratio (10.3 percent), for reasons of risk. Unlike the CFs and the CAVs, CFCs
cannot be owned by banks (except those specializing in leasing under Law 35,
1993). The bulk of their shares are in the hands of investment companies and
businesses of the productive sector.

The financial services organizations comprise leasing companies, bonded
warehouses and trust companies, whose basic statistics for 1991 appear in Table
4.1. In 1992, the unemployment funds were introduced to manage the social benefit savings provided to workers by businesses. The creation of pension funds as the
basis of an individual capitalization system is under discussion in the Congress. In
addition to these entities there are more than 1,000 first-grade savings and loan
cooperatives supervised by a body separate from the financial authorities. These
cooperatives possess capital comparable with that of the CAVs (Vesga and Lora,
1992). In 1992, the two largest cooperatives were turned into banks.

Leaving aside the funds and cooperatives referred to, and including the special entities enumerated at the end of Table 4.1, there are 160 entities in all, 23 of
them official and the rest private (including the mixed and foreign organizations
that operate only in the banking sector).[5] The system's capital and reserves are
equivalent to 3 percent of GDP, which in 1991 was shared equally by the public
and private sectors, and the assets equal approximately 50 percent of GDP, also
shared equally (plus the assets of the Bank of the Republic, which are worth 22.4
percent of GDP). The public sector's share is excessive in terms of capital and

---

4 The Herfindhal indexes for loans, assets, liabilities, and net worth are all 0.128 for 1991,
without any significant fluctuation at least since 1980.

5 The table does not include statistics for Finagro, Findeter, and Bancoldex, which are recently
created second-floor official institutions whose indicators are not available.

assets, and it is dispersed throughout the breadth of the system partly as a result of the preventive nationalizations during the crisis of the eighties. The opportunities opened up by Law 45 of 1990 resulted in four foreign entities joining the banking sector (three of them Venezuelan), and five entities being privatized. Thus public sector participation in the banking system has dropped from 60.3 percent of the assets in 1989 to 44.3 percent in December 1991 and 36.7 percent in November 1992.

Structure of Assets

The main component of the system's assets in the loan portfolio amounts close to 70 percent in the case of the CAVs, CFs, and CFCs, and 45 percent in the case of the banks (Table 4.2). The smaller share of credit in the banks' assets is due to the size of the liquid assets and the forced investments and of the reserve requirement (28.2 percent), compared to the 4.6 percent for the CFs, 9.5 percent for the CAVs, and 10.9 percent for the CFCs (rates determined essentially by the legal requirements governing cash reserves and investments). The CFs are the only segment of the system that makes capital investments (about 5 percent of its assets). This small difference in the structure of the balance sheet shows that few of the CFs' original objectives have been met. Voluntary investments, which were practically nonexistent until the mid-eighties, now represent 5 percent of the system's assets. This share depends, however, on strictly cyclical factors, owing to excess liquidity and the use of open market operations as a monetary management tool. Other investments (which include investments of cash reserves being dismantled and others of less value) represent 4 percent of the CAV and CFC assets, 3 percent of the banks' assets, and 1.6 percent of CF assets. The physical assets represent about 2 percent of the assets of the system and the unproductive assets (doubtful loans and accounts receivable) approximately 6 percent, (6.4 percent in the case of the banks) and lower rates in the CFs (3.8 percent) and CAVs (3.4 percent, while for the CFCs it is 9.4 percent).

Structure of Liabilities

For the system as a whole the deposits and current liabilities with the public account for 73.7 percent of the liabilities and the resources obtained from the central bank 7 percent (Table 4.3). The rest are debit accounts consisting of interbank funds, acceptances, accounts payable, remittances, bonds, and obligations with international or national lending institutions. The fact that the official institutions depend more on special liabilities (other current liabilities and the rest of the liabilities) is due to the operations to bail out and finance institutions nationalized during the eighties.

Table 4.2. Asset Structure of Major Colombian Financial Institutions, 1991
(Percentages)

Institutions	Liquid assets	Investments							Credit Portfolio[4]	Acceptance Debtors	Inactive assets		Other Assets	Total Assets	Assets/GDP
		Forced	Cash reserve	Voluntary	Capital	Others	Reserve	Total			Physical	Others[5]			
Banks	20.60	4.33	2.47	3.64	0.00	0.44	0.00	0.00	43.68	4.65	2.20	6.41	11.57	100.00	22.39
Private	19.76	4.75	2.23	3.57	0.00	0.36	0.00	0.00	45.24	5.63	2.23	5.35	10.89	100.00	10.49
Mixed	14.38	6.87	2.97	7.36	0.00	0.00	0.00	0.00	49.99	5.73	1.49	3.04	8.17	68.42	1.05
Foreign	18.96	4.05	2.34	8.02	0.00	1.15	0.00	15.57	46.73	5.16	1.90	3.92	7.76	65.47	0.94
Official	22.31	3.63	2.68	2.91	0.00	0.50	0.00	9.73	41.08	3.46	2.28	8.13	13.02	100.00	9.91
Financial corporations	2.23	1.22	1.13	1.86	4.98	0.45	0.66	8.98	70.59	0.20	0.84	3.79	13.37	18.20	4.55
Private	2.41	1.49	1.30	1.79	4.86	0.47	0.12	9.61	72.42	0.13	0.79	3.40	11.24	0.00	3.72
Official[1]	1.42	0.05	0.39	2.18	6.28	0.35	3.06	6.19	62.47	0.50	1.08	5.50	22.83	100.00	0.84
Savings and loan associations	1.47	3.77	4.01	9.90	0.00	0.00	0.00	17.69	72.76	0.00	2.02	3.40	2.66	8.08	8.35
Private	1.82	3.61	3.89	8.45	0.00	0.00	0.00	15.96	74.58	0.00	2.15	3.19	2.31	100.00	5.61
Official	0.75	4.10	4.26	12.88	0.00	0.00	0.00	0.00	69.04	0.00	1.74	3.83	3.40	8.97	2.73
Commercial financial companies	4.32	2.44	3.53	5.60	0.00	0.27	0.01	11.85	64.62	2.38	2.33	9.36	51.50	100.00	2.44
Private	4.39	2.57	3.23	4.70	0.00	0.30	0.01	10.78	65.72	2.40	2.42	9.48	4.81	0.00	2.22
Official	3.64	1.17	6.53	14.48	0.00	0.00	0.00	0.00	53.73	2.13	1.52	8.23	8.58	100.00	0.22
Others[2]	7.32	1.04	0.00	15.72	0.00	0.00	0.00	0.00	1.43	0.00	17.69	11.09	45.80	74.49	0.35
Private	4.48	0.80	0.00	15.55	0.00	0.00	0.00	0.00	1.29	0.00	18.84	10.47	48.56	100.00	0.25
Official	14.83	1.69	0.00	16.16	0.00	0.00	0.00	0.00	1.78	0.00	14.32	12.72	38.50	65.54	0.09
Total private[3]	11.13	3.81	2.58	4.99	0.72	0.30	0.02	12.38	57.86	3.12	2.13	4.83	8.55	0.00	24.27
Total official	16.42	3.46	2.90	5.12	0.38	0.38	0.19	12.05	47.85	2.55	2.17	7.15	11.81	0.00	13.80
Total	13.05	3.68	2.70	5.04	0.60	0.33	0.08	12.26	54.23	2.91	2.15	5.67	9.74	100.00	38.07

Source: Asociación Bancaria de Colombia, FEDESARROLLO calculations.
[1] Includes only IFI and Corfigan.
[2] Includes trust companies and bonded general warehouses.
[3] In the case of banks, includes mixed and foreign.
[4] It refers to active portfolio.
[5] Includes doubtful debts and accounts payable.

Table 4.3. Structure of the Liabilities of Major Colombian Financial Institutions, 1991
(Percentages)

Institutions	Current Liabilities										Banco de la República			Other Liabilities	Total Liabilities	Liabilities/ GDP
	Current account deposits	Bills payable	Certificates of deposit	Bonds	Ordinary	Time	Fixed rate savings account	Fixed rate savings certif.	Others	Total	Coupons	Financial Funds Rediscount	Total			
Banks	29.06	0.00	20.00	0.00	6.20	3.54	0.00	0.00	6.20	65.00	1.69	6.27	7.95	27.04	100.00	20.02
Private	30.14	0.00	21.18	0.00	5.17	4.56	0.00	0.00	4.92	65.97	0.52	6.63	7.16	26.87	100.00	9.09
Mixed	22.93	0.00	33.30	0.00	1.09	5.97	0.00	0.00	5.89	69.19	1.25	7.76	9.01	21.80	100.00	0.91
Foreign	21.70	0.00	34.14	0.00	6.85	4.88	0.00	0.00	5.07	72.64	3.52	7.63	11.15	16.21	100.00	0.82
Official	29.27	0.00	16.25	0.00	7.67	2.17	0.00	0.00	7.60	62.95	2.72	5.63	8.35	28.70	100.00	9.19
Financial corporations	0.00	0.00	43.78	8.37	0.00	0.00	0.00	0.00	0.84	52.99	0.19	22.25	22.44	24.57	100.00	3.50
Private	0.00	0.00	47.33	8.35	0.00	0.00	0.00	0.00	0.68	56.36	0.21	22.18	22.39	21.24	100.00	3.10
Official[1]	0.00	0.00	15.82	8.52	0.00	0.00	0.00	0.00	2.11	26.44	0.02	22.79	22.81	50.75	100.00	0.39
Savings and loan associations	0.00	0.00	0.00	0.00	4.03	0.00	74.72	17.50	0.02	96.28	0.00	0.00	0.00	3.72	100.00	7.90
Private	0.00	0.00	0.00	0.00	5.30	0.00	73.74	17.12	0.03	96.19	0.00	0.00	0.00	3.81	100.00	5.33
Official	0.00	0.00	0.00	0.00	1.40	0.00	76.76	18.29	0.01	96.46	0.00	0.00	0.00	3.54	100.00	2.57
Commercial financial companies	0.00	0.14	81.47	0.00	0.00	0.00	0.00	0.00	0.73	82.34	0.25	0.00	0.25	17.41	100.00	2.15
Private	0.00	0.15	80.63	0.00	0.00	0.00	0.00	0.00	0.81	81.60	0.00	0.00	0.00	18.40	100.00	1.92
Official	0.00	0.00	88.60	0.00	0.00	0.00	0.00	0.00	0.07	88.68	2.35	0.00	2.35	8.98	100.00	0.23
Others[2]	0.00	0.00	0.00	0.00	0.00	0.00	0.00	0.00	15.83	15.83	0.00	0.00	0.00	84.17	100.00	0.10
Private	0.00	0.00	0.00	0.00	0.00	0.00	0.00	0.00	8.93	8.93	0.00	0.00	0.00	91.07	100.00	0.09
Official	0.00	0.00	0.00	0.00	0.00	0.00	0.00	0.00	86.58	86.58	0.00	0.00	0.00	13.42	100.00	0.01
Total private[3]	14.70	0.01	25.99	1.22	3.85	2.39	18.48	4.29	2.77	73.71	0.44	6.70	7.14	19.14	100.00	21.27
Total official	21.71	0.00	14.16	0.27	5.98	1.61	15.94	3.80	5.77	69.23	2.06	4.90	6.96	23.81	100.00	12.39
Total	17.28	0.01	21.64	0.87	4.63	2.10	17.55	4.11	3.87	72.06	1.04	6.04	7.08	20.86	100.00	33.66

Source. Asociación Bancaria de Colombia, FEDESARROLLO calculations.
[1] Includes only IFI and Corfigan.
[2] Includes trust companies and bonded general warehouses.
[3] In the case of banks, includes mixed and foreign.

Only the banks have a relatively diversified structure for attracting deposits including current accounts (29 percent of liabilities), certificates of deposit, most of them with 90 days' maturity (20 percent), ordinary savings sight deposits (6.2 percent), term deposits (3.5 percent), and other current liabilities (6.2 percent). In addition, the banks depend on central bank resources for 8 percent of their liabilities. Their funding sources are fairly stable, both individually, and overall, which offers them the possibility (little explored) of changing maturities (Arciniegas, 1984; Rodríguez, 1991).

By contrast, the CFs depend on certificates of deposit (CDT) (43.8 percent), and resources from the Bank of the Republic (22.4 percent). Since the CFs' main discretional source of deposits consists of concentrated, and relatively unstable resources, they are poorly equipped to change maturities, so that long-term lending has depended essentially on the central bank and international organizations. However, financing by means of medium-term bonds doubled in 1992, increasing to almost 12 percent of the CFs' borrowing.

The CAVs obtain practically all their resources through savings deposits in three forms: ordinary (4 percent), constant value accounts (75 percent), and constant value term certificates (17 percent). Only the last-named have a repayment term, 90 days in virtually every case. The constant value accounts are the most stable form of borrowing in the system (despite their marked seasonality), so that CAV borrowings are rather stable. Nevertheless, their ability to compete depends crucially on the monetary correction of the UPAC, which determines the profitability of their constant value liabilities (in relation to the CDTs of other intermediaries and in relation to the traditional bank savings accounts, whose yields were liberalized in 1991).

The CFCs have the system's most concentrated borrowings: 81 percent consists of term certificates. The fact that their resources and borrowing costs are unstable severely curtails their investment opportunities. The trust companies and bonded warehouses depend crucially on resources of a nature specific to their activity.

Real Interest Rates and Spreads

The CDT, issued by banks, CFs, and CFCs, is the chief instrument for borrowing financial resources at market rates. Its yield has been positive with fluctuations of less than 10 percent since 1985 (Figures 4.1). Overall borrowing by CFCs has had a cost very similar to that of the CDT, since the latter has been their chief borrowing instrument. The banks also borrow CDTs in substantial amounts but have less costly resources such as savings accounts and the (unremunerated) current account. Hence their weighted borrowing cost has been constantly negative in real terms. Meanwhile, the chief borrowing instruments of the CAVs have been tied to monetary correction, plus a return that was fixed until 1991. The

Figure 4.1. Colombia: Real Borrowing Rates, 1983-92
(Percentages)

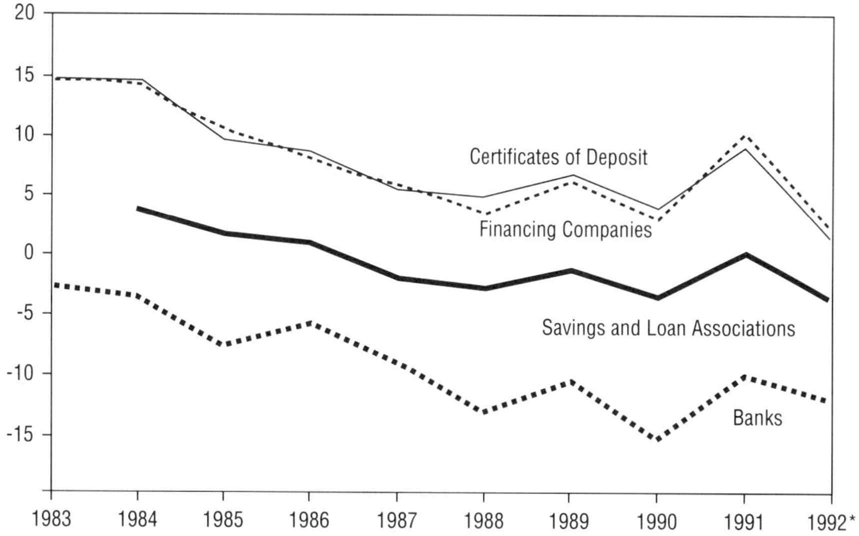

Certificates of Deposit

Financing Companies

Savings and Loan Associations

Banks

Sources: Clavijo (1991) and economic memoranda.
* As of September 1992.

correction has been below inflation, because of ceilings set for its calculation and the hybrid adjustment methods adopted from 1984 on.[6] As a result, the CAVs' cost of borrowing has tended to be negative.

Since 1985 there has not been any clear trend as regards real borrowing rates. In 1991 rates rose temporarily because of monetary sterilization policies, which were reversed in 1992.

The lending rates of all the financial intermediaries have been positive in real terms, and they have come down appreciably since the middle of the last decade, under the pressure of controls imposed in 1986 and 1988. In recent years, bank and CFC lending rates have followed the same pattern as borrowing rates, and in 1992 they also felt the effect of new controls. By contrast, the easing of CAV lending rates in 1991 led to a sharp increase that year, which was only partially reversed in 1992 (Figure 4.2).

---

[6] Since May 1993 the correction has been calculated as 90 percent of the weighted cost of the CAVs' borrowing resources in the preceding month. This method replaced the previous system, which combined inflation with a market interest rate indicator.

Figure 4.2. Colombia: Real Lending Rates, 1983-92
(Percentages)

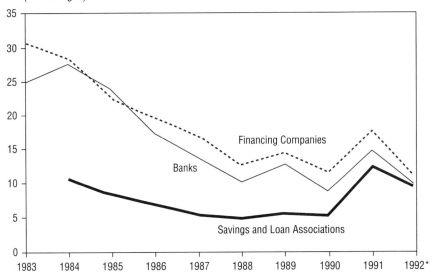

Sources: Clavijo (1991) and economic memoranda.
* As of September 1992.

Spreads, calculated as the difference between the (nominal) lending rate and the (nominal) weighted borrowing rate on the various resources, show appreciable fluctuations over time and enormous differences among intermediaries (Figure 4.3). Those of the banks and the CFCs have fallen since the mid-eighties. Those of the CAVs, on the other hand, have tended to rise, especially in the past few years in the wake of the easing of their lending rates.

Bank spreads can be broken down into an operating cost component, a policy cost component (because of the reserve requirements and forced investments), and a market structure component, which exists because the demand for credit from the banks is not infinitely elastic. The fact that of the three components only the last rose during the eighties suggests that limited competition was the chief factor preventing an even greater reduction in spreads (Barajas, 1992).[7]

[7] This study finds that the marginal operating costs trended downward in the eighties, suggesting improvements in efficiency not reflected in the traditional indicators. See Lora (1991a) for an estimation of the bank lending rate based on costs.

Figure 4.3. Colombia: Brokerage Spreads, 1983-92
(Percentages)

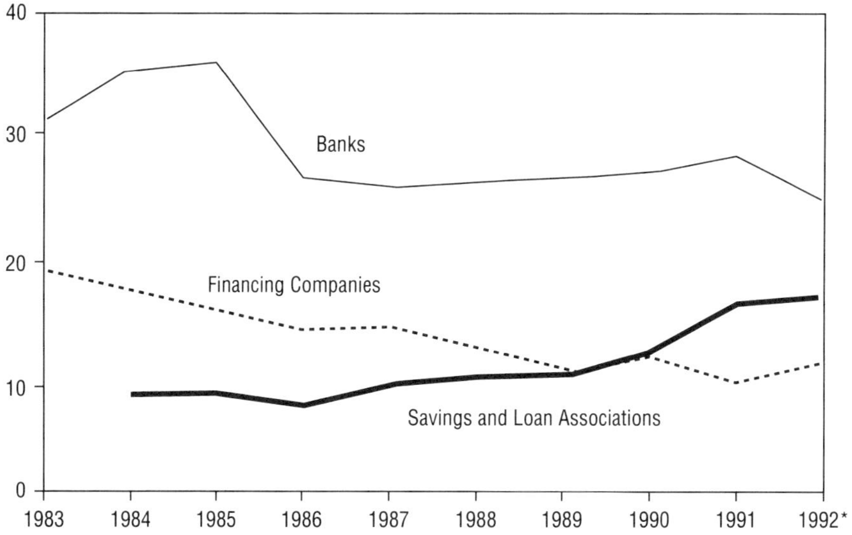

Sources: Clavijo (1991) and economic memoranda.
* As of September 1992.

Performance of the System

Gross Financial Productivity Indicators

The gross financial margin as a percentage of total assets shows appreciable differences between types of intermediary: 9.2 percent in banks, 7.1 percent in CFCs, 5.6 percent in CAVs, and 4.3 percent in CFs[8] (Tables 4.4 and 4.5)[9] There is no definite pattern by type of property: official CFs have greater access to cheaper official resources, which allows a greater spread, but this argument does not apply in the case of banks because of the smaller revenues produced by their assets. The differences of this indicator are strengthened when calculated with respect to productive assets instead of total assets (17.6 percent in banks, 9.8 percent in CFCs, and about 6 percent in CFs and CAVs). Banks are in a privileged position in terms of gross spreads because of their monopoly on unremunerated

---

[8] The variability (typical/average deviation) of this indicator is relatively moderate among the firms of each group: 19 percent for banks, 38 percent for CFs, and 10 percent for CAVs. This implies limited differentiation of the borrowing or lending interest rates among the firms of each group. (Tables 4.4 and 4.5).

[9] The series of Table 4.5 refer only to the private institutions. The indicators may show small differences with respect to Table 4.4 because of rounding in the original figures.

Table 4.4. Colombia: Major Financial Institutions Performance Indicators, 1991
(Percentages)

Groups	Financial Margin			Efficiency and Productivity Indicators					Profitability Indicators		Tax Indicators	
	GFM	(GFM/TA)	(GFM/AA)	FE/TA	Lab.exp./TA	Adm.exp./TA	Lab.exp./GFM	Adm.exp./GFM	Return on assets	Return on capital	Taxes/TA	Taxes/GFM
Banks	2.0	9.20	17.56	8.92	4.39	5.20	47.72	56.51	2.51	46.84	0.83	9.00
Private	2.1	9.47	17.29	8.30	4.09	4.75	43.16	50.09	2.90	61.38	1.14	12.03
Mixed	1.8	10.09	16.00	12.76	3.60	4.33	35.66	42.91	4.32	58.22	1.95	19.30
Foreign	1.6	10.98	17.98	16.92	4.94	6.13	44.99	55.83	2.80	31.86	1.20	10.92
Official	2.0	8.66	18.05	8.41	4.75	5.69	54.82	65.69	1.87	34.16	0.34	3.98
Financial corporations	1.3	4.31	5.52	17.12	1.40	1.76	32.53	40.89	3.45	33.13	0.68	15.83
Private	1.2	3.40	4.28	19.50	1.15	1.51	33.87	44.46	2.97	45.74	0.55	16.30
Official	2.3	8.34	11.62	6.52	2.51	2.87	30.10	34.42	5.60	20.08	1.25	14.97
Savings and loan associations	1.3	5.58	6.75	19.96	1.75	2.27	31.42	40.72	1.43	54.86	0.67	12.02
Private	1.3	5.81	7.00	19.54	1.74	2.28	29.91	39.18	1.58	58.22	0.76	13.11
Official	1.2	5.12	6.25	20.83	1.79	2.27	34.94	44.30	1.12	47.02	0.49	9.50
Commercial financial companies	1.3	7.10	9.75	21.97	2.38	3.01	33.51	42.45	3.24	31.51	0.90	12.67
Private	1.3	7.53	10.30	21.68	2.33	2.94	30.87	39.07	3.51	35.68	0.99	13.09
Official	1.1	2.84	4.04	24.75	2.92	3.72	102.68	130.83	0.64	4.30	0.05	1.77
Total private	1.5	7.58	11.23	14.43	2.93	3.54	38.68	46.64	2.72	51.50	0.98	12.98
Total official	1.7	7.84	13.86	11.04	3.99	4.80	50.91	61.26	1.93	30.23	0.42	5.40
Total	1.6	7.68	12.08	13.19	3.32	4.00	43.22	52.07	2.43	42.82	0.78	10.17

Source: Asociación Bancaria de Colombia. FEDESARROLLO calculations.
GFM: Gross financial margin = Financial income (FI) - Financial expenditures (FE).
Financial income (FI) = Interest + amortized discount + monetary correction + commissions.
Financial expenditures (FE) = Interest + amortized premium + monetary correction + commissions.
TA: Total assets.
AA: Active assets = Voluntary investments + capital investments + loans
Lab. Exp.: Labor expenses.
Adm. exp.: Administrative expenses including: labor, contributions and dues, leasing, taxes, maintenance, insurance, office improvements, etc.

current accounts. In 1991 spreads as a percentage of assets or as a quotient between financial inflows and outflows reached their highest level since 1980 for banks (Table 4.5). The same does not apply to CFs, where spreads stabilized after the crisis at moderate levels.[10] In the case of the CAVs, the gross spread has increased appreciably since 1989 but the ratio of financial inflows to outflows has remained constant.

Productivity and Efficiency Indicators

The financial cost of assets (financial costs/total assets) also shows appreciable differences among groups of institutions. In general, the official institutions tend to have more moderate financial costs, because of the low cost of official resources. The financial cost of the banks' assets in recent years returned to its levels before the crisis. That of CF assets, on the other hand, has shown a worrisome upward trend since 1987, owing to the higher cost of borrowing through CDTs and, to a lesser extent, the higher cost of lines of credit and credit funds. In the case of CAVs it has been very stable.[11]

The labor cost per peso of assets exceeds $0.04 in the banks, about twice that of the other intermediaries. Only in the case of the CFs are the labor costs of official institutions significantly higher than those of private institutions. Neither the crisis nor the subsequent recovery effort has succeeded in reducing the labor cost per peso of bank, CF, or CAV assets.[12]

As a percentage of the gross spread, labor costs account for 48 percent in the case of banks and about 32 percent in that of CFs, CAVs, and CFCs.[13] The higher labor costs of the banks are linked to their more extensive office networks, possibly greater staff seniority and, in some cases, the lower degree of systematization. With this indicator one finds higher labor costs for the official institutions among all types of intermediaries with the exception of the CFs (due in this case to the low financial cost, which is reflected in wider margins). By combining the labor cost indicator by peso of asset one finds that the low labor productivity in the official financial institutions is a result of the low gross profitability of those operations rather than of high labor costs, as will be seen below.

Administrative costs (current, excluding financial and labor) as a percentage of assets represent 5.2 percent in the case of the banks, 1.8 percent for the CFs, 2.3 percent for CAVs, and 3 percent for CFCs (Table 4.4). The banks' high costs seem to be due to their past practice of opening offices and incurring other

[10] The indicators in Table 4.5 refer to private CFs only.
[11] The variability of this indicator is 31 percent for banks, 32 percent for CFs and 3 percent for CAVs.
[12] The variability is 28 percent for banks, 40 percent for CFs, and 8 percent for CAVs.
[13] With variabilities of 35 percent, 25 percent, and 12 percent, respectively.

Table 4.5. Series of Indicators of the Major Colombian Financial Institutions
(Percentages)

Year	Capital Growth Rate	Capital Assets	Financial Margin			Efficiency and Productivity Indicators			Profitability		Liquidity	Portfolio	
			GFM FI/FE	GMF/TA	GFM/AA	FE/TA	Lab. exp./TA	Adm. exp./TA	Return on cap.	Return on assets	Curr. assets/curr. liab.	Bad debt reserve	BDR/Portfolio
Banks													
1980		5.88	1.88	6.83	11.73	7.72	3.88	4.19	27.62	1.62	40.81	33.91	3.96
1981	15.50	5.05	1.71	6.69	11.37	9.39	3.73	4.04	26.71	1.35	35.44	32.44	4.32
1982	14.13	4.71	1.60	6.28	10.37	10.40	4.02	4.37	12.81	0.60	30.56	37.25	7.99
1983	4.30	3.80	1.58	5.68	9.22	9.74	3.93	4.29	13.20	0.50	29.49	37.26	9.08
1984	-1.47	3.03	1.29	3.55	5.84	12.12	3.94	4.36	5.20	0.16	27.49	27.48	17.89
1985	14.90	2.84	0.96	-0.68	-1.12	16.41	4.00	4.46	-177.94	-5.05	19.54	63.71	24.08
1986	87.86	4.02	1.34	3.82	6.62	11.16	3.87	4.30	-7.06	-0.28	20.78	66.04	21.17
1987	28.34	4.02	1.37	4.16	7.13	11.15	3.78	4.22	7.59	0.30	20.66	73.11	16.18
1988	35.62	4.04	1.42	4.60	7.52	10.96	3.72	4.20	21.96	0.89	23.10	62.58	8.33
1989	25.90	3.84	1.72	7.12	12.42	9.94	3.64	4.23	42.87	1.65	27.23	86.50	3.46
1990	47.58	4.50	1.79	7.69	14.76	9.68	4.06	4.69	32.31	1.45	28.24	111.06	2.12
1991	41.30	5.35	1.93	9.00	17.16	9.72	4.39	5.20	47.87	2.56	35.00	115.24	2.24
Financial Corporations													
1980		8.69	1.73	7.72	11.63	10.64	0.85	1.04	22.55	1.81	1.81	0.00	1.76
1981	28.55	8.03	1.87	10.27	16.69	11.74	1.13	1.35	20.08	1.69	1.64	52.10	2.45
1982	8.25	8.42	1.39	5.65	9.31	14.49	1.22	1.47	8.46	0.68	2.87	8.13	2.54
1983	13.04	8.02	1.00	0.05	0.08	20.59	1.47	1.85	-27.60	-2.28	3.32	29.52	3.57
1984	5.87	8.27	0.91	-1.84	-3.15	20.17	1.35	1.74	-42.17	-3.29	1.70	49.54	13.65
1985	14.53	7.80	0.91	-1.62	-2.81	17.30	1.19	1.52	-18.15	-1.82	2.86	46.22	16.95
1986	83.98	10.01	1.18	2.63	4.03	14.84	1.10	1.34	22.38	1.30	4.06	57.21	20.34
1987	-31.46	5.81	1.21	3.39	5.24	16.40	1.05	1.29	43.94	2.13	3.28	45.28	4.07
1988	17.24	4.84	1.24	3.90	4.90	16.59	1.01	1.32	43.85	1.92	4.09	53.31	1.42
1989	33.21	4.37	1.16	3.05	3.77	18.58	1.03	1.35	50.62	2.33	2.50	73.13	0.58
1990	48.77	4.60	1.16	3.22	4.05	19.68	1.15	1.51	45.74	2.97	4.24	110.12	0.39
1991	74.79	6.49									3.81	134.23	0.28

(continues)

Table 4.5. Series of Indicators of the Major Colombian Financial Institutions (cont.)

Year	Capital Growth Rate	Capital/ Assets	Financial Margin GFM FI/FE	GMF/TA	GFM/AA	Efficiency and Productivity Indicators FE/ TA	Lab. exp./ TA	Adm. exp./ TA	Profitability Return on cap.	Return on assets	Liquidity Curr. assets/ curr. liab.	Portfolio Bad debt reserve	BDR/ Portfolio
Savings and Loan Associations													
1980		3.55									1.83		1.70
1981	40.20	3.36									2.20		0.89
1982	20.60	2.90									1.86		1.32
1983	22.31	2.59	1.20	3.83	4.37	19.20	1.39	1.65	26.23	0.68	1.65		1.63
1984	23.70	2.52	1.20	3.76	4.23	18.53	1.56	1.90	22.43	0.57	1.73		3.10
1985	31.14	2.32	1.18	3.60	4.14	20.00	1.45	1.75	22.10	0.51	1.52		3.01
1986	34.33	2.41	1.20	3.68	4.25	18.53	1.49	1.80	24.05	0.58	1.65		3.20
1987	31.21	2.49	1.21	3.86	4.45	18.76	1.55	1.86	30.76	0.77	2.14		2.75
1988	38.47	2.62	1.22	4.13	4.65	19.01	1.62	2.00	29.81	0.78	2.15		2.39
1989	43.35	2.90	1.25	4.80	5.52	19.52	1.71	2.20	36.79	1.07	2.36		2.37
1990	33.90	2.92	1.26	5.22	6.32	19.90	1.83	2.38	40.86	1.19	2.69	20.35	2.49
1991	32.80	2.60	1.27	5.37	6.50	20.18	1.75	2.27	54.85	1.43	1.61	27.06	1.87

Source: Asociación Bancaria de Colombia, FEDESARROLLO calculations.
GFM: Gross financial margin = Financial income (FI) - Financial expenditures (FE).
TA: Total assets.
AA: Active assets.
Lab.exp.: Labor expenses.
Adm.exp.: Administrative expenses, including; labor, contributions and dues, leasing, taxes, maintenance, insurance, office improvements, etc.
Curr. assets.: Current assets = Cash and deposits in the Banco República + Interbank Funds + Other debtors in M/L.
Curr. liabilities.: Current Liabilities = deposits and receivables + interbank funds.
BDR: Bad Debt Reserve.

costs in order to maximize their participation in the current account and savings deposit market (where interest rates are controlled and negative in real terms). Bank costs furthermore reflect the administrative costs of the national payments system and various administrative and control charges imposed by the economic authorities. It is nevertheless noteworthy that this category of other bank costs did not go down during or after the crisis, and in fact, has gone up in the last few years. No significant adjustment is discernible in the case of the CFs either, and in the CAVs the trend has been upward, at least since 1985.

Administrative costs represent 57 percent of the gross spread in the case of banks and around 41 percent in other groups of intermediaries (Table 4.4). This indicator's variability is very high within the group of banks (61 percent) and CFs (54 percent) and considerably lower in the CAVs (18 percent). The high variability for banks and CFs is consistent with the assumption of sizable inefficiency margins for the intramarginal units because of the possible existence of economies of scale and high barriers to the entry and departure of entities. Several econometric studies have in fact concluded that economies of scale exist with respect to production, size of accounts handled, and joint production of assets and liabilities in the Colombian financial system.[14] Since the economies of scale have not been exhausted, a trend toward concentration and operational cost-cutting should be apparent, but this has not occurred in practice (Arango, 1991). That could be due as much to the barriers just mentioned as to problems created by too much market segmentation. These reasons also appear to explain the rigidity apparent in the principal efficiency and productivity indicators analyzed in this section.

Profitability Indicators

The system's profitability indicators were negative during the crisis of the mid-eighties. After several years of recovery, they are now higher than at the start of the eighties. On average, the profitability of the banks is 2.5 percent with respect to assets and 46.8 percent with respect to capital (real on the order of 15 percent). Profitability is not uniform for the different types of institutions, which is a result of the lack of crossed competencies owing to specialization. In addition, the profitability of the official institutions is substantially lower than that of the private ones, because the objectives of some that are still being reorganized are other than economic. Profitability varies greatly (61 percent) among the banks and is more moderate among the CFs (28 percent) and the CAVs (32 percent).

The direct tax burden on the financial system does not appear excessive: 13 percent of the gross spread in the private institutions and 5.4 percent in the offi-

---

[14] Villegas and Acosta (1989); Bernal and Herrera (1983); Ferrufino (1991); Suescún (1987); and studies listed in Arango (1991).

cial ones (it does not differ substantially by type of institution). It absorbs 36 percent of the earnings of the private sector and 22 percent of the official earnings (the direct corporation tax in Colombia is currently 35.1 percent). It is important to note, however, that in 1992 a system of inflation adjustments went into operation for the financial statements of all types of businesses (Orozco and Pardo, 1992). This system requires that nonmonetary assets and liabilities be corrected for inflation, with the differences shown as profits. Nonmonetary liabilities include accounts that are indexed or subject to monetary correction (UPAC) and foreign currency accounts (like the institution's own position). The effect of the adjustments for the financial system as a whole in the first half of 1992 was to reduce its profitability from 30 percent to 20.4 percent (consequently diminishing the actual tax burden). The reduction varied greatly by groups of institutions.[15]

Portfolio Quality Indicators

Overdue accounts (including doubtful loans) of the system as a whole represent 6.2 percent of the total portfolio, but the figure is twice as high for the official as for the private intermediaries (9.9 percent versus 4.4 percent) (Table 4.6). This phenomenon is repeated in the case of the banks and the CFs, and it is the result both of inclusion within the official group of nationalized institutions that are not yet privatized and of the greater risk problems of the official agricultural development intermediaries (in particular the Coffee Bank and the Agrarian Bank, the latter not included in the calculations). By types of institution, the CAVs have the lowest levels of overdue accounts (3.4 percent) and the CFCs the highest (9.2 percent), because of the characteristics of their loans. Portfolio reserves exceed the doubtful loan portfolio, except in the case of the CAVs, where they cover barely 27 percent but are fully backed by mortgages. The current portfolio quality indicators represent very substantial improvements over the critical period of the eighties (Table 4.5).

The statistics on portfolio maturities (available only until 1988 and of dubious reliability) show a balanced maturity distribution for the system as a whole, with the banks specializing more in short-term loans (up to three years; 68 percent of their assets), CAVs in long-term loans (longer than five years; 86 percent), and the other intermediaries in medium-term loans (including the CFs, which were originally created to finance long-term investments.

---

[15] From 29.8 percent to 22.8 percent for banks, from 24.7 percent to 14.6 percent for CFs, from 43.7 percent to 26.8 percent for CAVs, and from 33 percent to 12.8 percent for CFCS. See *Revista del Banco de la República*, September 1992.

Table 4.6. Colombia: Structure of the Portfolios of Major Financial Agents, 1991
(Percentages of net portfolios)

Institutions	Active portfolio	Overdue portfolio[4]	Portfolio Reserve	Total net portfolio[5]	Total net portfolio/ GDP	Bad debt reserve (BDR)
Banks	93.86	8.72	-2.58	100.00	10.42	115.24
Private	95.96	5.76	-1.72	100.00	4.94	142.73
Mixed	97.45	3.49	-0.94	100.00	0.54	123.71
Foreign	97.48	4.37	-1.85	100.00	0.45	286.15
Official	90.75	13.04	-3.79	100.00	4.49	102.20
Financial corporations	98.67	2.04	-0.71	100.00	3.26	150.26
Private	98.80	1.58	-0.38	100.00	2.72	134.23
Official[1]	98.02	4.39	-2.41	100.00	0.53	166.27
Savings and loan associations	97.13	3.38	-0.50	100.00	6.25	27.06
Private	97.44	2.93	-0.36	100.00	4.30	25.65
Official	96.45	4.36	-0.81	100.00	1.96	28.62
Commercial financial companies	92.11	9.22	-1.33	100.00	1.71	116.68
Private	91.94	9.33	-1.26	100.00	1.58	108.30
Official	94.23	7.89	-2.12	100.00	0.13	271.64
Others[2]						
Private	95.21	5.22	-0.43	100.00	0.00	57.14
Official	100.00	0.43	-0.43	100.00	0.00	100.00
Total private[3]	96.59	4.40	-1.00	100.00	14.54	93.93
Total official	92.93	9.91	-2.84	100.00	7.11	87.38
Total	95.39	6.21	-1.60	100.00	21.65	90.00

Source: Asociación Bancaria de Colombia, FEDESARROLLO calculations.
[1] Includes only IFI and Corfigan.
[2] Only includes bonded general warehouses.
[3] In the case of banks, includes mixed and foreign.
[4] Includes portfolios more than twelve months overdue, which are considered bad debts (BDR).
[5] Total portfolio: active portfolio + overdue portfolio + reserves.

Regulation and Supervision of the System

Structure

The board of directors of the Bank of the Republic is responsible for managing monetary and financial policy. Under Law 35 of 1993 the following functions were shifted to the government: authorizing operations; determining maturities, guarantees, and levels of capital related to those operations; limiting the granting of endorsements or guarantees; determining margins of solvency, net worth, and investment of reserves; and setting the rules of prudential regulation. In open contradiction with the spirit of financial liberalization of recent years, the same law empowered the Ministry of Finance (through its new technical vice ministry) to intervene in the operation of the financial system by setting individual ceilings, the prohibition of reciprocities, and the imposition of credit allocation percentages for vital sectors (in all up to 30 percent of assets under equal conditions for all intermediaries).

The Banking Superintendency is responsible for oversight and administrative regulation of banks, CFs, CAVs, CFCs, leasing companies, second-grade financial cooperatives, and bonded warehouses. The Guarantees Fund, which was set up during the crisis of the eighties, operates deposit insurance and acts as ultimate guarantor of the rights of savers and depositors. During the crisis it acquired ownership and control of five banks, one CF and two CFCs, for the purpose of reorganizing and capitalizing them (three of the banks have already been reprivatized, the CF was taken over by a bank, and one of the CFCs was liquidated). Initially it operated with issues and forced investments of the financial system and the coffee sector. In 1989 its equity was strengthened in order to avoid this type of financing.

The regulation and intervention established in 1993 may give rise to decisional conflicts due to the overlapping of the technical vice ministry's functions with those of the securities and banking superintendencies, especially when it is not possible in practice to distinguish clearly between regulation and oversight. Moreover, regulatory decisions made by an agency not connected with bank operations can give rise to unsuitable rules, legal instability, and conflicts of interpretation and responsibility (Cabrera, 1992).

Policy of Reserve Requirements and Forced Investments[16]

Reserve requirements and forced investments relating to the different types of borrowings (not only current accounts) of the financial intermediaries have traditionally been the chief instrument of monetary control in Colombia and an expeditious channel for the development funds administered by the Bank of the Republic. In late 1979 they reached actual average levels of over 40 percent of the borrowings of banks, finance corporations, and commercial financing companies. In the eighties they fell and became less widespread, and greater importance for purposes of monetary control was given to open market operations (OMAs). However, in 1991, although OMAs were increased to unprecedented

---

[16] Basic data from Asociación Bancaria, *Manual de Tesorería Bancaria* (permanent updating) and "Notas Editoriales," *Revista del Banco de la República (May 1992)*.

levels in reaction to the accumulation of international reserves, the effective ratio of cash reserves and forced investments was raised again (to 30.6 from the 22 percent at which it stood in 1990) through the imposition of a marginal reserve requirement of 100 percent on all borrowings of the principal financial intermediaries (excepting only the CAVs). In May 1992 measures were taken to reduce the scattering of reserve requirements by type of financial instrument, but the actual average rates were not reduced.

At present, the reserve requirement applied to current accounts and other current liabilities of banks to private individuals is 41 percent. The figure is 70 percent on official current accounts and other current liabilities of banks up to 30 days, and 10 percent on savings or term deposits up to 180 days and savings accounts of banks and CAVs. The 10 percent rate also applies to all CF and CFC borrowing with maturities of under 180 days. A 5 percent rate applies to certificates of deposit with maturities of 180 days or more.

In view of the high reserve requirements of the eighties, the authorities at that time allowed investment of part of the cash reserve in certain remunerated securities (issued by the Banks of the Republic, financial funds, and other institutions), and computation of some loans as part of the cash reserves. These practices, which again came into use in 1991, were discontinued in 1992. Most of the investments that they computed for the cash reserves were frozen and will be phased out by the year 2000. For the rest, reserve requirements must be represented in unremunerated reserves in the Bank of the Republic or as cash held by the financial institutions. The cash position is calculated by two-week periods, and shortfalls or surpluses in excess of 1 percent are carried over to the following period.

Apart from the reserve requirement, the only current forced investment of a general nature with respect to current liabilities is intended for agricultural development through the Fund for the Financing of the Agricultural Sector (Finagro, currently separate from the Bank of the Republic).[17] It amounts to 7 percent of gross borrowing (with some minor exclusions and substitutions) by banks (except for specialized agricultural banks), CFs, and CFCs (and 2 percent for CAVs). Until 1990 forced investments for agricultural investments (received by the former FFAP) were based on lending, which is more stable (Revista del Banco de la República, August 1990). In 1990 all the amounts representing the innumerable previous forced investments were frozen until they fell due.

---

[17] The other rediscount funds operating in the Bank of the Republic suspended operations in 1991 and were transferred to other agencies. However, the bank acts as intermediary of external lines of credit for development (see "Notas Editoriales," *Revista del Banco de la República*, November 1991).

Interest Rate Policy

Practically all lending and borrowing rates were set by the economic authorities until the early seventies. Interest rates on loans (except those of the CAVs) were the first to be freed. The interest rate on the CDTs of banks and corporations, which was set by bank agreements, was freed in 1980, and was followed by vigorous growth of this instrument, given the high reserve requirement levels. The monetary correction (UPAC) which applies to all CAV lending and borrowing operations was partially tied to the CDT interest rate in 1984, thus giving it some flexibility. The returns on CAV term accounts were freed in 1989, and the returns on the remaining CAV borrowings were freed in 1991. Interest rates on CAV loans were also freed, except for the low-cost housing sector (for which 20 percent of the borrowings must currently be earmarked). Also freed at the end of 1990 were the returns on bank savings accounts, which until then had been kept at negative real levels, and in 1983 a gradual process was initiated to eliminate the subsidy to credits from financial funds, tying them for this purpose to the CDT interest rate (plus a few points). Despite this across-the-board freeing process, lending and borrowing rates overall have been subjected to sporadic interventions (the most recent in the first half of 1986, the second half of 1988, and from June to December 1992).

The freeing of returns has hurt the CAVs' competitiveness in relation to the other intermediaries because the CAVs have lost their exclusive right to offer attractive remuneration for highly liquid assets. The CAVs also had an exclusive right to make loans with implicit capitalization of interest (by virtue of the indexation of its transactions), which gave them a virtual monopoly on long-term credit. This exclusivity also disappeared when the capitalization of interest was permitted in 1989. The CAVs' future role is therefore under discussion (as part of the discussion concerning the universal banking system in relation to the affiliate banking system; see Peñalosa, 1992).

The freeing of returns has also caused financial resources to become more expensive, because of the tendency to remunerate highly liquid assets (Figures 4.1 to 4.3).

Linking the interest rate of directed credits to the CDT rate has made the cost of these resources unstable and uncertain, and may in 1992 have limited the demand for agricultural credit through Finagro as commercial credits became cheaper.

Policies of Access to Liquidity[18]

The instruments of access to liquidity include interbank credits, "repo" operations or swap contracts and rediscount rates in the Bank of the Republic.

---

[18] See Asociación Bancaria, *Manual de Tesorería Bancaria* and "Notas Editoriales," *Revista del Banco de la República* (August 1990, April and May 1992).

The cash surpluses of the financial intermediaries can be held in surplus (unremunerated) reserves, in reserves of the Bank of the Republic or the Treasury of the Republic (remunerated, and with maturities of seven days to 12 months), securities of the National Energy Financing Corporation (12–month maturities and up), banker's acceptances, CDTs of the financial institutions, and bonds and commercial paper of the private sector (more than three months). Until 1991 the CAVs could freely maintain and withdraw their cash surpluses in a fund of the Bank of the Republic, where they obtained a return (according to monetary correction). This mechanism constituted an expeditious channel that endogenized the money supply by preventing serious liquidity mismatches in the financial system, though limiting the effectiveness of the monetary and interest rate policy and reducing competition in the financial resources market.

All the financial intermediaries are authorized to carry out among themselves short-term loans and discount operations at such interest rates as may be agreed. These operations constitute the interbank credit that makes it possible to regulate the distribution of liquidity among institutions.

The "repo" operations or swap contracts are for the temporary acquisition of securities on dates and at prices previously agreed upon. They may not be used as a continuing source of funds, but they are permitted for the purpose of solving temporary cash flow problems. They are often carried out with securities issued by the central bank itself or by the Treasury of the Republic. When "repo" operations directly involve the Bank of the Republic to provide liquidity, they may only be performed for periods no longer than seven days and at market interest rates.

There are ordinary and special rediscount rates to give access to cash from the central bank to all the financial intermediaries. The former differences in access by type of intermediary were abolished in 1992. The ordinary rate is restricted to correcting temporary drops in deposits; it is immediately available (subject to subsequent verification) for up to 10 percent of current liabilities. It can be used three times per year, for periods of 15 days which may be extended once. Currently their cost is the effective 90-day borrowing rate for banks and corporations (DTF) plus seven points (for CAVs the terms are 30 days and the cost is the monetary correction plus 16 points). The special rate is reserved for critical illiquidity conditions and must be granted through a program between the financial institution and the Bank of the Republic and the Banking Superintendency. The maturity at this rate cannot exceed six months.

In 1992, imbalances in the system's financial flows arose as a result of the elimination in 1991 of the mechanism providing access to liquidity from the CAVs and the functional separation between the Bank of the Republic and the government.[19] This is a temporary source of vulnerability in the financial system.

Reorganization and Portfolio Quality Policies

The recession of the early eighties combined with inappropriate practices in the area of credit approval and portfolio risk control on the part of the financial intermediaries. As a result, doubtful assets mounted to 24 percent of the portfolio in 1985 in the case of banks and 20 percent for the CFs. To correct this situation and clear the balance sheets, a substantial increase in the system's reserves was required until those doubtful loans were covered. These requirements entailed writing down equity in order to reflect the true condition of the institutions (see the next section). Temporary incentives were granted to reorganize the portfolio in the form of special rates in the Bank of the Republic, and permanent limits were set for individual loans and those made to administrators, shareholders, and related parties. In 1990 credit risk qualification criteria were introduced, as a basis for the new equity requirements (see below). Thanks to improved debt quality, the reserve amount had already been reduced below 3 percent of bank assets since 1989 and to much lower figures for the CFs and CAVs (Table 4.5).

Capitalization Policies

The financial crisis of the early eighties gave rise to a severe decapitalization of the system, especially in 1985, when the banks' equity profitability was -178 percent and that of the CFs -42 percent (Table 4.5). As a percentage of assets the banks' net worth fell from 5.9 percent in 1980 to 2.8 percent five years later. The capitalization policies adopted at that time raised this figure to 5.4 percent in 1991. The previous leverage (debt/equity) limits (which arbitrarily defined the debt and the equity under consideration) were replaced in 1990 by capital requirements on the basis of assets weighted by risk (with capital requirements of 0, 10, 20, 50 and 100 percent according to risk), following the Basle Agreement guidelines (though with somewhat higher requirements than those of the OECD), and applying identical standards to the entire financial system, not

---

19 The problem is made more acute by the fact that, as the monetary authorities acknowledge, the Treasury's monetary operations are unstable and unpredictable (see "Notas Editoriales," *Revista del Banco de la República*, August 1990). In August 1992 the banks experienced serious cash shortfalls because of the massive subscriptions of compulsory fiscal bonds and insufficiency of the interbank credit market, despite the abundant money supply (see *Revista del Banco de la República*, August 1992).

only the banks. Additional capitalization requirements were 16 percent for commercial banks, 1.5 percent for CAVs, 4 percent for CFs, and 30 percent for CFCs (Watson, 1989). Finally, Law 45 of 1990 established minimum amounts of capital for each type of financial intermediary.

Regulation and Control Policies

The financial crisis of the eighties revealed the fragility of the existing regulation and control techniques and the need to strengthen them in order to later restart the process of freeing the financial markets (Montenegro, 1983). The advances in this area were reflected in the asset qualification standards already mentioned; in the Unified Accounts Plan (PUC) for all the financial intermediaries, which ensures the openness and comparability of information; and in a Bank Inspection Manual, which explains control procedures and provides instructions for carrying them out. The requirement to consolidate each institution's balance sheets was also established. In the administrative sphere the Banking Superintendency's functions were simplified, as were the procedures for authorizing changes in schedules, the opening of offices, and the creation of new services by the financial intermediaries (Fernández, 1991).

**Relationship between the Financial Sector
and the Remaining Economic Sectors**

The original balance sheets provide the most appropriate tool for summarizing the financial system's relationships with the rest of the economic agents (Table 4.7). From the consolidation of all the balance sheets one learns that the external sector is the most important financial agent in Colombia. Its financial assets in the country (as of 1991) represented 50 percent of GDP, made up basically of loans (41 percent) and foreign investment (8 percent). Its principal liability consisted of the country's international reserves (14.3 percent of GDP), which leaves a net financial position of 36 percent of GDP (without counting unregistered assets of Colombians abroad).

The financial assets of the entire financial system (without the Bank of the Republic) amount to 48 percent of GDP, with the banks accounting for a large portion (20 percent). Lending by the banks, CFs, CAVs, and CFCs is directed chiefly at the private sector (although the banks earmark funds worth nearly 4 percent of GDP as reserves in the Bank of the Republic). In the case of the "other financial intermediaries," which include entities of a special nature, many of them official, lending involves the private sector, the public sector, and the rest of the financial system in approximately equal parts. Most of the financial system's borrowing is also from the private sector (although the "others" group relies in considerable measure on external resources and on the rest of the financial intermediaries).

The private sector's financial assets amount to 38 percent of GDP. Of this total, more than 8 points represent central bank assets, 13 represent commercial bank assets, and 9 represent CAV assets. The rest are spread among the financial system's remaining segments (the public sector does not receive substantial funds from the private sector, and figures for private financial assets abroad are not available). The private sector's liabilities exceed its assets by 3 percent of GDP, so that it is a net debtor of the rest of the agents. This is to say that its physical capital exceeds its equity by that amount (without counting its financial assets abroad).

The public sector is also a net debtor, to nearly 40 percent of GDP, and most of its debt (34 percent) is financed with external funds and with credits from the special entities included in the "others" group (4 percent). Although the public sector owes 2.8 percent of GDP to the Bank of the Republic, it has assets in that institution worth 2 percent of GDP.

In this way, financial interrelationships in the Colombian economy fall into two groups, one consisting of the external sector and the public sector and the other of the main financial intermediaries and the private sector.[20] The external sector also lends on a considerable scale to the private sector and borrows from the Bank of the Republic. The "other intermediaries" group conducts more evenly distributed lending and borrowing transactions with the private and public sectors. The operations of the financial system as a whole total 13.4 percent of GDP, but of these slightly more than half (7 percent) take place between the central bank and the rest of the financial system.

From the point of view of financial instruments, the monetary assets (without international reserves) amount to 14 percent of GDP, supplied in practically equal parts by the Bank of the Republic and the commercial banks. Savings instruments total somewhat less than 20 percent of GDP. One quarter are non-monetary borrowings of the Bank of the Republic, a third are liabilities of the banks and the rest are spread among the remaining financial intermediaries. The financial depth measured by this indicator is modest by international standards and has not changed since the mid-eighties (Fernández, 1991). Domestic credit balances stand at 51 percent of GDP and external credit at 41 percent. International reserves equal 14 percent of GDP and the rest of the financial assets a scant 18 percent of GDP.

In summary, the structure of the financial operations is characterized by: (1) high concentration of financial relationships between two pairs of agents, the public sector and the external sector on the one hand and the private sector and the financial system on the other; (2) greater relations between the central bank

---

[20] In 1992, however, the public sector increased its direct link with the private sector by floating securities worth 1.8 percent of GDP (including treasury and Fen securities, but without including forced bonds of the government or the National Coffee Fund).

Table 4.7. Matrix of Financial Statements in Colombia, 1991
(Percentage of GDP)

		Banco de la Republica	Commercial banks	Financial corporations	Savings & loan associations	Comm. financial companies	Others	Public sector	External sector	Private sector	Net financial position	Totals
Banco de la Republica	M		3.88	0.01	0.02	0.03	0.04			3.82		7.80
	FS		0.33				0.31			4.66		5.30
	C								1.38			1.38
	O		0.48	0.07	0.36	0.12		2.06	0.90	0.04	0.00	4.02
Commercial banks	M									6.41		6.41
	FS									6.85		6.85
	C	0.32					2.02		1.23		2.63	3.57
	O						0.02	0.47		0.14		0.64
Financial Corporations	M											0.00
	FS		0.05							1.62		1.67
	C	0.63					0.79		0.40		0.90	1.82
	O							0.04				0.04
Savings and loan associations	M											0.00
	FS											0.00
	C						0.14			8.76		8.90
	O							0.09			0.20	0.09
Commercial financial companies	M											0.00
	FS	0.01								1.74		1.74
	C		0.01									0.02
	O						0.13			0.00	0.35	0.14
Other financial agents	M											0.00
	FS		0.23			0.14	0.05			3.51		3.93
	C	0.39	1.91						2.46		2.66	4.75
	O	0.02	0.40	0.04	0.12	0.13	0.18	0.14		0.07		1.12

Table 4.7. Matrix of Financial Statements in Colombia, 1991 (cont.)

		Banco de la República	Commercial banks	Financial corporations	Savings & loan associations	Comm. financial companies	Others	Public sector	External sector	Private sector	Net financial position	Totals
Official sector	M											0.00
	FS									0.40		0.40
	C	2.80	0.88	0.13	0.13		4.18		33.61			41.74
	O		0.31								−39.64	0.31
External sector	M											0.00
	FS											0.00
	C											0.00
	O	14.32	0.05								35.95	14.37
Private sector	M											0.00
	FS											0.00
	C		10.36	3.84	7.36	1.69	4.50		2.08			29.82
	O	0.03	1.21	0.33	1.20	0.14	0.08		8.26		−3.04	11.24
Total	M	0.00	3.88	0.01	0.02	0.03	0.04	0.00	0.00	10.23		14.22
	FS	0.00	0.62	0.00	0.00	0.13	0.37	0.00	0.00	18.78		19.89
	C	4.13	13.16	3.97	7.49	1.69	11.63	0.00	41.16	8.76		92.00
	O	14.37	2.45	0.44	1.67	0.40	0.42	2.80	9.16	0.26		31.96
Total		18.50	20.10	4.43	9.19	2.25	12.45	2.80	50.32	38.02	0.00	158.06

Source: Banco de la República Bulletin, June 1992, Tables 2.1.1 to 2.1.8.
Table 6.1.3. for economic and agricultural development bonds of public sector banks.
Banking and Finances, January-March 1992, balance sheets.
Banco de la República, Bulletin No. 196, Major monetary indicators and external sector: page 4, for Titulos de Ahorro Nacional (TAN) and financial assets of other financial institutions (cooperative agencies, ratable electric certificates and Titulos Energéticos [TER]).
M: Monetary assets; FS: financial savings; C: credits; O: Other financial operations.

and the rest of the financial system than within the latter; (3) little financial depth in the economy as a whole; (4) an important central bank role in the supply of monetary and nonmonetary assets; and (5) scant development of financial operations different from traditional ones involving monetary assets, savings instruments, and credit.

Outline of a Financial Reform

In the midst of an acute economic recession in 1982, the financial system went into crisis when portfolio quality deteriorated severely and the fragility of the control machinery, the vulnerability of equity, and the dangerous exposure of many intermediaries became evident. The crisis continued until 1985, driving several financial intermediaries into bankruptcy.

Ongoing Reforms

In response to the crisis, steps were taken to restore liquidity and shore up the equity of the intermediaries, and machinery was created to put assets on a sound footing. One bank was liquidated and several were nationalized and placed under the authority of the Financial Institutions Guarantees Fund set up in 1985.

Background and Objectives of the Financial Reform of 1990

Between 1986 and 1990 the Guarantees Fund led the process of restructuring and rehabilitating the institutions that had been taken over. During that time general measures were taken to deal with the bad debts, raise capital requirements and tie them to the risk structure, partially reopen the sector to foreign investment, monitor ownership changes in the system and reestablish deposit insurance, improve supervision and control mechanisms, and commence the dismantling of the myriad forced investments and the development credit subsidies (Fernández, 1991; Delgado and Roda, 1988). Although these measures brought a gradual return to market mechanisms in a context of macroeconomic stability, severe problems of inefficiency and lack of competition, which had been identified since the beginning of the crisis, remained unresolved (Montenegro, 1983).

In 1990 the restructuring of the financial system acquired special importance as one of the components of the ambitious economic modernization program of César Gaviria's new government. The program also promoted liberalization of external trade, simplification of labor rules, and partial liberalization of the exchange regime, giving the financial system an active role in exchange operation. (Fernández, 1991; and Zuleta, 1991).

The outline of the financial reform was drawn in Law 45 of 1990. The principal reform consisted of adopting the affiliate banking system as an intermediate solution between the multiple and specialized banking systems, in order to make the system more efficient and avoid the greater risks and conflicts that the extreme approaches would presumably entail (Arboleda, 1991). The banks, finance corporations and commercial financing companies were authorized to invest in affiliated financial services companies (trust companies, leasing companies, stock brokerage firms, bonded warehouses and companies administering unemployment and pensions) without exceeding 100 percent of their capital and reserves. Trust companies, brokerage houses, and fund administrators were not allowed to engage in credit operations between parent and affiliate (although, for no clear reason, leasing companies and bonded warehouses were allowed to). Nor were affiliates allowed to participate in the capital of other institutions. In order to make the system flexible, the law authorized credit establishments (but not affiliates) to engage in innovative transactions, and it regulated the relations between the parent and its affiliates in order to prevent conflicts of interest and abuses by financial interests.

The rules on mergers, conversions and breakups of institutions were eased to encourage competition and allow the entities to move more freely in the sector. Entry into the sector was based upon meeting capital and professional requirements, all restrictions to foreign investment in the sector were abolished, privatizations were regulated, and rules were issued governing the transparency of transactions and the monitoring and control of the entities (Arboleda, 1991).

Financial Reform since 1990

In 1992 the Congress and the government issued different provisions changing the structure and functions of the financial entities in a manner inconsistent with the terms of Law 45 of 1990 and with the system of affiliates established by it (Law 35 of 1993 and Decrees 1.135, 1.763, and 2.179 of 1992).

The most important changes to the structure of affiliates were made with regard to the leasing companies. Law 35 requires that they be converted into commercial financing companies, so that they can attract funds from the public. Once converted, they will be allowed to grant credit up to the limit set by the government, and within that same percentage existing CFCs will be allowed to lease with an option to buy. In addition, CFCs specializing in leasing may obtain capital from credit establishments.

Law 35 authorized CAVs to invest in any type of financial services company and to conduct operations they could previously not engage in, such as foreign currency transactions and short-term loans not backed by mortgages.

The functions of the CFs were modified by government decrees. Decree 1.763 authorized them to engage in factoring in foreign currencies and to grant credit for working capital to all sectors of the economy (not only to industry and mining). Decree 2.179 authorized them to raise funds through savings accounts, since their only source of funds from the public was CDTs. This decree also granted credit establishments "the use of their network of offices by financial services companies, insurance organizations, stock brokerage houses, capitalization companies, and dealers in insurance for the promotion and management of the authorized operation."

Despite the new functions authorized through these provisions, Law 35 specified that government could not reduce the operations which existing enterprises were currently authorized to perform, or authorize other types of entity to perform operations carried out by specialized enterprises.

These provisions were adopted as a response to various pressures from the financial enterprises for the purpose of broadening their business, offsetting the loss of some prerogatives—especially in the case of the CAVs— and eliminating some of the arbitrary restrictions on their operation (Peñalosa, 1992 and 1993; González, 1993). The final result, however, is far from coherent. Table 4.8 shows the investments in affiliates and other permitted entities. The existing approach is devoid of logic since no type of financial entity has the exclusive role of a financial holding company and crossed investments are possible (though not yet used in practice). This approach cannot prevent conflicts of interest in the conduct of operations, and the operations are not logically framed. In fact, as Table 4.9 shows, no system of specialized functions or multibanking is defined for the credit enterprises, nor for the financial services companies and institutional investors.

Road to Multibanking

The manner in which the financial system is currently organized has numerous shortcomings in addition to being arbitrary. First, it involves duplication of administrative and operating costs (although an attempt is being made to get rid of some duplications through the recently authorized use of the networks of credit enterprises by financial services companies, insurance companies, capitalization companies and insurance dealers). In addition, the legal protection of many market niches under the current system severely limits competition and works against fair treatment for all. The profitability of some operations is the result of legal decisions in the tax area (leasing with option to buy, in particular), restrictions on foreign currency operations (which not all the entities are permitted to conduct), and the existence of instruments restricted to certain entities (the UPAC, which is available only to CAVs). This creates an inherently unstable situation in which the survival of groups of entities depends on legal decisions, and pressures can lawfully be exerted in response to these decisions to maintain the areas of competence of the different groups of entities. This situation notwithstanding, the regulatory structure in Colombia has progressed to the point where

Table 4.8. Colombia: Investments in Subsidiaries and Other Institutions

Credit Institutions	Banks	Financial corporations	Savings and loan associations	Trust companies	Stock-brokers	Financial companies specializing in leasing	Bonded general warehouses	Pension and unemp. funds	Insurance companies	Investment fund mgt. companies
Banks		X	X	X	X	X	X	X	X	X
Financial corporations	(X)		(X)	X	X	X		X		
Savings and loan associations		(X)		X	(X)	(X)		X		
Commercial financial companies				X	X	X		X		

Source: Current legislation.
X: Investment permitted.
(X): Investment permitted since Law 35 of 1993 or Decree 1.135 of 1992.

a start is being made in basing standards on operations and not entities, in fields such as reserve requirements, forced investments, leverage ratios, and access to primary liquidity.

One feature of the multiple banking system is the inclusion of the investment banking system in the spectrum of services offered. In Colombia this mixture has traditionally been avoided in order to isolate this type of risk to savers, but with discouraging results, given the finance corporations' limited capacity for risk investment. These corporations have concentrated their investment on enterprises under their control, linked to their own economic groups. The capital requirements by levels of risk that already exist in Colombia are sufficient prevention against the risk problems whose avoidance has been sought.

Given the weaknesses of the current system, the multiple banking system could be instrumental in correcting the problems of inefficiency and oligopolistic structure that characterize the Colombian financial system and that have not yielded to other methods of financial reform adopted in recent years.

The combined output in a multibanking system helps to cut investment and operating costs, raises capacity utilization, reduces the cost of obtaining information and the average transaction cost, and is conducive to a better balance between market power and gains in productive efficiency as the level of output approaches optimum size (Khatkhate and Riechel, 1980).

By eliminating legal specialization by entities, one attempts to allow all the financial intermediaries to conduct the operations permitted in the marketplace, leaving it for them to determine where their competitive advantages lie. This should occur under a regulatory system based on type of operation, not institution, in an environment of strong, healthy domestic and external competition that discourages oligopoly. The entities that are now specialized could maintain their competitive advantage through operations if they achieve the cost and quality levels required by the marketplace, but they would not simply be protected by a legal authorization that somewhat arbitrarily embraces some but excludes others.

In addition, the universal banking system furthers the creation of enterprises by addressing across the board all the enterprises' financing and financial consultation needs, reducing credit risk through greater information and contact with businesses, cushioning the effects of external shocks on the production of a single product, and creating greater opportunities for international competition.

The adoption of a multibanking system in Colombia should then be governed by the following criteria:

•   Free competition in all operations involving borrowing, lending, administration and services (except insurance and management of forced savings resources), subject to meeting the requirements concerning professional exper-

Table 4.9. Colombia: Authorized Financial Agents and Operations

	Passive operations										Active operations						Administrative and service operations						
	Current account	Savings account	CD	Bond	Bills	Domestic credit	External credit	Fund rediscount	Primary liquidity access	Forced savings	Domestic credit	Credit cards	Direct investment	Financial invest.	Own foreign currency position	Leasing	Foreign currency	Trust	Debit card	Warehousing	Real Estate (corretaje)	Financial eng. services	Insurance
Credit institutions																							
Banks	X	X	X	X	X	X	X	X	X		X	X		X	X		X	X	X			X	
Financial corporations		(X)	X	X		X	X	X	X		X	X	X	X	X		X	(X)a	X			X	
Savings & loan associations		X	X	X					X		X			X			(X)		X		X		
Commercial financial companies			X	X					X		X	X		X	X	(X)	X	(X)a	X				
Financial services companies																							
Trust companies					X									X			X	X			(X)a		
Stockbrokers											(X)						(X)a	(X)a			X		
Leasing companies (CFC)					X						X			X		X						X	
Bonded warehouses																				X			
Unemp. funds management																							
Institutional investments																							
Insurance companies						X							X	X	X								X
Investment funds													X	X	X								
Pension and unemp. funds										X				X	X								

Source: Current legislation.
X: Operation permitted.
(X): Operation permitted since Law 35 of 1993.
a Investment trust through underwriting operations.

tise, minimum capital and leverage by lending operation according to risk (Basle Agreement) set by the Banking Superintendency. Each entity would decide the range of services it wishes to offer, based on its experience and actual or desired specialization (and advertise itself in accordance with its degree of specialization). Investment banking could be included. While a reasonable reserve requirement is being achieved and forced investment is being dismantled, a separation would be maintained between banking and nonbank credit institutions, based solely on whether current accounts are handled.

• Separation of insurance from financial business, though allowing the use of the networks of credit institutions to sell insurance and authorizing the insurance companies to invest in credit institutions (whether banks or non-banks) and vice versa (provided there are no direct and indirect crossed investments between them). Separating the insurance business respects the unpredictable nature of the risks assumed in it and the inadvisability of using the insurance system to cover financial risks, because of the possibility that moral hazards may arise.

• Separation of pension and unemployment fund management, because the resources administered in this case grow out of an official intervention for the generation of forced savings. Mixing them with other financial activities would give rise to conflicts of interest, restriction of competition, and instability discussed above, which should be avoided in the multiple banking system. With respect to property, credit institutions would be allowed to invest in enterprises administering pension and unemployment funds. The use of resources of such funds for capital investments in credit institutions would also be allowed, provided there were no crossed investments.

• Protection to savers from possible abuses of dominant power in the financial or investment markets by means of deposit insurance (already in place) and rules governing competition among the entities.

• Opportunity for any entity to carry out "innovative" operations, subject to authorization by the Banking Superintendency.

• Opportunity for any entity to use any of the existing financing methods for its lending or borrowing operations. Any transaction could call for a fixed or variable interest rate, with or without capitalization of interest, or it could be indexed. To that end the UPAC correction system should be applied strictly in accordance with inflation (Lora and Sánchez, 1992).

Tables 4.10 and 4.11 illustrate the proposed reform with regard to investments and operations. All that is needed to realize it is to refine the law and set a date on which the system will start operating. From that moment on, and indefinitely into the future, each entity would be able to carry out its current or new operations, meeting the relevant legal standards and the minimum capital requirements. It would not be necessary for the entities to change their firm names, but they would be free to do so to reflect their new range of services.

Reorganization of the Public Banking System

The entities nationalized during the crisis of the eighties are currently undergoing reprivatization. Three banks have already been sold: Trabajadores (now the Mercantile Bank,) Tequendama, and Comercio (merged with the Bank of Bogotá). Still to be privatized are Banco de Colombia, Banco del Estado, and the CFC Pronta. The government announced the privatization of the two banks in 1993 and the takeover of Pronta by the Banco de Colombia. The privatizations have given rise to inflows of foreign capital but the capital market has not been strengthened, nor has support been given to democratic capitalism. Law 35 of 1993 introduced these objectives as a requirement for future privatizations, which may complicate the process since in earlier privatizations the bidders clearly sought total control of the entities' stock.

In addition, although law 45 of 1990 gave the government the power to reorganize the traditional banking system that had evolved in Colombia since the 1930s, little headway has been made in that direction. Thus far, the stock of Banco Ganadero and Corporación Financiera Popular have been sold to the private sector. The privatization of Banco Cafetero has been announced, but there is still no sales program for the remaining institutions: Caja Agraria, Banco Popular, Banco Central Hipotecario, Concasa, and other financial institutions with shares owned by the National Coffee Fund, Corpavi, and La Previsora. The only one of these having a clear reason to remain in the public sector is the Caja Agraria (Agrarian Bank), since the monetary and credit system in the country's rural areas would be severely restricted in the hands of the private sector. Even in this case, however, it is open to discussion whether the bank should be replaced by a new organization free of the benefits-related and operating burdens and the organizational rigidities which hobble the bank (Hernández, 1992; and Steiner, 1992). Apart from these financial entities, there are various official agencies (IFI, Findeter, Finagro, and FEN) that channel resources from multilateral organizations and in some cases from domestic capital or the forced investment market (Finagro). For reasons of risk perception on the part of multilateral organizations and domestic investors, and because of the requirements imposed by those organizations to ensure control and efficient use of resources, there are no immediate prospects for privatizing these agencies.

Sectoral and Macroeconomic Problems and Distortions

Excessive Reserve Requirements and Compulsory Investments

As a result of recent decisions, the reserve requirement regime has been standardized for instruments of a similar nature (regardless of the issuing institution), investments substituting for cash reserves and the crossed subsidies to

Table 4.10. Colombia: Authorized Financial Agents and Operations under the Proposed Reform

	Passive Operations									
	Current account	Savings account	CD	Bond	Bills	Domestic credit	External credit	Fund redis-count	Primary liquidity access	Forced savings
Banks	X	X	X	X	X		X	X	X	
Nonbanking institutions		X	X	X	X		X	X	X	
Insurance companies						X				
Pension and Unemployment funds										X

Table 4.10. Colombia: Authorized Financial Agents and Operations under the Proposed Reform (cont.)

	Active operations							Administrative and service operations						
	Domestic credit	Credit cards	Direct investment	Financial invest.	Own Foreign currency position	Leasing	Foreign currency	Trust	Debit card	Leasing	Factoring	Real estate	Financial engineering services	Insurance
Banks	X	X	X	X	X	X	X	X	X	X		X	X	X
Nonbanking institutions	X	X	X	X	X	X	X	X	X	X		X	X	X
Insurance companies				X										X
Pension and Unemployment funds				X							X			

Source: Author's calculations.
X: Operation permitted under proposal.

Table 4.11. Colombia: Authorized Investment under Proposed Reform

	Banking	Pension and unemployment funds	Insurance companies
Banks	X	X	X
Nonbanking institutions		X	X

Source: Authors' calculations.
X: Investments permitted under proposal.

which they gave rise have been abolished, and forced investments are being phased out (except for the one designed for Finagro).

Colombian reserve requirements are very high by international standards,[21] and the economic authorities intend to start reducing them in 1993. However, international comparisons should not be relied upon without correcting for inflation, which implies subsidizing the banks that have a monopoly on unremunerated current accounts. With this factor in mind, a reserve requirement of 54 percent would be consistent with parity of interest rates for loans given the assumption that the condition of parity of borrowing rates is being complied with and the levels of banking efficiency are in line with international ones.[22] This cash ratio would not be very far from its present levels (62.6 percent at year-end 1991, including compulsory and cash reserve investments). However, with the current borrowing rate (27 percent), which corresponds approximately to the international real interest rate, given domestic inflation of 25 percent, the reserve requirement would have to be negative (-6 percent). The distortion springs from the fact that the devaluation rate is below the spread between domestic and external inflation. Under these circumstances, current reserve requirements are too high. However, it would be impractical to try to eliminate them because the distortion cannot be permanent, while on the other hand the reduction of the reserve requirements would be irreversible. Hence it would be more advisable to follow a policy of gradual reduction of the reserve requirements consistent with expectations of devalua-

---

21 Reserve requirements for current accounts are 6.2 percent in Austria, a maximum of 12.1 percent in Germany, 22.5 percent in Italy, as low as 2.5 percent in Japan, 4 percent in Sweden, 18 percent in Spain (partly remunerated), up to 12 percent in the United States, 10 percent in Chile, 25 percent in Uruguay and 15 percent in Peru.

22 This calculation takes into consideration forced investments offering 7 percent of current liabilities to Finagro as part of the reserve requirement. The calculating formulas are contained in the technical report submitted to the IDB and may be requested from the authors.

tion (which must eventually correspond to the inflation spread). With an expected devaluation of 8 percent (and an inflation rate 3 points higher), the reserve ratio would have to be 42 percent (more than 20 points lower than current levels, including investments).

There has also been a simplification process with respect to forced investments. The only forced investment that is not being phased out is the one designed for Finagro. The return on these investments has gradually been coming into line with the market rate, and the difference that still exists for the regular subscription issues should be eliminated. The cost of rediscountable credits in Finagro has also been raised and now stands above the financial system's borrowing rates, even for small producers (Hernández, 1992).

In the past there were several reasons to justify a rediscount fund for the agricultural sector, as it prevented the chronic shortage of credit and instability of monetary policy from affecting agricultural supply (Lora, 1991a). Although these two reasons no longer carry weight, Finagro is justifiable as a conduit for external credit for the sector and as a financing mechanism (through the forced investments) of the banking system specialized in providing credit to small farmers, especially the Agrarian Bank. Because of the high risks and low profitability of this business, the Agrarian Bank would incur higher borrowing costs which it would be unable to shift to farmers (through adverse selection risk). However, no justification exists for rediscounting aimed at financing agribusiness, which has access to regular credit.[23] Therefore, the forced investment designed for Finagro should be reduced by 70 percent, in order to be concentrated exclusively on the financing of small producers.[24]

Conflicts between Macroeconomic Stabilization and Financial Reform

The year 1990 began the last phase of the financial restructuring process with the legal approval of a very ambitious reform framework designed to improve the

---

[23] Directed credit does not change the lender's perception of risk. Since the lender risks not only his own resources but also rediscounted ones, yet has a limited operational margin, the rediscount mechanism can in practice lead to rationing which would not otherwise exist. This situation would be corrected if the margin granted offset the operation's greater risk. Although this would entail interest rates on the loans higher than the usual market   rates for other activities, given the greater risk of farming activity and considering that the cost of the rediscount resources for the intermediary is the same DTF which corresponds to the cost of its own borrowings.

[24] Credit to small producers represents 28.2 percent of Finagro-approved credit (Hernández, 1992). To keep the rediscount rate charged to intermediaries on credits to small farmers low (that rate is currently the DTF market rate minus 7 points), it would be necessary also to reduce the profitability of the securities.

sector's competence and efficiency. Also begun was the process of reprivatizing the banking institutions nationalized during the crisis, and the financial sector was given a more active role in the foreign exchange market in conjunction with the substantial liberalization of the currency market. All this happened in the course of an economic restructuring that included the total freeing of imports, the elimination of restrictions on foreign investment, labor reform, and the reorganization of the state administrative system (Lora, 1991b).

It is interesting to note that, despite currency liberalization and the active role given the financial system in private sector exchange transactions, the reform of the financial system did not permit dollarization of domestic financial transactions. The prohibition on any kind of borrowing in foreign currency was maintained, although loans in foreign currency were allowed.[25]

In the short-term macroeconomic context, the reforms gave rise to inconsistencies deriving from the conflict between the monetary control objectives and the results of structural reforms in the fiscal and exchange areas, as the fiscal deficit mounted and an exchange surplus formed. In order to avoid this conflict in practice, a backward step was taken in the financial liberalization process: in early 1991 marginal reserve requirements of 100 percent were imposed on the financial intermediaries and interest rates on central bank securities were hiked to unprecedented levels.

The monetary control policies of the first half of 1991 proved unworkable, which prompted the central bank's new board of directors, constituted in August of that year, to establish lower interest rates as a policy objective, followed by the winding down of open market operations to contain the inflow of foreign exchange. In October, however, again counter to the general objectives of liberalization, the maturity of the exchange certificates issued in exchange for foreign currencies purchased by the central bank was lengthened from 3 to 12 months. These therefore soared from 2.9 percent of the money supply at year-end 1990 to 15.6 percent at year-end 1991 and 27.1 percent in 1992. In order to moderate the monetary effects of the inflow of foreign exchange in October and November 1991, the banking system was obliged to purchase foreign exchange through the "internally generated position" in an amount equivalent to 30 percent of its borrowings in foreign currencies (which rose to 45 percent in 1992, equivalent to $112 million for banks and CFCs). This move was at odds with the intention of eliminating all forced investment. Furthermore, in contradiction of the intention to contain the inflow of foreign capital, but with the objective of forcing greater competition in the financial system and lower-

---

[25] The net amount of foreign currency transactions is regulated by the limits of the "internally generated position in foreign currency," which currently require banks to hold foreign exchange. Over this limit, domestic credits in foreign currency must be backed by external resources of correspondent banks, which are usually short-term.

ing interest rates for loans, direct external financing of businesses was authorized in the early months of 1992.

Finally, the measure most at variance with the objectives of financial liberalization was adopted in June 1992, when controls were imposed on lending rates. These controls, which were maintained until the end of the year, consisted of a ceiling on the weighted average interest rate on loans up to 18 months of each financial intermediary. Paradoxically, however, the controls did not produce either the rationing or the distortions that would have occurred in a context of financial repression and control of monetary aggregates. The controls actually reinforced the already noticeable trend toward lower credit costs resulting from abundant liquidity and greater competition with resources of foreign origin.[26] The larger reductions favored large businesses, because of their greater ability to negotiate and their access to external credit, but the availability of domestic credit improved for businesses of all sizes.[27] The new market conditions moreover required that the financial system offer longer-term credit in order to avoid formerly uncommon restrictions, in many cases with variable interest rates. During the period when the controls were in effect, bank assets grew 16 percent in real terms and assets of the financial system as a whole 14 percent. Assets had fallen 7.7 and 4.4 percent, respectively, in the preceding 12 months.

As we have seen, macroeconomic stabilization was carried out simultaneously with the reform of the financial system, which led to conflicts between the two. The roots of the conflict, however, lie in the sequence in which the macroeconomic reforms were applied rather than in the simultaneous implementation of the financial system reform. In particular, the premature liberalization of the exchange market complicated macroeconomic management because of high interest rates and the stability of the current account of the balance of payments. The problems were aggravated by the delay in reorienting monetary policy to management of the interest rate, given the impossibility of controlling the money supply in the new conditions under which the economy was operating.

With monetary policy reoriented, the possibilities for restarting the reforms have improved. The reason is that the endogeneity of the money supply

---

[26] According to Banking Superintendency statistics, lending rates fluctuated between 33 percent and 35 percent imposed as a ceiling, as compared with 44 percent and 48 percent in the preceding six months. According to 128 industrialists surveyed by FEDESARROLLO, the average effective rate of bank loans in domestic currency fell from 42.4 percent in December 1991 to 32.7 percent in June 1992.

[27] The average cost of bank loans in domestic currency fell 12.9 percent for large businesses, 9.2 for medium-sized ones and 7.1 percent for small ones. Access to credit sources of the national financial system improved for 60 percent of large businesses, 75 percent for medium-sized ones, and 61.5 percent for small ones.

(through the mobility of capital and the changes in the central bank's nonmonetary liabilities balance) allows lower reserve requirements and makes it easier to keep interest rates low (given the stability of the country's external accounts and their relative macroeconomic stability). In addition, the increase in domestic financial savings as a result of the capital inflow facilitates the introduction of new financial instruments, such as government and corporate bonds and various borrowing instruments of the banks and other intermediaries, which improve the operation of the financial system and make its reform possible.

The economic authorities are beginning to explore these possibilities. In 1992 the government floated $750 million in bonds on the domestic market with maturities of three to seven years. The regular placement of Colombian treasury issues intended for fiscal financing was begun at the start of 1993. The floating of Venezuelan treasury bonds in Colombia was also authorized. On other fronts the new possibilities have not yet been attempted. Reserve requirements are still high, for fear that their liberalization might trigger an excessive expansion of the money supply and raise costs of the open market operations that would have to be undertaken in order to sterilize it.

Expectations Concerning Devaluation and Stabilization
of International Reserves

From mid-1991 to mid-1992, expectations of a real revaluation of the exchange rate mounted on account of the rapid accumulation of international reserves and the instability of monetary policy. The devaluation expected by the public during the first half of 1992 was 7.5 points less than the official devaluation rate of 14 to 15 percent (Cárdenas, 1992). Accordingly, foreign currency loans gained favor because their cost was substantially below that of peso loans.[28] As a result, the portfolio of the banks and the financial system as a whole contracted in real terms until May 1992, as discussed above. As expectations of a revaluation and inflow of capital moderated, the demand for credit revived in the second half of 1992, fostered also by the interest rate controls. As discussed in an earlier section, the slower pace of devaluation would require the total elimination of the reserve requirements in order to achieve parity between domestic and external lending rates. With the current reserve requirement levels, the financial system is in a weak position to compete with external borrowing (although its efficiency might be at a level with the international banking system).

---

[28] In a sample of 40 large-scale industrial enterprises it was found that foreign currency loans as a share of total credit grew from 35.6 percent at year-end 1991 to 42.4 percent in June 1992 (Business Opinion Survey, FEDESARROLLO. Findings of the special industrial sector survey on effects of controlled interest rates).

Expectations of moderate devaluation and the changes in the international reserve position will continue to influence the performance of the financial system for the rest of the decade, especially owing to the prospects for increasing oil exports. The effects will depend on the stabilization policies adopted for the current account and international reserves. A recent FEDESARROLLO study (ANIF and FEDESARROLLO, 1993) considered four strategies for managing the current account until the year 2000 and assessed its macroeconomic effects. In a strategy based on neutral exchange and fiscal policies, the current account would remain permanently in surplus. The other strategies would incur a current account deficit of 0.5 percent of GDP through one of the following options: changing the real exchange rate, raising intensive public investment in imports, or raising public consumption (fiscal, economic growth, and inflation forecasts are shown in Figures 4.4 to 4.6).

On the basis of these simulation exercises, financial effects can also be analyzed with the aid of a simple financial programming model.[29] That model assumes perfect mobility of international capital to make the real results compatible with the liquidity and financing needs of the public and private sectors. Consistent with the assumption of capital mobility, the money supply is endogenous in order to meet the nominal demand for money (which depends on GDP and the interest rate). Total (domestic plus external) credit demand depends exclusively on nominal GDP[30] and it is balanced with the endogenous behavior of remunerated borrowing of the financial system.

Also consistent with the previous assumptions, the domestic interest rate is equivalent to the external interest rate combined with the devaluation rate and a risk premium.

The trends regarding international reserve accumulation will be a result of the economy's need for liquidity. Since inflation implies an erosion of monetary balances, there will be continuous pressure to accumulate reserves (which entails paying an inflation tax to the rest of the world). Thus maintaining the same (end-1991) level of OMAs and reserve ratios, if policies to revaluate the exchange rate are not implemented, international reserves as a share of GDP will tend to rise from 15.3 percent initially (Figures 4.7 to 4.8) to between 17.4 and 19.7 percent of GDP in the year 2000, according to the income elasticity of the money demand (1 in the high option, 0.4 in the low). An exchange rate revaluation policy (establishing 0.5 percent of GDP as the current account deficit) would reduce the pressures to accumulate reserves, but less through its effect on

---

[29] Detailed specifications for the model are contained in the technical report submitted to the IDB and are available from the authors.
[30] There is no evidence to support the theory that the demand for credit in Colombia depends on the interest rate.

Figure 4.4. Colombia: Macroeconomic Results of Medium-term Simulations: Fiscal Deficit, 1992-2000
(Percentage of GDP)

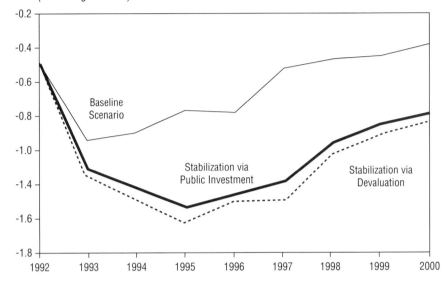

Source: ANIF-FEDESARROLLO.

the current account than because it would curb inflation (Figures 4.4 to 4.6). In this case the year 2000 would see balances of 14.8 to 18.2 percent of GDP. A policy designed to reduce OMAs would also help stabilize international reserves, by raising the degree of monetization of the reserves. Reductions in the reserve ratios would work in the same direction. Without revaluation policies, the phasing out of OMAs would make it possible to stabilize the balance of international reserves as a proportion of GDP for several years (indefinitely in the option of low elasticity of demand). With policies designed to revalue and reduce OMAs, pressure to accumulate reserves would be moderate or nonexistent.

The behavior of the interest rate will depend on exchange management. The resulting real interest rate will be stable if the constant real exchange rate is maintained, but it would have to post abrupt fluctuations from year to year if the decision were made to stabilize the current account through variations in the real exchange rate (Figures 4.7 to 4.9). The instability of the real exchange rate would increase the financial system's vulnerability as it seeks to compete with the rest of the world because of the difficulty of synchronizing the fluctuations of domestic financial returns with the expectations of devaluation. The instability

Figure 4.5. Colombia: Macroeconomic Results of Medium-term Simulations: Economic Growth, 1992-2000
(Percentages)

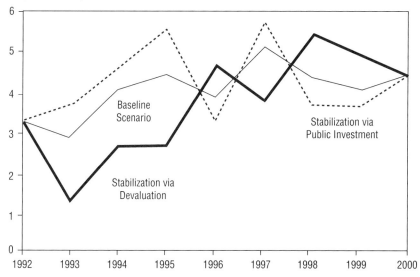

Source: ANIF-FEDESARROLLO.

Figure 4.6. Colombia: Macroeconomic Results of Medium-term Simulations: Inflation, 1992-2000
(Percentage changes)

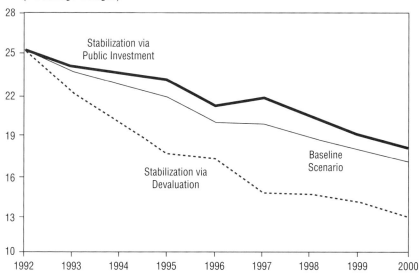

Source: ANIF-FEDESARROLLO.

Figure 4.7. Colombia: Changes in International Reserves and Interest Rates According to Medium-term Simulations: International Reserves without Reduction of Open Market Operations (OMA), 1992-2000
(Percentage of GDP)

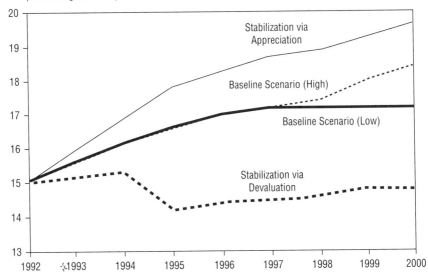

Source: FEDESARROLLO estimates.

Figure 4.8. Colombia: Changes in International Reserves and Interest Rates According to Medium-term Simulations: International Reserves with Reduction of Open Market Operations (OMA), 1992-2000
(Percentage of GDP)

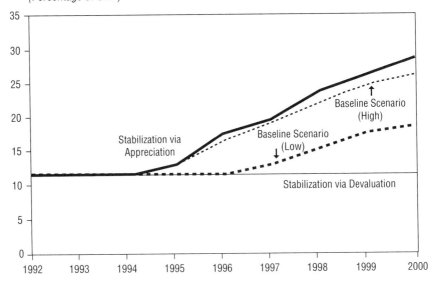

Source: FEDESARROLLO estimates.

Figure 4.9. Colombia: Changes in International Reserves and Interest Rates According to Medium-term Simulations: Interest Rates, 1992-2000
(Percentages)

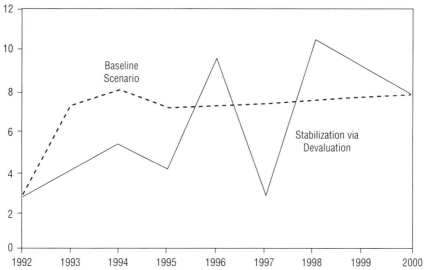

Source: FEDESARROLLO estimates.

of real returns would moreover affect the portfolio risk and could produce periods of financial disintermediation.

Outlook Regarding Sector Performance

The financial system's performance will depend on the handling of the main variables of macroeconomic policy as well as microeconomic and sectoral factors. The influence of these factors can be examined on the basis of the same model described above.

Table 4.12 presents some simulations of financial system growth, measured by its lending. Case 1, which constitutes the basic case, assumes unitary inflow-elasticities of the monetary demand and the demand for credit. It also assumes that the current nominal levels of the domestic public debt and of the open market operations remain unchanged, and that there is no modification of the real exchange rate. In this baseline scenario the financial sector grows by an average of 3.2 percent annually until the end of the century, slightly below average economic growth (4.1 percent). The reason is that part of the demand for credit from

Table 4.12. Simulations of Financial System Growth
(Based on real credit variation)

	Case 1	Case 2	Case 3	Case 4	Case 5	Case 6	Case 7	Case 8
				A. Parameters				
Monetary demand income-elasticity	1.0	0.4	1.0	1.0	1.0	1.0	1.0	0.4
Credit demand income-elasticity	1.0	1.0	2.0	1.0	1.0	1.0	1.0	2.0
				B. Policy variables				
Public debt bonds	Constant	Constant	Constant	Financial deficit	Constant	Constant	Constant	Financial deficit
Open market transactions	Constant	Constant	Constant	Constant	Reserve stabiliz.	Constant	Constant	Reserve stabiliz.
Real exchange rate	Constant	Constant	Constant	Constant	Constant	Curr. acct. stabiliz.	Constant	Curr. acct. stabiliz.
Public investment	Constant	Constant	Constant	Constant	Constant	Constant	Curr. acct. stabiliz.	Constant
				C. Growth results				
1993	4.7	5.4	8.0	-1.4	9.6	2.6	4.8	-0.3
1994	4.3	5.4	9.1	-0.4	7.7	3.7	4.4	1.9
1995	3.8	5.2	9.4	1.1	5.4	2.9	0.9	-1.1
1996	3.2	4.3	7.9	0.6	1.4	5.9	3.0	8.9
1997	4.3	5.3	10.3	4.0	2.8	1.5	4.5	3.5
1998	2.1	3.3	7.7	2.5	1.0	5.6	2.0	12.7
1999	1.5	2.7	7.0	1.7	0.7	2.5	1.5	10.3
2000	2.0	3.3	8.2	2.8	1.3	2.0	2.1	8.1
Average	3.2	4.4	8.5	1.4	3.7	3.4	3.3	5.5

Source: FEDESARROLLO's calculations.

the private sector is met by the rest of the world, given the economy's needs for liquidity.

Case 2 shows that if those liquidity needs respond less than proportionally to economic growth, the possibilities for expansion of the financial sector are greater. The modernization of payment systems and improved banking efficiency, which make for more efficient management of liquid resources, will thus further a growth in lending by the financial system. The same will occur if the demand for credit responds more than proportionally to productive activity. If the demand for credit reaches an elasticity of 2, the sector can grow at an average rate of 8.5 percent to the end of the century in case 3, as against 3.2 percent in the baseline case. Again, this will depend on the sector's success in diversifying its financial products and in increasing its efficiency in such a way as to improve financial intermediation, which is discouraged at present by high spreads and the absence of comprehensive customer services.

The policy adopted by the government in 1992 to finance the fiscal shortfall in the domestic bond market will help expand the capital market and facilitate macroeconomic management, as discussed, but it will limit growth of the financial system. In this case, average growth would drop to 1.4 percent for the rest of the decade and could be negative the first few years. This is because the private sector would use part of its lending capacity to acquire official bonds and replace the resources with greater external finances (given the assumption of an infinite supply of external credit). For similar reasons, the policy of reducing the balance of the OMSs to help stabilize the international reserves, which the monetary authorities have proposed since late 1991, would allow greater growth of the financial system, especially during the first few years, when the liquidation of securities of the Bank of the Republic would have to be greater in order to stabilize the reserves.

A policy of revaluation over the next few years, aimed at generating a deficit of 0.5 percent of GDP, initially would reduce the sector's growth rates and make them more unstable throughout the period (case 6). It could also, as previously mentioned, destabilize real interest rates with negative effects on the sector. By contrast, a policy of stabilizing the current account by greater public investment (case 7) would do very little to change the financial sector's growth pattern compared with the baseline case.

Finally, it is useful to examine a probable combination of the two preceding cases, assuming an improvement in financial efficiency reflected in the elasticities of demand for money and of lending operations, and the adoption of the following policy mix: (1) financing of the fiscal shortfall by placing bonds on the domestic market; (2) reduction of open market operations in order to stabilize international reserves as a proportion of GDP at their present levels; (3) reduction of the real exchange rate in the first years to stabilize the current account at a deficit of 0.5 percent of GDP; and (4) a stable public spending policy (with 5 percent growth for investment). In this case, the outlook regarding average growth for the financial system is fairly favorable (5.5 percent), but growth is very low or negative until 1995 because of the revaluation and domestic financing of the fiscal deficit (case 8).

The level of financial deepening in Colombia is very low by international standards. The M2 to GDP ratio of 17 percent in 1990 and 1991 is lower than the 23.8 average calculated by the World Bank (1989) for low-growth countries, and far from the Asian exporting countries (Naya, 1989). This ratio is also low compared with Latin American countries such as Chile, Mexico, and Venezuela (32, 30 and 24, respectively).

The reduced intermediation will tend to correct itself in the future if the reforms of the sector facilitate the development of new financial instruments and reduce the spreads.[31] The larger current supply of official paper will also make for higher intermediation, as will the possible creation, currently under discussion in Congress, of pension funds to manage social security savings. The chief threat to financial deepening is not, as in the past, the risk of financial repression or the instability of monetary policy but the tendency to revaluation of the exchange rate. As we have seen, the present slow pace of devaluation would entail the abrupt lowering of reserve requirements in order to make competition with external financing possible. A policy of revaluation to stabilize the current account would furthermore reduce economic growth and lower the sector's performance and, in the end, lead to destabilization of the interest rate.

---

[31] However, some of the new instruments will work against traditional banking intermediation, such as the direct securitization of obligations of nonfinancial enterprises, the development of mutual investment funds and the systems of direct credit of some large businesses (Cabrera, 1992).

BIBLIOGRAPHY

Arango, C. A. 1991. "Economías de escala en el sistema financiero colombiano: Revisión de la evidencia empírica." *Banca y finanzas* 22.

Arango, C. A. and H. Piñeros. 1992. "Notas sobre los determinantes de las tasas de interés: El ajuste de corto plazo." *Banca y finanzas* 24.

Arboleda S. 1991. *Ley 45 de 1990. Reforma financiera y de seguros.* Bogotá.

Arciniegas, P. 1984. "La estabilidad de las captaciones de los intermediarios financieros colombianos." *Ensayos sobre política económica* 6.

Asociación Bancaria de Colombia. *Manual de tesorería bancaria.* Bogotá.

———. "Del Fondo Financiero Agropecuario a Finagro: Pocos avances y muchos retrocesos." *Banca y finanzas* 19.

Asociación Nacional de Instituciones Financieras (ANIF) and FEDESA-RROLLO. 1993. *Informe Macroeconómico y Sectorial. Actualización.* January. Bogotá: ANIF-FEDESARROLLO.

Avella, M. and E. Lora. 1991. "El dinero y el sistema financiero colombiano." In *Introducción a la macroeconomía colombiana, 3rd Edition,* eds. E. Lora and J. A. Ocampo. Bogotá: FEDESARROLLO/Tercer Mundo Editores.

Banco de la República. *Revista del Banco de la República,* various issues.

Barajas, A. 1992. "El comportamiento del sector bancario y los determinantes de las tasas de interés en Colombia." In *Apertura: Dos años después,* ed. A. Martínez. Bogotá: Asociación Bancaria de Colombia.

Bernal, O. and S. Herrera. 1983. "Producción, costos y economías de escala en el sistema bancario colombiano." *Ensayos sobre política económica* 3.

Cabrera, M. 1992. "La apertura y la liberación financiera en Colombia." In *Apertura: Dos años después,* ed. A. Martínez. Bogotá: Asociación Bancaria de Colombia.

Cárdenas, M. 1992. "Flujos de capitales, diferencial de rentabilidad y estabilización macroeconómica en Colombia, 1991–92." *Debates de coyuntura económica.* October.

Clavijo, S. 1991. "El margen de intermediación en Colombia." *Banca y finanzas*. January-March.

Delgado, L. F. and P. Roda. 1988. "El apoyo del Estado al sector financiero en su reciente crisis: recursos dirigidos y costos asociados." *Banca y finanzas* 1. January-February.

FEDESARROLLO. 1988. "La inversión privada en la coyuntura actual." *Coyuntura económica*. March.

Fernández, J. 1991. "Un marco para el desarrollo del sector financiero." In *Apertura y modernización: Las reformas de los noventa,* ed. E. Lora. Bogotá: FEDESARROLLO/Tercer Mundo Editores.

Ferrufino, A. 1991. "Reestimación y ampliación de la evidencia sobre las economías de escala en el sistema financiero colombiano." *Ensayos sobre política económica* 19.

González, C. 1993. "La organización del sistema financiero colombiano y el debate sobre la multibanca." *Debates de coyuntura económica*.

Hernández, A. 1992. "El crédito rural y el mercado de capitales." In *Apertura: Dos años después,* ed. A. Martínez. Bogotá: Asociación Bancaria de Colombia.

Inter-American Development Bank. 1990. *Economic and Social Development in Latin America: 1989 Report.* Washington, D.C.: Inter-American Development Bank.

Khatkhate, D. R. and K. W. Riechel. 1980. "Multipurpose Banking: Its Nature, Scope and Relevance for Less Developed Countries." *Staff Papers.* September. International Monetary Fund, Washington, D.C.

Lora, E. 1991a. "Políticas monetarias y comportamiento financiero en Colombia: un modelo financiero de equilibrio general." *Monetaria* 1. January–March.

———. 1991b. "Reformas para la modernización de la economía." In *Apertura y modernización: Las reformas de los noventa,* ed. E. Lora. Bogotá: FEDESARROLLO/Tercer Mundo Editores.

Lora, E. and F. Sánchez. 1992. "Indización de activos monetarios en Colombia." Research Report. Bogotá: FEDESARROLLO.

Memorando Económico. Bermúdez y Valenzuela. Various issues.

Montenegro, A. 1983. "La crisis del sistema financiero colombiano." *Ensayos sobre política económica.* December.

Naya, S. 1989. *Lessons in Development. A Comparative Study of Asia and Latin America.* Panama and San Francisco: CINDE/ICEG.

Ocampo, J. A., ed. 1987. *Historia económica de Colombia.* Bogotá: FEDESA-RROLLO/Siglo XXI Editores.

Orozco, A. and S. Pardo. 1992. *Ajustes integrales por inflación en la tributación colombiana.* Bogotá: CIJUF.

Peñalosa, E. 1992. "El UPAC maniatado." *Estrategia económica y financiera.* October. Bogotá: Servicios de Información, Ltda.

———. 1993. "Revolución en el sector financiero." *Debates de coyuntura económica.* Bogotá: FEDESARROLLO-FESCOL.

Rodríguez, C. A. 1991. "La estabilidad de las captaciones del sistema financiero colombiano." *Ensayos sobre política económica* 19. June.

Steiner, R. 1992. *Apertura: Dos años después,* ed. A. Martínez. Bogotá: Asociación Bancaria de Colombia.

Suescún, R. 1987. "Nueva evidencia sobre economías de escala en la banca colombiana." *Ensayos sobre política económica* 12.

Vesga, R. and E. Lora. 1992. "Las cooperativas de ahorro y crédito en Colombia: Intermediación financiera para sectores populares." Research report. , Bogotá: FEDESARROLLO.

Villegas, L. B. and C. E. Acosta. 1989. "Eficiencia y economía a escala en la Banca." *Revista Superintendencia Bancaria* 1 (2). January.

Watson, N. 1989. "Indicadores de solvencia del sistema bancario: Aplicación de la propuesta de Basilea a Colombia." *Ensayos sobre política económica* 16. December.

The World Bank. 1989. *World Development Report. Financial Systems and Development.* Oxford: Oxford University Press.

Zuleta, L. A. 1991. "Una reforma financiera para la década del noventa." In *Apertura y modernización: Las reformas de los noventa,* ed. E. Lora. Bogotá: FEDESARROLLO/Tercer Mundo Editores.

Zuleta, L. A. and M. Maurer. 1992. "Bases para una negociación de Colombia en una agenda de integración financiera." In *Apertura: Dos años después,* ed. A. Martínez. Bogotá: Asociación Bancaria de Colombia.

CHAPTER FIVE

URUGUAY

Nelson Noya and Daniel Dominioni[1]

This chapter describes the manner in which financial intermediation is conducted in Uruguay and the type of agent active in the system. It examines the amounts and allocation of the funds traded as well as the costs of intermediation, and seeks to determine the chief problems faced by the system in achieving a better allocation of resources. The time frame encompasses the eighties, but the emphasis is on the last few years. An effort is also made to assess the most recent policy changes affecting the financial sector, and to analyze the influence of the macroeconomic situation on the sector's performance. Finally, some policy recommendations for resolving the problems are put forward.

The Uruguayan financial system's specific characteristics—high dollarization, great freedom and openness, presence of a sizable banking system, and absence of significant domestic private agents—are of interest not only in a Uruguayan context but also to other Latin American countries that apparently are beginning to evolve along similar lines.

This chapter consists of three sections. The first examines the organization and operation of the financial intermediation system as well as the recent changes in banking policy. The second analyzes surpluses and financing needs of major institutional agents. The object is to link macroeconomic performance with financial intermediation. The last section contains two sets of policy recommendations, one linked to macroeconomic policy and its consequences on the financial system and the other referring to aspects of sectoral banking policy.

[1] Fernando Correa participated as research assistant. The authors wish to thank several persons for their comments, particularly Roberto Frenkel and his colleagues at the Center for Economic Research (CINVE).

Structure and Evolution of the Financial System

Institutional Structure

By the end of 1992 the Uruguayan financial system was made up of public and private institutions. The public institutions were the Central Bank of Uruguay (BCU), the Bank of the Eastern Republic of Uruguay (BROU), and the Mortgage Bank of Uruguay (BHU).

BCU performs the traditional central bank functions of acting as monetary authority and overseeing the financial system. It was created in 1967 and gradually took over the central bank functions previously carried out by BROU.

BROU is the leading commercial and development bank in the marketplace. (The proportions of the various agents per financial instrument are shown in Table 5.1.) It performs the functions of a development bank by making long-term loans to the productive sectors, particularly agriculture. However, its funds are raised on a short-term basis, in its capacity as a commercial bank. In addition, it functions as controller of external trade, and until very recently had a monopoly on the deposits of public enterprises and the central government.[2] It also channels international financial cooperation funds for promotional loans. Until the recent amendment of the financial intermediation law (in November 1992) it was largely autonomous from the central bank, not being subject to the same regime of compulsory reserve requirements and supervision as the private banks.

BHU is a development bank designed to channel funds for the construction or purchase of housing. Basically it lends long-term and takes in funds short-term and medium-term. In addition to this difference in terms, BHU deals in different units: it lends in unidades reajustables (URs) or readjustable units—units of account indexed according to nominal wages with two months' lag—and borrows URs,[3] pesos and dollars.

Private institutions in the Uruguayan financial system include commercial banks, financial houses, and financial intermediation cooperatives. There currently are 23 commercial banks. As a result of the reorganization carried out

---

[2] Until January 1991 that monopoly enabled it to attract those deposits at rates below the market, which gave it a source of income to subsidize credits.

[3] Strictly speaking, the units in which BHU borrows are not the same as those in which it lends, for deposits are readjusted monthly to the value of the UR and loans were readjusted annually until 1992, when the readjustment period was changed to four to six months. This fact is of some importance because, obviously, the risk of BHU rates is thus linked to the acceleration or deceleration of inflation. In fact, rather than being a "risk", that change is a key determinant of the bank's results, since by its nature it cannot change its active portfolio swiftly.

Table 5.1. Holdings of the Various Groups of Uruguayan Institutions by Type of Financial Instrument, June 1992
(Percentages)

| Financial instruments | BROU | BHU | Private Banks | | | Financial | |
			Managed	Other	Total	Companies	Cooperatives
			Credits				
National currency	52.9	0.0	8.4	31.5	39.9	0.2	7.0
Adjustable units	0.0	100.0	0.0	0.0	0.0	0.0	0.0
Foreign currency	36.5	0.0	4.7	45.7	50.4	11.3	1.8
Residents	49.0	0.0	n.a.	n.a.	45.6	3.0	2.4
Nonresidents	0.0	0.0	n.a.	n.a.	67.7	32.3	0.0
Total	28.2	28.9	3.8	30.6	34.4	6.5	2.0
			Deposits				
National currency	40.9	0.0	16.4	45.9	52.2	0.0	6.8
Demand	30.5	0.0	n.a.	n.a.	69.5	0.0	n.a.
Savings bank	68.7	0.0	n.a.	n.a.	31.3	0.0	n.a.
Fixed term	49.4	0.0	n.a.	n.a.	50.6	0.0	n.a.
Adjustable units	0.0	100.0	0.0	0.0	0.0	0.0	0.0
Foreign currency	29.8	6.4	7.6	42.6	50.1	12.8	0.9
Residents	42.6	11.2	n.a.	n.a.	44.5	0.0	1.6
Nonresidents	13.1	0.0	n.a.	n.a.	57.4	29.5	0.0
Total	29.7	9.7	8.2	41.1	48.2	10.8	1.5

Source: Based on Central Bank of Uruguay, *Boletín Estadístico,* various issues, and unpublished data.
n.a. Not available.

from 1982 to 1987, there are two subgroups in terms of property: banks whose capital is of foreign origin and those known as "managed banks." The foreign banks are either branches or locally established corporations whose shares are held by nonresident firms.[4] The "managed" banks started as private banks, with local or regional capital. Having fallen into difficulties, these banks were taken over by the state for purposes of rehabilitation and reprivatization.[5] The banks

---

[4] There is only one case in which a majority of the shares are in the hands of nonresident firms not engaged in banking abroad.

[5] There were four such "managed" banks, all taken over between 1985 and 1987: Italia, Pan de Azúcar, Comercial and Caja Obrera. In those years they accounted for approximately 30 percent of the private banking system's deposits market. The smallest, Italia, was taken over by Pan de Azúcar in 1989 and the largest, Comercial, was reprivatized in October 1990. Comercial was purchased by a regional group associated with a consortium of first-line transnational banks. Milnitsky (1989) and Banda (1990) describe how these banks were purchased.

can borrow and lend in domestic or foreign currency, without any restriction as to interest rates. Both groups of banks operate almost exclusively with short-term loans and deposits, in domestic or foreign currency, and with residents and nonresidents.

Financial houses are institutions that exclusively attract deposits of nonresidents and engage in offshore transactions, although banks may also do so.[6] They may, however, lend to residents. All offshore business is exempt from compulsory reserve requirements and from taxes on financial assets. The 12 existing houses are all owned by foreign capital.[7]

There are presently eight financial intermediation cooperatives.[8] They can only carry out intermediation transactions among their members, with cooperative companies, or with the rest of the financial system. Until recently they could not be active in the market of sight deposits with drafts. They account for a sizable share of domestic currency transactions, with 7 percent of the market (see Table 5.1).

Each of these institutions conducts transactions with a broad range of financial assets denominated in both domestic and foreign currency, primarily dollars. However, a certain differentiation by type of institution is observed (Table 5.2). For example, the official banks handle a larger share of credits in domestic currency than the private banks. At one end, BHU does not lend in foreign currency (except in the UR described previously), and at the other the financial houses operate almost exclusively in foreign currency. In addition, although deposits are highly dollarized, such dollarization is very low in BHU, a little lower in the cooperatives, and much greater in BROU and the private banks.

---

[6] Before 1981 they were called "banking houses" (*casas bancarias*). Only one such institution existed until 1976. Development of this group was swift from 1978 on, spurred by the fact that they did not fall under the legal prohibition from entering the system as decreed after a banking crisis in 1965. A peculiar interpretation in 1977 of the 1938 banking law excluded nonresident deposits from the legal definition of "public savings." This enabled the BCU, which was interested in promoting offshore operations, to expand the number of institutions without amending the law. This detail points out the rather weak legal basis and the scant political support for the construction of a "financial marketplace." Our hypothesis is that Uruguay became an international financial (or at least regional) marketplace in spite of itself, a few years after the financial opening, with very little thought given to the matter by the authorities at the time—except for the board of directors of BCU. The process of capital flight from Argentina was of some relevance to this development.

[7] The term "private banking system" is normally used in reference to the entire body of private commercial banks and financial houses.

[8] They are also known as "savings and loan cooperatives." They play a particularly important role outside the capital, where they replaced the now-extinct "popular banks" (*cajas populares*). Their share of agrarian and consumer credit is considerable.

Table 5.2. Structure of Credit and Deposits by Type of Institution, June 1992
(Percentage of total credits and deposits)

Financial instruments	BROU	BHU	Private Banks Managed	Private Banks Other	Private Banks Total	Financial Companies	Cooperatives
			Credits				
National currency	25.6	0.0	29.9	14.0	15.8	0.4	48.4
Adjustable units	0.0	100.0	0.0	0.0	0.0	0.0	0.0
Foreign currency	74.4	0.0	70.1	86.0	84.2	99.6	51.6
Residents	74.4	0.0	n.a.	n.a.	56.8	20.0	51.6
Nonresidents	0.0	0.0	n.a.	n.a.	27.3	69.0	0.0
Total	100.0	100.0	100.0	100.0	100.0	100.0	100.0
			Deposits				
National currency	14.8	0.0	21.5	12.0	11.6	0.0	48.1
Demand	4.1	0.0	n.a.	n.a.	5.8	0.0	n.a.
Savings bank	2.5	0.0	n.a.	n.a.	0.7	0.0	n.a.
Fixed term	8.1	0.0	n.a.	n.a.	5.2	0.0	n.a.
Adjustable units	0.0	44.3	0.0	0.0	0.0	0.0	0.0
Foreign currency	85.2	55.7	78.5	88.0	88.4	100.0	51.9
Residents	69.0	55.7	n.a.	n.a.	44.5	0.0	51.9
Nonresidents	16.2	0.0	n.a.	n.a.	43.8	100.0	0.0
Total	100.0	100.0	100.0	100.0	100.0	100.0	100.0

Source: Based on Central Bank of Uruguay, *Boletín Estadístico*, various issues, and unpublished data.
n.a. Not available.

The Financial System Since the Early Eighties

From Liberalization to Financial Crisis

In 1974 liberalization of the Uruguayan economy was set in motion across the board. A hallmark of this reform process was its great speed in liberalizing and opening up finance. Deregulation of the exchange market and the unrestricted opening up of international capital movements were already underway in October 1974. Milestones such as the deregulation of interest rates and the elimination of restrictions on bank assets were in place by the end of 1977. Other equally important aspects of that process, which continued until 1979, were the elimination of legal obstacles to the use of foreign currency in contracts (elimination of the compulsory exchange rate for domestic currency), the abolition of capital requirements and customer portfolio ceilings in the banking system, and the easing of requirements for the entry of new institutions into the system.

At the same time the level of economic activity rose at a rate without precedent in the preceding 20 years, during which it had been virtually at a standstill. That result, together with the financial opening and liberalization, the liquidity on the international credit markets, and the greater regional mobility of capital, gave a strong boost to financial intermediation. However, the rise in the financial deepening index—although it was a result expected by the literature underpinning the reforms (McKinnon, 1973 and Shaw, 1973)—came about not through a rise in the savings rate but through a reallocation of private sector assets.

Deposits in domestic currency and, primarily, in dollars in the financial system, increased as a result of the repatriation of capital and the elimination of informal dollar markets. The degree of dollarization of the public's financial assets did not change substantially from the beginning to the end of the seventies; dollarization preceded financial liberalization.[9]

Credit to the resident private sector in real terms in 1981 was around two and a half times as much as in 1975, which raised the credit-to-GDP ratio from 17.7 percent to 38.7 percent in that period. At the same time, deposits (without counting those allocated to transactions with nonresidents) multiplied by 3.5, so that their ratio to GDP rose from 10.8 percent to 32.8 percent (Table 5.3). Both levels are similar to those prior to the "financial repression," i.e., those of the forties (Noya, 1988).

The abandonment in late 1982 of the stabilization policy based on prior announcements of the exchange rate ("tablita") had important consequences for the financial system. Beginning in mid-1981 the country moved into an acute recession, while a growing lack of confidence in the prior exchange announcements was reflected first by deposits in the banking system moving rapidly into foreign currency and then, in 1982, by capital flight. Overindebtedness to the financial system on the part of businesses was already evident before the recession, with a resulting high degree of delinquency. Then the banks, seeing their deposits change to those denominated in dollars, obliged their debtors to refinance in dollars a sizable part of their borrowings originally taken out in domestic currency. This change aggravated insolvency problems when devaluation occurred in late 1982.

When the crisis struck, the state's policy was to reorganize the system, and BCU acquired a substantial volume of the irrecoverable portfolios of the private banking system (approximately 8 percent of GDP).[10] The banks owned by

---

9 See Noya (1988) on the reallocation of private sector assets between the late sixties and the mid-seventies.

10 It should be noted that many of the portfolio purchases by BCU were not intended to support insolvent entities but were part of a combined operation to obtain external financing in foreign currency at the time of the Mexican crisis. Some of the international banks that intervened, external creditors of the public sector, expressly encouraged the operation from their home offices. See Banda (1990), Roldós (1991), and Pérez-Campanero and Leone (1991).

Table 5.3. Uruguay: Credits and Deposits as Percentages of GDP, 1975–91
(Percentages)

Year	Credit to the private sector					Deposits from the private sector			
	BCU	BROU	BHU	Private banks	Total	BROU	BHU	Private banks	Total
1975	0.5	7.6	3.3	6.3	17.7	2.2	1.1	7.5	10.8
1976	0.6	8.2	3.6	7.7	20.1	2.8	1.4	10.7	14.9
1977	0.2	8.5	3.7	9.8	22.1	3.1	1.3	13.8	18.4
1978	0.1	8.5	3.9	12.6	25.1	3.5	1.3	17.3	22.1
1979	0.1	7.5	3.4	15.0	25.9	3.8	1.2	18.4	23.4
1980	0.0	7.8	4.3	19.9	32.1	3.8	1.1	20.7	25.4
1981	0.0	8.3	6.2	24.1	38.7	5.1	1.7	26.0	32.8
1982	0.4	10.9	9.6	30.5	51.4	7.2	2.7	33.6	43.5
1983	4.1	13.5	9.6	31.9	59.1	9.2	2.9	30.9	43.1
1984	8.8	12.9	9.1	23.4	54.2	10.9	3.3	28.9	43.1
1985	7.5	13.5	10.0	19.0	49.9	13.0	3.5	24.5	41.0
1986	5.1	12.6	10.3	15.8	43.8	13.1	3.6	22.8	39.5
1987	3.6	12.0	10.1	14.3	39.9	12.8	3.4	20.9	37.2
1988	2.6	13.0	10.5	14.6	40.7	14.5	4.3	22.4	41.2
1989	1.9	13.7	10.4	13.6	39.6	16.8	4.9	26.1	47.8
1990	0.4	15.0	10.6	12.0	38.0	20.2	6.0	32.5	58.6
1991	0.7	11.4	10.5	13.8	36.4	19.6	6.2	30.3	56.1

Sources: Based on data from the Central Bank of Uruguay, *Boletín Estadístico*, various issues and unpublished data.
Note: End-of-month annual balance averages divided by GDP at current prices. Deposits include demand deposits, in savings banks and at fixed term, in national and foreign currency, excluding deposits made to the accounts of nonresidents. Credits include credits to residents only.

domestic capital and some banks owned by regional capital, without strong external credit support, were not included in the operation but were kept in an insolvent but liquid condition, typical of banking crises, well into the eighties. Among them were the system's two largest banks, Comercial and Caja Obrera. The domestically or regionally owned private banks disappeared completely in the late eighties.

From 1982 to 1989: Contraction and Concentration of Credit

At the time of the crisis of 1982, credit to the resident private sector fell sharply. In 1990 this credit stood at 71 percent of its 1983 figure. The drop was steeper in the private banking system, with credit in 1990 at only 41.7 percent of the 1983 volume. The same did not happen to deposits, which continued to grow and in 1990 totaled 48.6 percent more than in 1983.

There are several reasons for this. First, the change in credits was tied to the greater risk of nonperformance by businesses. This risk of nonperformance was of two kinds: one traditional, stemming from the increase in business bankruptcies due to the recession and the unexpected changes in relative prices, and the other institutional, inasmuch as the financial crisis prompted the state to save businesses by taking steps, starting in 1981, that restricted creditors' powers of execution. From 1985 on it was primarily the legislative branch that pursued this effort by imposing successive compulsory refinancings of delinquent portfolios, as well as different suspensions of judicial executions. Each of the refinancings has been presented as definitive, but this situation was prolonged until 1992, when the last compulsory refinancing was enacted. This reduced the value of guarantees and blurred the definition of property rights.

Second, the inconsistency between the movement of the deposits and the investments stemmed from the central bank's policy of implicit deposit insurance (losses occurred only in the case of the Banco de Italia, the smallest). After the initial stage, this policy generated confidence, particularly attracting Argentine capital that found the Uruguayan marketplace safer.

As the system continued to attract funds but channeled less of it to the resident private sector, it necessarily increased its lending elsewhere. The fiscal crisis, combined with cuts in external funding, drove up the public sector's financial needs, displacing the private sector's demand for credit. The total balance of lending to the public sector and to nonresidents increased sixfold in real terms from 1983 to 1990.

Nontraditional activities such as offshore intermediation and other banking services expanded hand in hand with the retraction of credit and changes in borrowers. Those activities rose by a factor of 2.6 in real terms between 1983 and 1990, while revenues from services were 63 percent higher in real terms in 1989 than in 1983. One possible cause of this diversification of activities may be the sector's relative labor rigidity. The strong union presence has in fact made it almost impossible to dismiss bank employees because of agreements that are very favorable to wage-earners. Manpower thus incurs a sunk cost, so that an optimal management strategy, given the declining level of activity, consists of diversifying output.

The banking system shows a clear trend toward concentration in both lending and borrowing. From 1980 to 1990 the Herfindahl index applied to deposits by institution rose from 0.06 to 0.14. Credit per debtor is moreover concentrating appreciably within each sector, owing to the banks' growing specialization. The firms of each branch are faced with a steadily declining number of providers of credit. In 1982 the average share of the five major customers of each bank stood at 17.8 percent of its portfolio, with the twenty largest customers accounting for 36.2 percent. In 1990 these figures had climbed to 24.9 percent and 49.4 percent, respectively, with the phenomenon reflected most conspicuously in the branches of foreign banks. By the same token, in 1990

37.7 percent of businesses (accounting for 27.3 percent of total lending) were in debt to a single bank.[11]

BROU's participation in this period rose from 3.8 percent of GDP in the deposits market and 7.8 percent in the credit market in 1980 to 20.2 percent and 15 percent, respectively, in 1990 (Table 5.3). This is due to the greater fragility of the private banking system and the public's perception that the public banking system was backed by the state. In addition, BROU enjoyed a good image of financial strength thanks to its high ratio of deposits to capital.

Trends of the Nineties

In the eighties a system took shape in which the private banking system fell back almost exclusively to wholesale business (deposits from large customers, few branches and little staff, a few highly creditworthy customers, etc.). BROU, the managed banks, and the cooperatives provided retail intermediation and served large and high-risk enterprises (basically domestically owned, attuned to the domestic market, or exporters with various problems).

Towards 1989, however, the pattern showed signs of change. Some institutions began to take an active interest in the retail market. In some cases these were new institutions (such as the only reprivatized bank) and in others past strategies were being continued (as in the case of the cooperatives). Banks under typically transnational management were also turning to the retail credit market.[12]

One indication of these changes is the expansion of credit to consumers (mainly in pesos) and to wholesale trade (mainly in dollars). Between 1987 and 1992 the former went from 6 percent to 16 percent of bank credit in pesos to the private sector, and the latter rose from 22 percent to 30 percent in the foreign exchange portfolio with the private sector. However, total credit to the private sector fell 30 percent in real terms (Figure 5.1). This is even more striking if one considers that the level of activity grew 1.2 percent in 1991 and 7.4 percent in 1992. The counterpart of that trend was that credit to the manufacturing and agricultural sectors continued to shrink both in proportion to the total and in real terms. Therefore, there were no new loans to goods-producing sectors, particularly those producing tradable goods.

A second sign of change is the reversal of the fall in physical plant and staff at some banks. Almost all the banks had reduced plant and staff during the crisis.

---

[11] Dominioni and Vaz (1991) present abundant data on these changes.

[12] There are signs that the trend will persist: the reprivatization of the other managed banks will probably prompt them to enter this segment (one of the cooperatives, associated with regional and European capital, is a serious potential buyer of the largest one); the new financial law is more favorable to cooperatives; and other banks are investing in fixed assets.

Figure 5.1. Uruguay: Private Sector Borrowing, 1984-92
(Billions of 1982 N$Ur, adjusted by wholesale price)

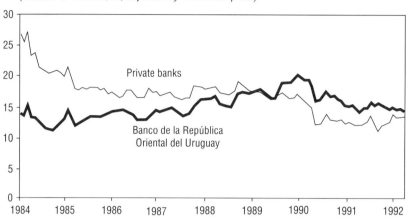

Sources: Banco Central del Uruguay, *Boletín Estadístico,* various issues; and unpublished data.

However, an expansive trend began in 1987, led by the banks of North American and European origin (except Spanish), and is clearly evident in increased hiring.[13] This expansion is reflected in the number of establishments one or two years later (Tables 5.4 and 5.5). More important than aggregate bank movements—which are strongly affected by staff cuts at the managed banks—is the fact that the type of bank that is expanding is the prototype of the wholesaler, in accordance with the ideas current in the mid-eighties.

Another sign of the recent changes appears in the declining participation of the public banking system, especially BROU (a development examined below).

Finally, new financial instruments, issued by this emerging bank, have begun to appear. These instruments, which make it possible to finance long-term credits in foreign currency, are three-year negotiable dollar certificates. They have been used primarily to finance housing loans. The significance of these operations is minimal, but they matter because of their novelty in a bank credit market that had never used long-term instruments.

---

[13] Of course there are exceptions attributable to the specific situation of each firm at the international level: the Bank of America decided to leave in 1987, the NMB maintained an expansive policy throughout the decade, and Lloyds underwent permanent downsizing (the possibility of its closing has been mentioned a number of times).

Table 5.4. Uruguay: Employment in Private Banks by Source of Bank Capital, 1975–91
(Number of individuals)

Years	Spanish	Other European	Latin American	North American	Others	Total
1975	1,138	1,041	162	281	2,720	5,342
1976	1,194	1,103	236	312	2,822	5,667
1977	1,303	1,150	289	347	2,855	5,944
1978	1,352	1,199	345	365	2,908	6,169
1979	1,454	1,285	417	425	3,028	6,609
1980	1,552	1,353	486	513	3,186	7,090
1981	1,626	1,383	493	598	3,423	7,523
1982	1,548	1,354	482	615	3,361	7,360
1983	1,483	1,309	470	613	3,231	7,106
1984	1,429	1,283	447	636	3,208	7,003
1985	1,432	1,270	430	661	3,064	6,857
1986	1,288	1,196	415	663	3,055	6,617
1987	1,124	1,144	412	532	2,928	6,140
1988	1,071	1,163	423	562	2,923	6,142
1989	993	1,206	399	597	2,815	6,010
1990	1,502	1,242	388	645	2,473	6,250
1991	1,317	1,242	353	667	2,402	5,981

Source: Asociación de Bancos del Uruguay, *Memoria Anual,* various issues.

Several factors are behind this change. Of the drop in credit in real terms in 1990, at least 20 percent is due to the introduction of new rules on writing off assets in 1989, which forced swift reduction of the credits inherited from the crisis.[14]

The expansion of consumer credit as a proportion of the total, which began in 1986, got fully underway in the nineties. The following factors explain that trend. First, personal credit is highly spreadable and low-risk, but very costly to select; lower international and local real financial costs in the nineties, coupled with changes in management technology, prompted banks to displace as purveyors of consumer loans finance companies not engaged in intermediation or retail companies actually supplying the goods. Second, the institutional risk entailed by refinancing and suspensions of activities imposed by successive laws creates an advantage in favor of personal loans. Another factor was BHU's withdrawal from the market in housing loans for middle- and high-income families.

In summary, by 1987 a situation had come about in which the banks were doing substantially less intermediation and developing nontraditional activities. Though continuing to attract funds, they were transferring them not to the pri-

---

[14] See Table 5.8. The changes in the rules are described below.

Table 5.5. Uruguay: Number of Private Banking Establishments by Source of Bank Capital, 1974–91

Years	Spanish	Other European	Latin American	North American	Others	Total
1974	63	30	3	8	134	238
1975	63	31	3	8	134	239
1976	63	31	3	9	132	238
1977	63	32	9	8	133	245
1978	65	35	14	10	133	257
1979	66	36	14	11	138	265
1980	68	41	19	13	139	280
1981	69	44	20	13	145	291
1982	69	44	20	13	144	290
1983	73	45	19	20	147	304
1984	76	43	19	24	141	303
1985	85	43	19	26	136	309
1986	80	38	17	26	143	304
1987	69	36	18	19	135	277
1988	58	36	18	21	135	268
1989	56	37	18	22	131	264
1990	52	37	16	21	127	253
1991	37	36	13	25	126	237

Source: Asociación de Bancos del Uruguay, *Memoria Anual,* various issues.

vate sector but to the public sector or the rest of the world. Until that time, customers actively borrowing from the public banking system were the safest and lending was largely focused on them. The riskier customers and small depositors were served only by the public banking system, the managed banks and cooperatives. The market was splitting into clear segments. Some changes since 1989 indicate a partial halt to this segmentation.

Nevertheless, the new credit of this emerging banking system is of low volume. More important, it is not channeled to businesses but to households and trade, financing the expansion of consumption, basically of durable and imported goods.

Costs of Intermediation and Bank Profitability

The previous section described the trends in the "quantities" transacted by the system. This section will assess the costs of that process. The real rates of interest on loans and deposits will be considered first, and then the spread charged by the banks. The spread is measured in two ways: by calculating the difference between lending and borrowing rates, and in accordance with the data of the accounting income statements and the banks' overall situation.

Real Interest Rates

As shown in Table 5.6, borrowing rates, whether on domestic currency or dollar deposits, have been negative or zero since 1985. The rates in dollars have been lower in the last five years. Nevertheless, the corresponding real rates on credits have been high, except for preferred customers. This last fact is even more evident from 1990 on for credits in pesos; since then the real lending rates have ranged from 8 percent to 45 percent annually, depending on the type of customer. By contrast, real lending rates on dollar loans are not high.

In other words, the costs of credit in domestic currency have become very high, but not the costs of credit in dollars. Those high peso levels are explained partly by higher borrowing rates, but spreads also began to increase in the nineties. These wider margins are analyzed in the two following points.

Interest Rate Differential[15]

The gross spread is the difference between rates corrected by the financial costs of freezing the compulsory reserve requirements. This calculation has two advantages, apart from its simplicity: first, it permits the inclusion of a long period, and second, the cost of financial intermediation in pesos and in dollars can be separated. However, it has the disadvantage that average interest rates are not necessarily representative of what happens either in the spread or on average. Nor does it serve to assess the significance of operating costs.

The results appear in Figures 5.2 and 5.3 for the period 1984–92. Six spreads are calculated, corresponding to three lending rates for each type of currency intermediated (pesos and dollars): maximum, minimum (preferred customers) and average. Yields from the most common maturity (three months) are used. It is assumed that the rates of return of remunerated cash reserves are identical to the borrowing rates of the respective deposits.[16] The rates for marginal reserve requirements were taken where these exist, so that the calculated spread approximates the marginal one. To discount the effects of inflation and at the same time make the spreads in the two currencies comparable, the domestic currency rates were made into equivalent rates in dollars on the basis of the devaluation that actually occurred.[17] For the same reasons, the effect of losses through

---

15 In large measure, this part follows the works of Fernández and Pereira (1992) and Gagliardi (1992).

16 The figure of Fernández and Pereira (1992) was adopted. They consider it reasonable over a long time period. The cumbersome nature of the rules on reserve requirements makes it rather pointless to examine this point in greater depth.

17 Obviously, this entails some distortion of the calculations insofar as there are differences between the actual and the expected devaluations.

Table 5.6. Real Interest Rates of Private Banks in Uruguay, 1984–92

	Lending Rate						Borrowing Rate	
	Credits in national currency			Credits in dollars			Deposits	
Year	Max.	Average	Min.	Max.	Average	Min.	In pesos	In dollars
1984	13.2	12.4	9.0	42.7	36.3	30.3	3.8	26.8
1985	6.2	6.0	1.5	7.4	1.8	-3.8	0.2	-6.4
1986	16.7	9.4	2.0	5.2	-0.6	-5.0	-3.2	-7.8
1987	28.2	15.1	8.7	20.0	12.8	8.7	3.9	5.6
1988	19.8	10.8	3.8	11.1	5.0	1.1	-2.4	-1.6
1989	22.2	9.9	2.4	14.0	9.2	5.5	-17.3	-12.1
1990	27.5	12.3	-0.9	3.0	-0.7	-4.4	-25.3	-23.4
1991	45.5	29.0	12.3	1.8	-1.3	-4.7	0.3	-7.5
1992	37.3	22.8	7.8	-0.9	-3.6	-6.6	0.1	-8.8

Sources: Oikos, *Panorama Financiero*, various issues, Central Bank of Uruguay, *Boletín Estadístico*, various issues, and unpublished data.
Note: Annual averages of monthly values, in annualized percentages, deflated by consumer prices.

devaluation on the unremunerated cash reserves in domestic currency were taken into account. Thus the spread in domestic currency can be expressed as:

$$(ia-d) \ x \ (1-er-n)/(1+d) + (er-1) \ (ip-d)/(1+d)en \ x \ d/(1+d)$$

where *ia* is the lending rate, *d* the actual devaluation rate, *er* the remunerated cash reserve rate, *en* the unremunerated cash reserve rate, and *ip* the borrowing rate. The net spread thus calculated should cover the opportunity cost of capital and operating costs. The same formula was applied for the spread in dollars, except that in this case the devaluation adjustment is not called for. The results appear in Figures 5.2 and 5.3.

Thence flow the following facts. The existence of spreads below 5 percent in dollars for almost the entire period, even with maximum rates, would indicate low-cost intermediation. Intermediation in pesos, on the other hand, was always more costly, but even more so in the nineties, with spreads of more than 17 percent charged to average customers in the nineties and more than 30 percent to the riskiest or costliest ones. By contrast, spreads in dollars are on a slight downward trend and are always narrower and more stable. The domestic currency spreads are more volatile and widen when inflation speeds up (as in the 1989–90 period). There were zero or negative spreads in domestic currency until 1990 for preferred customers.[18]   But these customers saw an increase in the spread

---

[18] A zero or low spread for preferred loans is consistent with the results of a recent opinion survey of bank managers, who say that adjustment occurs predominantly with respect to the

Figure 5.2 Uruguay: Private Bank Spreads on 90-day Deposits in Local Currency, 1984-92
(Annualized rates)

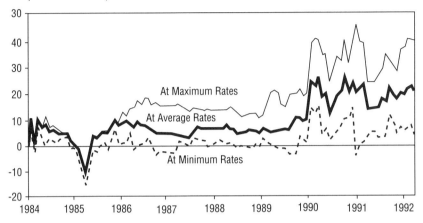

Sources: Banco Central del Uruguay, *Boletín Estadístico*, various issues; Oikos, *Panorama Financiero*, various issues; and unpublished data.

Figure 5.3. Uruguay: Private Bank Spreads on 90-day Deposits in Dollars, 1984-92
(Annualized rates)

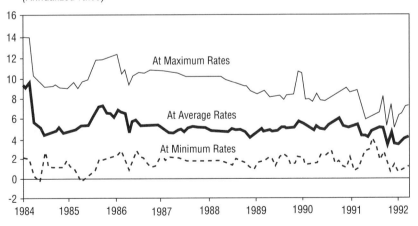

Sources: Banco Central del Uruguay, *Boletín Estadístico*, various issues; Oikos, *Panorama Financiero*, various issues; and unpublished data.

Table 5.7. Uruguay: Average Bank Margins, 1986–92
(Annualized percentages)

Period	National currency with lending rates			Dollars with lending rates			Difference national currency vs dollars with lending rates		
	Max.	Average	Min.	Max.	Average	Min.	Max.	Average	Min.
1986–89	13.5	5.2	-0.6	9.8	5.0	1.7	3.7	0.2	-2.4
1990–92	31.4	17.4	4.6	7.6	4.7	1.7	23.8	12.7	2.8
1990–92 difference with respect to 1986–89	17.9	12.2	5.2	-2.2	-0.3	0.0			

Sources: Oikos, *Panorama Financiero*, various issues, Central Bank of Uruguay, *Boletín Estadístico*, various issues, and unpublished data.

applied by the banks after that date. Also from that year forward, the differential between preferred and nonpreferred rates in domestic currency increased greatly, whereas it diminished slightly in dollars.

The size of these differentials and their relative changes are summarized in Table 5.7. What is the reason for these trends and the differences between peso and dollar spreads? There are three factors to which they can theoretically be attributed. First, the differences (or the changes of a given spread over time) can reflect different costs. Second, if we assume that the banks are risk-averse, the arbitrage could not occur if they perceive that one operation is riskier than the other: they would demand a risk premium to offset the differences. Finally, there can be conditions of disequilibrium or increases in the power of the market.

We shall try to break down those variations in spreads into different factors. To that end we shall assume that the differences in spreads charged to preferred customers cannot reflect different levels of risk, as explained by the following factors:

(1) A combination of changes in reserve requirement policy and the issuance of drafts between 1990 and 1991, which made transactions in domestic currency less profitable. Until mid-1990, drafts in pesos and in dollars were issued at a rate set at the beginning of each day by BCU, which accepted the entire demand. After that date, the rate of the drafts was subject to weekly

---

borrowing rate, while the lending rate comes given to them (Fernández and Pereira, 1992). This can be interpreted to mean that the risk-free lending rate (preferred customers) comes given to the banks. It should be noted that the negative and very similar spreads for the whole spectrum of lending rates between 1984 and 1985 are the result of the regulation of maximum lending rates in domestic currency which was applied temporarily in that period. The quality of the information of that period should therefore be treated with some skepticism.

auction, without it being known how much the amount accepted would be. In addition, the banks conducted present selling transactions with future purchase of drafts with the public for only one day, thus avoiding the reserve requirement rules. This enabled them to offer greater profitability to preferred customers on sight deposits. A part of the increased profit was appropriated by the banks. This explains the zero or negative spread charged to preferred customers in domestic currency in the eighties. With the introduction of the auction system, this operation became less profitable because it increased the risk of staying liquid and added uncertainty concerning the returns on cash reserves.[19] This possibility was eliminated in July 1991 when present sale transactions with future purchase of public securities were included in the transactions subject to compulsory reserve requirements.[20] This factor explains the modifications in the spread in pesos charged to preferred customers in the nineties, as well as part of the difference in the eighties with respect to the dollar spread.

(2) The differences between peso and dollar spreads throughout the period are due in part to the volatility of inflation.[21] The higher the inflation, the more volatile it is, which creates a risk that does not exist (or is negligible) in dollar transactions. Let us suppose that the differences between peso and dollar spreads for preferred customers reflect a premium for the greater inflation in pesos. Let us further suppose that there was only one jump in this premium in the nineties, corresponding to the greater inflation of this last period. Between 1986 and 1989 there was another factor that explains this difference: the profits attracted by the banks through the factors mentioned in (1) above. The difference in the spread charged to preferred customers in the nineties between pesos and dollars would then reflect that premium: 2.8 percent. Another procedure produces the same

---

[19] The fact that the rates of dollar drafts rose by a few percentage points when the bidding mechanism was introduced buttresses this idea. Before the bidding, treasury drafts in dollars were sold at the LIBOR window; then they routinely exceeded that rate. The new procedure applies to drafts in either pesos or dollars. However, it is obvious that alternative short-term investments exist for cash surpluses in dollars on the international market, but not for pesos.

[20] One piece of evidence that these transactions existed is the rapid growth in real terms of the sight deposits. In addition, the drafts are replaced by profitable deposits in BCU, at a rate determined by the latter. In principle, this last change should have had opposite-sign effects on the spreads. On the one hand, the banks would lose profits as the rate of return of the drafts was greater than the rate set by BCU. On the other, as that rate fluctuated more, when it was set by weekly bidding, the banks would reduce the risk. Since it is not possible to gain access to information on the rates of return of the cash reserves, no detailed assessment of this point can be made.

[21] Hernández (1992) presents theoretical arguments and evidence on the relationship between the greater volatility and financial intermediation spreads.

result. Let us suppose that the premiums are additive. Then the difference between the spread in pesos for preferred customers in the nineties and the spread in the eighties reflects the rise of inflation and the disappearance of the factors cited in (1). Then the subtraction of the increase of the spread in pesos between 1990 and 1992 and between 1986 and 1989 (5.2 percent) from the difference between the peso and dollar spreads between 1986 and 1989 (-2.4 percent) would also be the premium for the greater inflation of the nineties, which happens to be 2.8 percent. This may give an idea of the effect of the factor cited in (1): it would be between 2.4 percent and 5.2 percent.

(3) The increase in the BROU lending rate. As noted, this public bank is especially important in domestic currency transactions. A series of changes in its regulatory framework and in its management prompted it to raise its lending rates in domestic currency (as will be seen further on). At the same time its participation in the credit market was curtailed (Figure 5.1), as the increased rates drove customers to the private banking system, customers whose cost of opportunity of the credit, given by the BROU rate, went up. This would account for the widening spreads in domestic currency for non-preferred customers. For the banks it would be best to raise the rates to the point where they compete with the marginal bank, in this case BROU. The private banks' widening spreads coincide with BROU's raising of the nominal lending rate: the spreads increased by 12 percent to 18 percent, while BROU raised the rate 20 percent, making it equal to the private banks' average rate.

(4) Higher cost because of the shifting of assets to consumer credit, low-risk because it is highly diversifiable but more expensive to select. Since consumer loans are not preferential, this only explains the greater increase in the spreads on the highest rates. Nevertheless, the cost pressure hypothesis is not consistent with the idea expressed in point (3) above. But the same argument could be applied as in that case, with the banks raising the rate on consumer loans to the same level at which they compete with the consumer finance companies, whose highest rates make up the opportunity cost of borrowers. The following section will deal with the changes in operating costs.

(5) If the situation is one of disequilibrium, the banks may no longer be able to raise the rate for peso deposits in order to attract deposits in that currency, even though they are facing unsatisfied demand for peso loans. In fact, as will be seen, the returns on the peso deposits have in recent years consistently surpassed dollar returns, which has not generated a significant change in the portfolio of the private sector toward assets in pesos. However, the persistence of these large peso spreads makes it difficult to explain the slow adjustment of nominal lending rates.

(6) The fact that banks limited themselves to the safest customers, reducing the risk as loan activity contracted, could account for the slightly narrower range of dollar spreads throughout the period.

In conclusion, in the nineties the real lending rate in pesos rose sharply and stayed at high real levels because of higher profit margins resulting from a permanent spread (in the order of 10 percent per year) in favor of peso deposits. The margins rose mainly because of BROU's higher rates and because they began to compete with nonbank segments with higher costs of lending (consumer finance). Other lesser factors would be the greater volatility of inflation in the nineties and the changes in the reserve requirement regime and the auctioning of drafts. Intermediation in dollars, moreover, is done at low cost.

If the bulk of the increase in peso rates reflects the customer's higher opportunity cost for borrowing outside the private financial system, the banking system would be appropriating intramarginal revenues. If the reference were the consumer loans of the finance companies, the displacement of the latter by the banks would result in improved social efficiency. But where businesses, and nonpreferred businesses in particular, are concerned, the higher cost of private credit in pesos would reflect BROU's higher cost. As we saw, this last effect has not resulted in an expansion of credit but simply in a shifting of borrowers from BROU to the private banking system.

Factors (1) and (2) are too small to have much impact. In terms of efficiency, however, the changes in the reserve requirement rules mean that the inflation tax base was expanded, so that these rules have two contradictory effects: they diminish distortions by eliminating the discriminated evasion by businesses, and they augment them by expanding the tax base. The changes in the form of draft auction created some room for the conduct of monetary policy, instead of higher financial cost, although inasmuch as they made drafts more illiquid they may have increased the money supply, offsetting that higher cost.

Income Statements[22]

Consulting the statements of aggregate results of the private banks to measure the cost of intermediation requires allocating the operating costs between the financial intermediation activities and the rest, and between fixed and variable costs. This last is useful for estimating the marginal cost of intermediation. Three assumptions were used. The first or high assumption was extreme in that, given the rigidities mentioned in variable costs, all the costs are fixed. A low-spread assumption allocated them according to the quantifiable proportion between earnings from services and financial revenues (adjusted for devaluation). An intermediate assumption assigns to variable costs the average result of the extreme positions.

---

[22] Here Dominioni and Vaz (1992) were followed, with modifications.

Table 5.8. Uruguay: Private Bank Margins According to Profit and Loss Statements, 1987–92

(Annualized percentage rates converted to dollars)

		1987	1988	1989	1990	1991	1992a
(1)	Average return on credits	7.4	11.6	11.4	17.9	18.4	16.9
(2)	Average financial cost	3.8	5.9	4.7	6.7	5.2	3.5
(3)	Gross brokerage margin (1)–(2)	3.6	5.7	6.7	11.2	13.1	13.4
(4)	Credits/deposits ratio	67.6	65.5	56.2	44.7	39.7	39.6
(5)	Yield on other assets	0.4	2.0	3.8	5.4	4.3	5.6
(6)	Average variable operating cost						
	a) Low hypothesis	6.9	6.6	6.1	7.3	7.6	8.9
	b) High hypothesis	4.1	4.5	4.7	5.8	6.1	5.6
	c) Average hypothesis	5.5	5.6	5.4	6.6	6.8	7.2
(7)	Variable brokerage margin (1)*(4)/100–(2)+(5)–(6)						
	a) Low hypothesis	-5.3	-2.9	-0.5	-0.6	-1.2	-0.1
	b) High hypothesis	-2.4	-0.9	0.8	0.9	0.2	3.1
	c) Average hypothesis	-3.8	-1.9	0.1	0.2	-0.5	1.5
(8)	Net earnings from deposit services	1.8	2.0	1.8	1.9	1.8	1.8
(9)	Variable bank margin (7)+(8)						
	a) Low hypothesis	-3.4	-1.0	1.3	1.3	0.6	1.7
	b) High hypothesis	-0.6	1.1	2.7	2.8	2.1	4.9
	c) Average hypothesis	-2.0	0.1	2.0	2.1	1.4	3.3
(10)	Fixed costs per deposit						
	a) Low hypothesis	1.4	1.5	1.1	1.0	0.8	0.5
	b) High hypothesis	4.2	3.5	2.5	2.6	2.2	2.1
	c) Average hypothesis	2.8	2.5	1.8	1.8	1.5	1.3
(11)	Total bank margin (9)–(10)	-4.8	-2.4	0.2	0.3	-0.2	1.2

Sources: Central Bank of Uruguay, *Boletín Estadístico*, various issues, unpublished data, and Dominioni and Vaz (1992).
aThe data for 1992 are for the second six months; the rates of return were annualized.

The estimates for the period 1987 to the second half of 1992 are presented in Table 5.8.[23] All the relationships are calculated in reference to the average annual amount of the deposits (converted to dollars). Returns on other assets include remunerated and unremunerated cash reserves, as well as investments with correspondents abroad and assets against the public sector. Instead of correcting the income statement for inflation, adjustments for inflation were made to the returns and financial costs of assets and liabilities in pesos, so that the returns shown in Table 5.8 are denominated in dollars.

The measure comparable to the rates differential calculated in the previous section is the gross spread (row 3) plus the return from other assets (row 5); that

---

[23] The data prior to 1987 do not follow the same accounting practices, which invalidates any comparison with them. Similarly, the lack of public records regarding BROU's statements of results, even in 1992, prevents their comparison with those of the private banks.

sum has a similar tendency to and even approximates their mean levels. The low level of 1987 and 1988 is certainly influenced by the managed banks, given the poor quality of their portfolios, so that there are negative spreads, followed by a positive financial and banking spread. The loans to deposits ratio falls and the returns on loans rise as a result of the writing off of assets and the allocation of new loans at higher rates. As a consequence of these movements, the gross spread has risen considerably, so that financial intermediation for the private sector has become more expensive.

The impact of the variable operating costs (for any assumption) is growing, which is consistent with the idea that the costs of selection of the new loans will rise. These costs are high in absolute terms: between 4 percent and 6 percent of the deposits (according to the various assumptions). If the increase of the consumer loan portfolio justifies those rising costs it can be seen in the following manner: operating costs rise 6 or 10 percent of the credits to 14 or 22 percent, and if we keep in mind that the banks' domestic currency credits are barely 15 percent of their total credits, the rise in costs cannot be attributed to this reason alone.

However, the trend also could be related to the fact that personnel costs in the Uruguayan system are relatively high because of union pressure. The wage bill accounts for 40 percent to 50 percent of the variable costs and in recent years has equaled some 4 percent of deposits. According to Bucheli (1992) the salaries of bank employees are about 216 percent above those of people in similar education and age groups, that is, discounting the possible effects of differences due to education or experience. With the available data it is impossible to determine what part of that differential is due to a union-led capture of monopolistic bank revenues.

The variable spread (row 7) can be taken as a measure of the marginal cost of intermediation: it is zero or negative through almost the entire period. The total profitability of the banks is almost zero or negative, except in the last year, for which data, because it is not final yet, must be viewed with greater caution. Finally, the strong influence of the performance of the other assets (row 5) in widening the spreads should be noted. Not considering the effects of profitability on deposits of correspondents would indicate that the net balance of the changes in the reserve requirements has been highly favorable to the banks since the beginning of the nineties.

Financial Assets and Returns

In this section we will try to identify the main historical features of the public's demand for financial assets, with particular emphasis on how the rates of return and the speeding up or slowing down of inflation causes changes in the portfolio structure of private agents.

As we have already mentioned, the extreme dollarization of the Uruguayan economy's financial relations gives it a unique character. The dollarization not only affects the deposits and loans of the financial system but also encompasses the public debt. The treasury has issued debt in dollars since the early seventies, in the form of bills as well as bonds. A part of the bonds and bills in dollars is in the portfolio of the financial institutions, another is held by the public, and an undetermined share is held by nonresidents.[24] Bills are also issued in domestic currency and, with the exception of those placed in the financial system, are assumed to be held by the resident public.

Figure 5.4 shows the composition of the volume of financial assets held by the resident public. It is evident that foreign currency assets have been growing, particularly since 1983. Their growth received new impetus from 1989 to 1990, when inflation approached three digits annually. In general, the volume of financial assets in relation to GDP has remained stable, even during the crisis, and it has been growing since 1985.

The differential between the return on deposits in domestic currency and that on dollar deposits is presented in Figure 5.5. If one takes the interest rate on dollar deposits as a reasonable measure of the profitability of all foreign currency-denominated assets, the following generalizations can be deduced.

The differential in favor of peso assets has been negative throughout almost the entire period. It was clearly positive only during the "tablita" period (1978 to 1982), during 1985 and 1986, and from mid-1990 on. That is, the positive differential coincides with periods of real appreciation in relation to the dollar. The periods of high instability of this differential coincide with those of its negative value. There are also times when inflation accelerated and exchange policy was more erratic.

When that differential is highly negative the portfolio shifts toward dollar-denominated assets. That phenomenon is generally associated with bursts of rapid inflation. This occurred between 1982 and 1983 and at the start of the nineties. Except in the tablita period, the positive and relatively stable differentials (e.g., those between 1985 and 1986 and since 1990), although ranging between 5 to 10 percent annually, have not caused significant changes pointing to a dedollarization of assets.

It can therefore be said that dollarization has shown a certain irreversibility. The demand for domestic currency-denominated assets tends to be asymmetrical in its movements with respect to differences in returns: a pronounced and, above all, unexpected reduction in relative returns in pesos triggers a fall from which no recovery is possible, at least not immediately.

---

[24] A reasonable assumption, which probably overestimates the proportion of bonds and bills in the hands of residents, is that this proportion of the total amount of bonds and bills is the same as that of residents' deposits in relation to the total amount of deposits in foreign currency. That is the assumption used in this paper.

Figure 5.4. Uruguay: Financial Assets Held by Residents, 1976-92
(Percentages of the total)

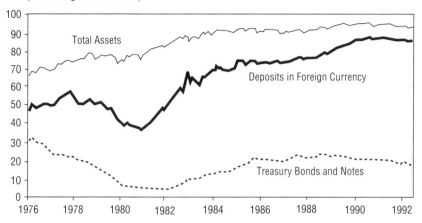

Sources: Banco Central del Uruguay, *Boletín Estadístico*, various issues; and unpublished data.
Note: "Treasury Bonds and Notes" refers to the proportion of treasury bonds and bills in foreign currency. "Deposits in Foreign Currency" means the degree of dollarization of assets (with the difference between these two lines indicating the portion of deposits in foreign currency). "Total Assets" shows the total interest-bearing assets (with the difference between "Total Assets" and "Foreign Currency" indicating the interest-bearing assets in local currency and in UR). Finally, the difference between the last line and the 100 percent total represents the portion of currency in circulation and demand deposits (M1).

Figure 5.5. Rate of Return Differential in Pesos, 1978-92
(Ex post over 90-day deposits)

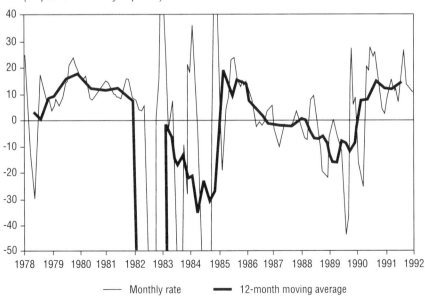

Sources: Banco Central del Uruguay, *Boletín Estadístico*, various issues; Oikos, *Panorama Financiero*, various issues; and unpublished data.

Proposed and Ongoing Financial Reforms

Reforms to the system have been implemented since mid-1989, based on the recommendations in the structural adjustment agreements with the World Bank (SAL I of 1987, and fundamentally, SAL II of 1989) and the technical and financial assistance agreement with the IDB. These changes encompass the rules of prudential policy, reserve requirements, BCU's treatment of the public banking system, changes in the latter's management, and the recapitalization of the managed banks.

Changes in Policies Concerning Regulation of the Private System

In the third quarter of 1989 new regulations governing prudential standards were put into effect whereby the Basle Committee's recommendations were progressively adopted. Changes were made to the way an institution's minimum equity was set, the manner in which risks were classified and evaluated, as well as forecasting procedures.[25] The fixing of minimum net worth liability per institution was modified: under the new rules, it was based on asset quality instead of, as previously, on the bank's legal status, its plant, and inflation. The former prudential regulation instrument, now replaced, was the limit of aggregate borrowing as a multiple (by 20) of equity, cash reserves, and the public securities portfolio.

Based on these changes, the minimum net worth requirements were raised to 8 percent of risky assets net of bad debt reserves. According to Amoroso and Xavier (1988), the implicit coefficient in the prior system was 4.78 percent, so that the application of the new system should have entailed a capitalization of the banks.

Furthermore, as the earlier rules for classifying risky assets depended on whether or not the debtors were meeting due dates, a risk classification system was established on the basis of objective and subjective criteria emanating from BCU. The classification is reviewed twice a year by each institution. Loans can be found to be of normal risk, potentially troublesome, of doubtful recovery, and unrecoverable.

As a result of these new rules, the net worth of the private banking system in current dollars rose in 1990. By the same token, the leverage ratios of each bank changed significantly from 1987 to 1991, particularly in the system's weaker banks (the managed banks), which were also the biggest.[26]

As was already pointed out, the reduction in the proportion of overdue assets in the total portfolio is one of the most important changes in financial statements starting in 1987 (Table 5.9).

---

[25] See Amoroso and Xavier (1988) and Banda (1990).

[26] It must be taken into account that, although it is good approximation, the net worth is not exactly the objective variable of the regulation.

Table 5.9. Uruguay: Delinquency and Leverage by Bank, 1987–92
(Percentages)

Banks	Overdue credit as a percentage of total credit				Liabilities as a percentage of net worth			
	December 1987	December 1990	December 1991	June 1992	December 1987	December 1990	December 1991	June 1992
BROU[1]	n.a.	n.a.	15	n.a.	n.a.	n.a.	3	n.a.
Caja Obrera[2]	18	13	5	4	28	25	14	18
Comercial[2]	50	1	0	0	6	9	12	14
NMB	2	3	1	0	24	18	23	25
de Credito	24	9	1	1	30	28	9	12
Montevideo	29	6	5	3	34	19	13	15
Trade Development/ American Express	7	0	0	0	11	19	12	8
Exterior	5	5	3	4	19	19	27	53
Discount	9	1	1	1	9	13	14	11
Santander	8	0	0	0	9	16	24	18
Pan de Azúcar[2]	44	22	5	3	66	207	4	30
De Italia[2]	68				43			
Real	44	17	6	4	11	22	23	24
UBUR/Banesto	23	12	6	6	13	40	13	12
National Republic of NY	0	0	0	0	47	27	19	34
Surinvest			3	2			8	8
do Brasil	30	2	2	1	5	6	6	8
Citibank	6	1	0	0	13	5	8	9
Sudameris	13	0	0	0	18	20	19	22
Holandés	2	0	0	0	17	15	19	22
Boston	0	0	0	0	13	20	19	18
Lloyds of London	8	0	0	0	19	20	22	26
Centrobanco	19	8	2	4	11	7	7	7
Nación Argentina	12	1	1	1	6	10	9	12
Total private banks	21	6	2	2	16	18	12	17

Source: Based on unpublished data from the Central Bank of Uruguay.
[1] The dates for BROU are for the month of September.
[2] "Managed" banks.
n.a. Not available.

The changes in the reserve requirement regulations were carried out mainly in 1991 and consisted of substituting a deposit remunerated at a rate fixed by BCU for the share of monetary regulation bills that constituted remunerated compulsory cash reserves.[27] In addition, the same reserve requirement rules are

---

[27] The consequences of these new regulations were examined in an earlier section of this chapter entitled "The Interest Rate Differential."

applied to the banking system and BROU, as will be examined in the following section.

Changes in the financial intermediation law approved in November 1992 enhanced BCU's power to penalize public banks and individuals for irregularities, gave BCU clearer authority to grant licenses and allow the opening of branches (separating such authority from that of the Executive Branch), and limited financial assistance to troubled institutions to the maximum determined by their equity liability. It was further explicitly established that the state would not be liable for the liabilities of institutions and in that connection would not act as insurer. In summary, apart from the enhanced enforcement power, the principal changes relate to deposit insurance and licensing.

The most important element in licensing policy is implicit and relates to the rules for entering the system. BCU's licensing policy has had an unwritten rule which the last two boards of directors (1985–89 and 1990 to the present) have consistently followed: not to authorize the establishment of new banks unless they are institutions backed by leading international banks. Domestic and even regional groups are not admitted to the system unless they form an association with some bank capital that is solidly backed in developed countries.[28]

This licensing policy is designed to enable BCU to dissociate itself from covering deposits in case of a crisis. One consequence is that if forms of management vary with the type of ownership, the institutions comprising the system become more risk-averse inasmuch as the acceptable entrants are banks with high ownership by transnational banks. Therefore the policy has consequences on resource allocation. This point will be discussed further toward the end of the chapter.

Restructuring BROU

The restructuring guidelines were defined in the agreements mentioned with the IBRD and the IDB and, as regards the public banking system, are designed to standardize the criteria governing the treatment of these banks with respect to the private banks. With regard to BROU, that standardization encompassed the compulsory reserve requirement regime, including the harmonization of the regime with respect to deposits attracted from the rest of the public sector under a monopoly; it also encompassed the treatment of nonperforming loans and accounting practices.

BROU's size, history and nature set a peculiar stamp on its management. It is generally accurate to say that its loan portfolio is made up of two parts. The first part consists of lesser risks, where the criteria for access to credit are based on the

---

[28] Licensing policy has been cautious pending the reprivatization of the managed banks.

evaluation of guarantees. This part is regulated by the bank's technical staff, which finds in the demand for guarantees an objective procedure for minimizing losses due to its decisions. A second part is composed of sizable risks, almost exclusively of enterprises of domestic groups, where access to credit is regulated by its board of directors (composed of five members appointed by Parliament at the beginning of each period of government). Under these circumstances, it is not surprising that only the private banking system participates financially in projects with a high potential for short-term reimbursement, albeit with low guarantees. It is not surprising that BROU has many delinquent accounts in its portfolio of large business sectors and a high recovery of loans in the more diversified sectors.[29] Nevertheless, BROU continues to be the only available source of long- or medium-term credit with which to purchase capital goods.

It has been maintained that BROU had the ability to set a lower lending rate in domestic currency than the private banks (and thus to displace them). That ability would be based on three factors: the collection of some taxes; a calculation of costs according to average and not marginal cost; and the subsidy implicit in a monopoly on access to public sector funds, with lower reserve requirements than the funds of the private sector. The program introduced two measures to correct those sources of competitiveness not tied to the logic of the market: harmonization of reserve requirements for the public and private sectors, and changes in the costing system. After these were applied, lending rates in pesos and in dollars rose significantly.

The following considerations show that although subsidies deriving from public funds were the chief factor financing that divergence of rates, the full set of changes in BROU policy indicate that the bank is seeking increased profitability.

First, the taxes are not significant, for the principal revenue is a commission of one-tenth of one percent on almost all the country exports and imports of merchandise. This input is from the sixties, when BROU was tasked with recording foreign trade transactions. It is therefore questionable whether this charge is actually a tax. BROU receives annual revenues from it on the order of $12 million to $15 million. That gross income represents less than 1.5 percent of its loans (and not more than 2.5 percent of domestic currency loans), so it cannot be

---

[29] As Table 5.9 shows, BROU has a larger percentage of overdue assets than private banks (15 percent versus 2 percent). One piece of evidence in support of the text's argument is the larger proportion of the delinquent portfolio in dollars, where large customers predominate: 15 percent as against 4 percent in domestic currency (the private banking system does not show significant differences between the two currencies). This results both from the type of management and from the delay in adjusting its accounting practices to those of the rest of the system, which makes the comparison less reliable (there is probably a tendency to underestimate the portfolio's poor quality).

Table 5.10. Transfers Received by BROU for Inflation Tax, 1982–91
(Percentage of GDP)

Year	Demand deposits (1)	Net credit to the government (2)	Reserve requirement and currency issue (3)	Total (1)+(2)–(3)
1982	0.1	-0.3	0.1	-0.2
1983	0.8	-0.5	0.2	0.1
1984	0.4	-1.1	0.3	-1.1
1985	0.4	-1.1	0.4	-1.1
1986	0.4	-0.3	0.4	-0.3
1987	0.0	0.0	0.0	0.0
1988	0.4	0.3	0.3	0.4
1989	0.5	0.5	0.3	0.7
1990	0.7	0.4	1.1	0.1
1992	0.5	0.6	0.5	0.6

Sources: Central Bank of Uruguay, *Boletín Estadístico*, various issues, and unpublished data.

considered an important source of subsidies, especially if the record-keeping costs were included.

The importance of the differential reserve requirements and, in particular, the maintenance of the public sector's current accounts would represent a significant figure prior to 1991. An approximate estimate based on the inflation tax which BROU succeeds in collecting as a percentage of GDP showed that, in some years, that figure was the equivalent of 10 percent of credits in domestic currency (Table 5.10).[30]

This situation changed as of January 1991, when deposits of public enterprises and municipal governments, and a 100 percent reserve requirement, were applied on the increase in central government and Social Reserve Bank deposits over December 1990.

Under the terms of the agreements with the IBRD and the IDB, BROU should have changed the standards governing its lending rates and started using the marginal cost. It is not possible to quantify the impact of this change, because there are no official data. However, given the lack of infrastructure for generating information with which implementation continues to go forward, it seems

---

[30] Again, the lack of data on the ad hoc reserve requirement regime prior to 1991, subject to much negotiation, prevents any firm conclusion from being drawn on this subject. The figures in Table 5.10 must be regarded with caution because while there was a certain reserve requirement, part of the inflation tax was collected by BROU.

safe to say that this was not a factor that would operate effectively in setting lending rates and spreads.[31]

Additional evidence that the source of funding with which BROU was subsidizing credits until 1991 was the special treatment of its reserve requirements springs from the fact that the relationship among lending rates in pesos changes drastically only when that reserve requirement regime is modified: the average rate rises from 20 percent lower to the same as the private banking system's average rate in 1992. Nevertheless, as almost all public sector accounts subject to the 1991 change in regime are in domestic currency, this does not explain the rise in BROU's gross spread in dollars. BROU's dollar lending rates are 2 percent above those of the private banks beginning in mid-1991. All of this leads us to the hypothesis that the danger inherent in no longer being able to collect the transfers on public sector accounts prompted the decision to increase the profitability of lending in general. As the agreements with the IBRD and the IDB specify that the bank must be profitable and not encroach on the sphere of the private banking system, the higher rates should be seen in the light of those commitments.

Table 5.11. Participation of BROU in the Uruguayan Market, 1982–92
(Percentage of balances in December of each year as a percentage of the total for each type of instrument)

Years	Deposits in national currency			Deposits in foreign currency		Credits	
	Demand	Savings Bank	Fixed term	Residents	Nonresidents	National Currency	Foreign Currency
1982	22.0	30.0	15.0			30.7	23.8
1983	20.3	31.7	21.4	24.4	16.3	40.9	28.8
1984	21.1	31.4	26.9	31.7	17.1	36.6	33.5
1985	17.4	38.3	28.5	40.4	23.4	49.2	35.0
1986	19.7	45.4	33.8	37.1	21.8	50.6	33.5
1987	20.6	54.9	41.1	41.2	22.1	53.2	35.9
1988	29.7	59.7	42.5	43.9	19.1	59.4	34.0
1989	25.6	65.1	44.9	45.4	17.3	65.3	38.5
1990	28.8	69.7	50.0	47.0	16.3	66.9	41.1
1991	25.7	69.1	49.3	48.3	15.9	58.9	40.6
1992a	16.7	68.9	47.3	46.8	14.5	53.4	40.1

Source: Central Bank of Uruguay, *Boletín Estadístico,* various issues, and unpublished data.
a Balances in October.

---

[31] In several personal communications, the bank's technical staff tend to minimize the effect of the costing change.

The rate changes entailed a loss of credit market share (Table 5.11 and Figure 5.1), particularly in domestic currency. BROU's market share tends to drop in all instruments. If we bear in mind that BROU loses share in periods when confidence in the private system is high, and that the emerging bank strategies of the nineties may consolidate, BROU's position in the market looks even more threatened.

In summary, for the first time in many decades, if not its history, BROU is being subjected to some rules of the other commercial banks. The same happened with BHU,[32] more swiftly and with a clearer idea of its function: to provide long-term credit for housing, subsidizing only low-income sectors with treasury funds. No similar project guides BROU in this new situation. The idea that it should be converted into a commercial bank seeking to optimize its profits involves too great a break with its past and would surely take a long time to carry out. Given its weight, its decision-making machinery, the party-political character of its board of directors, and the diverse range of social agents involved with the bank (small agricultural businesses, large domestic capital not associated with foreign capital, depositors in areas where it is the only bank, depositors who cannot meet the minimums of other banks, and almost 6,000 employees), this or any other transformation is bound to create formidable difficulties.[33]

Some of the policies implemented are signs that BROU does not appear to have a clear policy. One example is the handling of the foreign exchange operation. As we saw, lending rates in dollars were raised together with those in domestic currency. However, borrowing rates have been kept above those of the private banks, which perpetuates the situation prevailing in the eighties. This is particularly puzzling in that the bank has difficulty making loans in that currency. A look at the monetary balance sheets shows how the increased amounts of foreign exchange raised almost all end up as cash and overnight deposits in New York.

Other Aspects of Restructuring the System

As regards the managed banking system, capitalization and reprivatization were chosen as the objectives. With respect to the first objective, the banks have been capitalized in amounts corresponding to the irrecoverable assets, but operational equilibrium still has to be achieved.

---

32 The restructuring of BHU has been carried out to a large extent with respect to its current financial equilibrium and the elimination of crossed subsidies on its balance sheet.
33 Although BROU employees are paid not quite half as much as those in private banks, an agreement has been signed which is intended to bring them to parity in two years.

Banco Comercial was reprivatized in October 1990, while by early 1993 the process of reprivatizing Pan de Azúcar was well advanced. The reprivatization of Caja Obrera is expected to pose more difficulties, since it has lost market share and qualified management staff and the market is rather small for an additional bank specializing in retail operations.

Parliament is considering a bill giving the central bank a new charter under which its board of directors would be politically independent by making member terms of office the same as those for the executive and legislative branches. In addition, a classification of the Superintendency of Banks would be established, and BCU would be given greater supervision and enforcement powers over the private and public banking systems.

The Financial Sector and Macrofinancial Relations

Three items on the policy agenda for the Uruguayan financial sector are interesting from a macroeconomic standpoint: the consequences of a stabilization policy, the impact of the public sector's financing needs on asset allocation, and the fluctuations in the real exchange rate and in the exchange risk.

The first point matters because a financial system does not allocate resources properly if inflation is not predictable, which requires that it be low, while inflation in Uruguay has run between 50 and 90 percent annually, with spikes of 130 percent. The second point is of interest in connection with efforts to prevent savings and the accumulated volumes of the private sector's financial assets from being shifted to the public debt. The third point is important because in a financial system functioning with two currencies, devaluations have consequences on the solvency of businesses and therefore that of the financial system. Moreover, this last issue affects the conditions of access to credit. The three points are interrelated in the following manner.

Permanent stabilization requires matching the public sector's financing needs to the long-term growth rate of the demand for lending. In addition, the relative size and stability of the demand for base money limit the ability to collect seigniorage and the inflation tax. This also influences the decision of what would be the policy's nominal anchor: issuance or the exchange rate. As discussed, that demand is small with respect to GDP, so that stabilization has always tended to be based on the nominal exchange rate. A basic question is why public deficits or surpluses are so dependent on conditions exogenous to economic policy.

The exchange risk is conditioned by the level of inflation and the antiinflation strategy. The dollarization of financial relations brought a change in the distribution of this risk. Previously, only agents involved in external trade or with access to the international capital market were affected by the devaluations. Now, as the local financial system intermediates in dollars but does not accept exchange risk, this risk is assumed by businesses. This introduces macroeconomic instability, by making credit conditions, and thereby the level of activity, more dependent[34] on shocks that affect the balance of payments or on faulty exchange rate policy.[35]

It is obvious that unforeseen shocks in the real exchange rate alter the relationship between borrowing and the internally generated capital of businesses. But even if adverse shocks are foreseeable, the rationing of credit in domestic currency and the absence of futures or options markets deprive businesses of a safe haven. An unexpected devaluation generates transfers of wealth among the agents, but so does an advance devaluation.

If there is macroeconomic concern for the system's solvency or the level of economic activity, the exchange rate must address not only competitiveness or capital movements but also the solvency of the financial system. Accordingly, it is important to know whether the magnitude of those wealth transfers is such as to jeopardize the system's stability and whether some form of countervailing policy is possible.

Meanwhile, any stabilization policy based on the nominal exchange rate as anchor tends—at least temporarily—to generate a real revaluation of the currency and a higher level of activity.[36] This occurs because the policy brings down nominal interest rates more rapidly than the increase in the prices of goods, so that the real interest rate falls and spending rises. These phenomena are clearly discernible in the Uruguayan case. In a highly dollarized system those effects are more pronounced: the lowering of the interest rate does not require perfect arbitrage, because financial assets are very largely in dollars and, moreover, the lowered ratio of dollar-denominated debt to prices eases the debt in both the public and private sectors. In this last case, it improves the debt to equity ratio of firms and enables them to seek more credit. In other words, in a dollarized economy stabilization through the exchange rate has an expansive effect on supply addi-

---

[34] This is consistent with Stiglitz's (1992) argument that the macroeconomic fluctuations are basically due more to the effects of credit than to effects more commonly discussed in macroeconomics, such as that of the interest rate on cost, or unexpected movements in real wages. Movements in the risk of noncompliance would be those that took such fluctuations into account.

[35] What is important here is the exchange rate with respect to the U.S. dollar and not with respect to a basket of trading partners' currencies as used in measuring competitiveness. Financial assets and liabilities are denominated almost exclusively in dollars. Trade takes place with partners who do not maintain constant real parity with respect to the dollar, so that, if Uruguay maintains the average real exchange rate, the fluctuations between the dollar and the remaining currencies have consequences in terms of transfer of financial wealth. See Noya and Rama (1987).

[36] See Végh (1992) for an overview of several stabilizations and an abundant theoretical bibliography of the subject.

Table 5.12. Savings and Financial Surplus by Institutional Sector in Uruguay, 1980–91
(Percentage of GDP)

Year	Public savings	Private savings	National savings	Primary results	Fiscal results	Private results	Results for the rest of the world
1980	5.8	4.4	10.2	0.4	0.1	-7.0	6.9
1981	5.3	6.6	11.8	0.2	-0.1	-4.1	4.2
1982	-0.9	12.3	11.4	-8.1	-9.5	4.4	5.2
1983	2.2	11.9	14.1	-3.0	-7.7	3.3	4.4
1984	1.3	13.0	14.4	-3.1	-9.3	6.6	2.7
1985	2.4	10.1	12.5	-1.1	-6.5	4.0	2.5
1986	5.3	11.1	16.5	1.7	-3.8	4.9	-1.1
1987	4.1	9.1	13.2	0.1	-3.5	1.7	1.8
1988	4.0	12.2	16.2	-0.1	-3.9	4.3	-0.4
1989	3.2	14.4	17.6	-1.1	-5.3	7.2	-1.9
1990	6.5	11.6	18.1	3.0	-1.2	3.9	-2.7
1991	8.3	8.3	16.5	4.1	0.6	0.5	-1.1

Source: Central Bank of Uruguay, *Boletín Estadístico,* various issues, and unpublished data.

tional to that of demand and, at the same time, the effects of an incomplete fiscal adjustment are concealed.

If stabilization fails there is a real devaluation, so that the risk of failed stabilization is also a risk of insolvency for businesses and the financial system.

Dynamics of the Public Deficit

The public sector ran a deficit during the eighties, accumulating debt with the rest of the world and with the private sector (Table 5.12). By contrast, the private sector accumulated net assets against the rest of the world throughout the period following 1982. Around 1986–87, the savings trend in the rest of the world changed. That situation changes in the nineties: the public sector comes into balance, and private savings decline.

The origins of the public deficit are similar to those of other Latin American countries: adverse trade shocks, unexpectedly rising international interest rates, real devaluation which increased the burden of the public external debt, reorganization of the private financial system by the central bank, falling tax receipts in relation to the GDP because of the recession, etc. In institutional terms, two components are paramount: BCU's parafiscal shortfall and the central government deficit.

The dynamics of BCU's shortfall are simple: since it was caused by the purchase of almost completely irrecoverable bank portfolios financed with borrowed dollars, it was tied to international interest rates and to the real dollar exchange rate. In addition, BCU purchased reserves through almost the entire period, which increased its financing needs outside those arising from its current account.

The dynamics of the deficit of the rest of the public sector involve several elements. The high elasticity of collection to the GDP makes it very sensitive to the business cycle.[37] The rigidity of expenditure on supplies leaves only two short-term adjustment variables: real wages and investment. The social security deficit is a basic component which, in addition to having a structural genesis, varies with the rate of inflation. Thanks to a constitutional amendment, retirement benefits have since 1990 been indexed to the past course of nominal wages. Thus, when inflation slows, social security outlays rise (producing a negative Olivera-Tanzi effect). In 1992 those outlays were equivalent to 12 percent of GDP at 60 percent inflation; if inflation declined by 20 percent in 1993, those outlays would increase to 16 percent of GDP. This implies that the indexing mechanism works against shock treatment by swiftly and significantly raising public spending in real terms. Hence the adoption of "gradualist" policies is widespread, sometimes regardless of the intentions of policymakers.

Other specifically Uruguayan phenomena spring from the maintenance of access to sources of funding in foreign currency: this explains why inflation has not gotten out of hand despite an average monetary base of only 3.5 percent of GDP. Those sources were securities issues in dollars and the financial system's reserve requirements. On the other hand, the fiscal adjustment continued and public debt accumulated.

A fiscal adjustment implemented since 1990 has cut the deficit substantially. The results are due both to tight fiscal policy and favorable exogenous developments. Fiscal adjustment was based on tax increases, which were supposedly temporary pending a real cut in spending. However, spending cuts helped the adjustment in 1990 in an unexpected way. When the stabilization policy was unsuccessful and inflation accelerated, social security outlays and real public wages fell. The stabilization policy sought to act swiftly on the indexation mechanisms by setting rate and wage increases and devaluation guidelines consistent with the deficit monetization forecasts. However, the persistence of indexing added to an external price shock caused by price rises in the two neighboring countries militated against quick results. When inflation began to slow in late 1990, spending rose in real terms.

In 1991 and 1992 the public sector practically achieved equilibrium. Continuing increased tax pressure and expanding GDP were factors, as well as

---

[37] Different estimates place it at around 1.7 to 2. See Noya (1989) and de Haedo and Sapelli (1989).

the reduction of the external debt because of the Brady Plan,[38] the lowering of the international rate, and the appreciation of the peso against the dollar. In this way, estimates of discretional fluctuation of aggregate fiscal policy indicate that it had little significance (Roldós, 1992). That is to say, factors external to fiscal policy are the deficit's chief determinants. Thus the current fiscal balance is very dependent on external shocks, be they favorable or adverse. Public borrowing is declining in real terms, but the monetary expansion financing the acquisition of reserves continues.[39]

The outlook depends heavily on international real interest rates and the real exchange rate. Meanwhile, the expansion of GDP will be difficult to sustain at its present pace. Without those exogenous elements the current deficit would not be zero. However, the factors casting the most doubt on the sustainability of the current fiscal situation pertain to the high tax burden and the fact that, as noted, real spending on social security rises inexorably as inflation continues to decline. Nevertheless, the reduction that has been achieved in public borrowing should ensure that in the short term there will be no substantial pressures on the financial market.

Transfers of Wealth and the Real Exchange Rate

As we have seen, a number of things can happen to the financial sector in the course of a stabilization plan: wealth is transferred among holders of financial assets, and the exchange rate lag distorts measurement of the fiscal adjustment. To give an idea of the scale of those variations, let us analyze the transfers of financial wealth caused by changes in the relative prices of financial assets and liabilities and by variations in the real exchange rate. The aim is to have an idea of the order of magnitude of those transfers, in order to see if it affects the net worth of firms and could drive them and the financial system into bankruptcy. That order of magnitude would in turn provide a quantitative approximation of the funds necessary to avoid acute financial crises.

Given an efficient financial market, transfers through anticipated fluctuations in the exchange rate would be offset by the spreads between interest rates

---

[38] This reduction, accompanied by the rescheduling of the rest of the debt to international banks, caused the subject of renegotiating that debt to fade to the background. However, problems in administering the public debt may surface with the renewed rise in the volume of bonds and bills.

[39] There are two reasons for the continuing accumulation of reserves: (1) the persistent increase in dollar deposits, which necessitates growing reserve requirements in that currency, which is reflected in the cash reserves of BCU and the private banking system; the same need is created by the growth of the public debt in foreign currency until 1989; and (2) the stabilization initiated in 1990 has resulted in real appreciation of the domestic currency; the BCU intervenes in the market in order to keep the real exchange rate from falling further.

Table 5.13. Transfers through Changes in Relative Prices between the Financial System and the Private Sector, 1982–91
(Percentage of GDP)

Year	Transfers through changes in the CPI/US$ ratio			Transfers including the effect of the real interest rate			CPI/US$ ratio 1982=100
	Through financial system assets	Through financial system liabilities	Net total	Through financial system assets	Through financial system liabilities	Net Total	
1982	22.7	-16.3	6.4	34.6	-21.1	13.5	100.0
1983	-0.2	3.3	3.1	11.8	-0.4	11.4	100.0
1984	0.7	2.2	2.9	7.5	0.0	7.5	102.3
1985	-2.4	6.0	3.6	2.2	4.1	6.3	95.5
1986	20.1	-21.6	-1.5	0.3	7.7	8.0	79.5
1987	-0.2	2.7	2.5	0.6	0.1	0.7	79.5
1988	-1.1	4.4	3.3	4.1	3.2	7.3	77.3
1989	-1.3	5.1	3.8	3.5	3.7	7.2	72.7
1990	-3.4	10.1	6.7	1.1	10.2	11.3	61.4
1991	-2.5	8.2	5.7	4.6	6.6	11.2	52.3

Sources: Central Bank of Uruguay, *Boletín Estadístico*, various issues, and unpublished data.
Note: CPI/US$ is the consumer price index compared to the exchange rate (in pesos for dollars).

in pesos and dollars. However, inefficiencies can prevent this offset from taking place. As will be seen, interest rate fluctuations do not offset those transfers.

Table 5.13 shows the transfers that took place among private parties and the private financial sector. Two measurements of the transfers have been considered: in the first place, computing only those due to changes in the exchange rate to price ratio, leaving aside any compensations due to changes in real interest rates, so that the transfers result from the application of the real depreciation affecting the original volumes, and, second, these transfers include the effect of the interest rate, i.e., they apply the real interest rate to loans and deposits. The table shows that the private financial sector has received transfers from the private sector, and that those transfers have moved in the same direction as the exchange rate with respect to the consumer price index. It is evident that, including the effect of the interest rate, this transfer is not compensated.

It is important to mark a difference between the nineties and the eighties. The private sector's position with respect to the banking system changed to the point where, starting in 1986, private individuals became lenders of foreign currency and borrowers of domestic currency. As this trend intensified in 1990, the course of the exchange rate with respect to prices began to reverse itself, and, beginning in that year, the fall of the exchange rate in relation to prices caused an increase in transfers from the private sector to the financial agents.

The scale of net transfers is such that any countervailing fiscal policy designed to cover insolvencies of the financial system must be very exacting.

Table 5.14. 1991 Public Deficit: Composition and Simulation of Increases in the Exchange Rate and Interest Rate
(In billions of new pesos)

Income and expenditures by institution	Figure for 1991	Simulation of increases of:	
		10% exchange rate	10% exchange rate and 100% interest rate
Central Bank			
Foreign currency outflows	323	356	356
Foreign currency inflows	63	69	69
National currency outflows	205	205	205
National currency inflows	19	19	19
Central government			
Taxes	3243	3328	3328
On domestic sales	2507	2563	2563
On income	224	224	224
On equity	216	216	216
Export receipt documents	-139	-153	-153
On foreign trade	436	479	479
Expenditures	7848	7917	8676
Current	3924	3959	4338
Interest	345	380	759
Others	3579	3579	3579
Investments	343	352	352
Public sector deficit	-1285	-982	-1362

Sources: Central Bank of Uruguay, *Boletín Estadístico and Boletín de Prensa*, various issues, and unpublished data.

The second point to be underscored is the real exchange rate's impact on public sector accounts. Table 5.14 shows the composition of the 1991 public deficit, and a simulation is run on the primary effects of a fluctuation in the real exchange rate or in the interest rate. An important find is that the chief effect of real devaluation on public finance is positive in nature. Given the current structure of the public sector's expenditure and revenue in foreign currency, a rising real exchange rate translates into a shrinking deficit. This situation changes, however, if one considers—as shown in the last column—the possibility of a rise in international interest rates. In this case, a duplication of the rate reverses the trend because of changes in the real exchange rate. In this way the sustainability of the present situation is conditional upon the international exchange rate levels. Nevertheless, it should be pointed out that we have considered only the immediate impacts on fiscal accounts, not analyzing, for example, what would happen to collection should real devaluation affect the level of activity.

Outlines of Policies and Proposed Reforms

As noted in the preceding sections, the Uruguayan financial system has not channeled savings to businesses in any substantial volume since the 1982 crisis. The reason lies in macro and microeconomic problems. The former include the distribution of the exchange risk, which limits the allocation of dollar credits to sectors where the banks do not do business. Until 1990, the expansion of the public debt meant strong competition for funds: as long as the public sector demanded funds, the system acted like another window for the placement of public debt, while it was restructuring its network and redirecting its efforts at nontraditional areas. Troubled banks which were taken over by the state and the public banking system, facing little in the way of competition, increased market share thanks to the safety that state backing gave them.

The situation changed in the late eighties. The public sector achieved equilibrium, prudential rules were tightened, treatment of the public banking system was brought into line with that of the private system, and signs emerged of changes in banking strategy. However, none of that generated intermediation directed at businesses.

The lack of credit to firms has not been noted in recent years because the fall of real interest rates to international levels triggered an inflow of capital partly aimed at financing the little private investment which, according to some indicators, capitalized firms by means of self-financing.[40]

Recent changes in bank policies indicate that a sizable proportion of the high cost of intermediation is due to the modification of BROU's rate policy. This places the subject of the public banking system's efficiency at the forefront of the debate.

In addition, the discussion of microeconomic or sectoral problems centers on three interrelated topics: licensing policy (which turns attention to the segmentation of the credit market as a consequence of the type of financial agents and their strategies), the system's safety, and the role assigned to the public system.

Macroeconomic Problems

As we have seen, the existence of a system that intermediates largely in dollars but assumes no exchange risk compels businesses to assume that risk. This creates a substantial asymmetry between the agents, because while the public may be capable of swiftly reallocating its assets when devaluation seems likely, busi-

---

[40] According to a survey conducted in late 1991, about 80 percent of investment undertaken in the manufacturing industry was financed with internally generated funds. See Torello and Noya (1992).

nesses cannot react as fast. As businesses are owned by the public, a devaluation increases the financial assets of households, at the cost of a loss of capital by businesses. If the real devaluation is large enough to drive firms to bankruptcy, households have an incentive to make firms fall.

These problems also occur when there are stabilizations. As curbing inflation is a necessary condition for the efficient functioning of the system over the long run, the adoption of a stabilization policy is inevitable. Stabilization policy however, tends to trigger real currency revaluations and transfers to businesses in its initial phase. Thus the risks of failed stabilization become a danger to the stability of the system.

In the context of implicit insurance of dollarized deposits, that causes the public sector's contingent external debt to grow at the start of a stabilization. The immediate consequence is that an accurate assessment of the fiscal policy situation must take account of the changes in that contingent debt.[41] The policy recommendation prompted by this consideration is that fiscal policies should be tighter, in order to build up international reserves in case of a devaluation. Similarly, deficits should be measured with reference to real parity exchange rates. Increased systemic risk from stabilization dictates that the only agent capable of covering it—the state—seek a self-insurance mechanism with the build-up of international reserves. Given the difficulties of implementing tighter adjustments, it would seem well to seek other mechanisms for diversifying risk.

Two mechanisms for reducing exchange risk are regularly mentioned: spurring the development of contingent asset markets, and imposing restrictions on private investment in foreign currency.

The implementation of policies to foster ways whereby the private sector could cover exchange risks (futures and options markets) seems difficult unless the public sector were to grant implicit subsidies. A futures market in domestic currency is practically nonexistent in Uruguay. It appears poor even in relation to other financial markets in the region. In any case, the need to make these operations more widespread and to train the necessary personnel seems to be the main focus, in connection with the lack of legal provisions.

Not to stimulate borrowing in dollars (for example, by establishing some kind of tax) runs up against the many opportunities for evading a measure of this

---

[41] This topic is particularly important if the fiscal situation is not put on a sound footing and a strategy of stabilization by shock therapy is followed. As Calvo and Végh (1992) point out, if inflation is high and climbing, the temptation may arise to increase the degree of dollarization or even to move on to convertibility. However, if the fiscal imbalance persists, the banks will feel pressured to lend to the government and businesses, which previously benefited from the inflation tax. The quality of the banks' loan portfolio will thereby tend to deteriorate and financial runs or collapses will become a possibility, in turn endangering stabilization.

nature in an economy as liberalized as the Uruguayan one. The great mobility of deposits and their arbitrage between local dollar rates and international rates suggests that it would tend to reduce intermediation. The imposition of additional costs on lending rates in dollars would surely affect nonpreferred customers, since the preferred customers may have several means of access to external credit.

Microeconomic Problems

The Uruguayan experience yields two lessons. One is important for countries that have macroeconomic instability, a certain amount of currency substitution, implicit deposit insurance or no insurance, and that have not undergone a macroeconomic crisis jeopardizing the financial system: although prudential regulations are being satisfactorily applied, major systemic risks are, in the long run, making the local agents fall. The second lesson pertains to the local situation, after the domestic private banking system has disappeared.

With regard to the first lesson, the dollarization of the economy creates a set of incentives in which banks that are not public or associated with strong international banks cannot survive strongly adverse external shocks. Therefore, prudential measures should not be relied on too heavily. If the risk is systemic or macroeconomic, in the sense that it affects almost all businesses that operate with the system, prudential regulations cannot diversify it. They can only require that the financial intermediaries assume losses by contributing capital preventively. Suppose, for example, that the prudential regulation system succeeds in giving the alert with sufficient advance notice concerning a case of risk of insolvency generated by a potential real devaluation. Only institutions with access to external credit or, more precisely, institutions able to obtain capital in response to the forecasts, could adjust to the situation required by the Superintendency. The other two forms of ownership have implicit insurance mechanisms. In this way the system raises a barrier to the entry of certain kinds of agents.

One solution would be to impose explicit, compulsory deposit insurance for privately owned local banks, charged to those banks. The insurance would have to be optional for foreign-owned banks and mandatory for the public banking system.

The disappearance of the domestic banking system is essential if we assume it to have negative allocation effects. Behaviors restricted by the goals of multinational banks, turnover of management staff, relations with local affiliates based on business dealings in the parent company, and substantial portfolio write-offs by the monetary authorities of the developed countries on investments in developing countries are inspiring great aversion to risk in the management of this type of banking agent.[42] In this way, projects that are profitable but risky, or expensive to monitor or select, are passed by, with resulting loss of efficiency.

Two items must be considered with respect to the recommendations for the present Uruguayan situation: whether or not to continue the current implicit licensing policy and the consequent changes to replace its function concerning the system's safety if it is deemed advisable to abandon it, and the role to be played by the public banking system.

As we have seen, the problem of the Uruguayan banking system's safety since 1985 has been tackled with an implicit restricted admission policy. That makes for a system with particularly risk-averse agents. The recent admission of a "mixed" banking system, with domestic or regional capital associated with first-line bank capital, suggests the possible existence of a banking system designed to finance projects which are riskier but profitable in the long run or in large numbers. Although it may still be premature to evaluate this emergent banking system's degree of aversion to risk, its recent performance supports this idea. We maintain that the stockholding participation of the "ensuring" partner does not take place without certain restrictions on the level of risk that it is prepared to accept. Compared with a domestically or regionally owned banking system, this mixed banking system could plausibly be regarded as more risk-averse. The cost of having an "external insurer" is to limit the level of risk which the banking system is prepared to assume.

The assumption that there will be no private banking agent to assume major risks with the present admission rules is impossible to verify fully in reference to the new banking system, not only because of the short time since that system's inception but also because of the presence of other factors that prevent any type of financial intermediation of average efficiency: the existence of institutional risk of forced nonperformance of debt contracts legislatively imposed. If there are no clearly delimited property rights, the market cannot function. No matter what the approach, this is a basic problem that must be resolved.

Reforms to expedite arrangements between insolvent debtors and creditors and bankruptcy proceedings, and to strengthen the judicial branch, intended to streamline the process of reorganizing or liquidating overindebted enterprises, are important but not decisive. Measures of this type are contained in a recent agreement signed with the IDB to improve the "investment climate." Apart from the fact that those procedures are generally designed for localized and not general capital losses of the system, what is most important is the design of institu-

---

[42] Many examples exist of these characteristics of foreign bank management. See Germidis and Michalet (1984), chapter 2, for underdeveloped countries and Grosse and Goldberg (1991) for the United States.

tional mechanisms which "tie the hands" of the public authorities when they try to prevent the breach of private contracts by legal mechanisms or to reach a credible undertaking that modifications of private contracts will not be resorted to by legal means.

Two general avenues to reform of the system then present themselves: either the current policy is maintained, with its allocation costs and its safety advantages, or the licensing policy is changed. In the first case, it should be pointed out that any prudential regulation policy like the one recently adopted is relative. In that context the concern regarding unequal information flows between banks and the public is pointless. It is not the specifics of the local situation that ensures the system's stability in the long run, but the status of its external partners. If the prestigious parent companies cover local firms, depositors have no incentive to distinguish between them, or to learn more about the status of the local banks.

With this system, and according to our assumptions, only the public banking system could occupy the place of the domestic private banking system. In BROU's case, this poses requirements with respect to loan portfolio management that are not currently being met.

If our reasoning is accepted, the right approach would be to change the licensing rule and admit domestic private agents. Then, as a substitute for the role of "external insurer," some kind of deposit insurance mechanism ought to be adopted. As we stated in connection with other countries, this insurance should be explicit and mandatory for domestic banks, including the public ones, and charged to them.

In that case the requirement for transparency of information becomes absolutely essential. The machinery for disclosure of information on the soundness of business projects and the solvency of the banks by the Superintendency, perhaps supplemented by private audits, would have to be strengthened. Despite some progress, the Uruguayan financial system is hardly transparent: no financial data are published on banks, public or private, or on businesses. Not even aggregate results are disclosed. This does not stem from any need for protection from competition, for some information is disseminated to financial institutions by BCU. In that sense, the existence of bank secrecy concerning the institutions' lending operations has no economic basis. The explicit abolition of that secrecy concerning lending operations would eliminate the legal doubts about the scope of this rule.

Finally, the restructuring of the public banking system, with particular reference to BROU, is key to any approach to regulating the private banking system. As noted, that process is not without difficulties. The main problem is lack of clarity as to the economic meaning of the proposed objective. Stated in more abstract terms, BROU's case exemplifies the problem of what the role of the public banking system should be in a context of open, liberalized financial markets. In a system of stringently rationed credit, its function was clear. In the new situation, it is not clear what shortcoming in the market this public enterprise should address. The question therefore arises why a public, apparently less efficient, institution has to exist in a presumably competitive marketplace.

The answer is twofold. Should the present restrictive admission rule be maintained, the task would be to assume the risks not taken by the transnational banks or the emerging "mixed" banking system. If, on the other hand, a less risk-averse domestic banking system is admitted, its function should be to provide long-term financing, since no private market exists.

In any case, BROU's transformation implies that it should be a bank whose core activity is lending. The extensive and costly borrowing network would be pointless under all the alternatives. The importance of cost reduction is obvious, given the problems generated with the raising of its lending rate. In addition, it should have in place extremely refined and public evaluation procedures to prevent it from being subjected to the activities of businesses in search of income. In that connection, the role of the board of directors composed of political representatives should be reduced to supervisory or control functions, while operations should be led by managers independent of the board of directors and new rules concerning the granting of loans. The new loan criteria should minimize the role of guarantees. Concomitantly, bureaucratic success in portfolio management should be measured in terms not of each particular case but of a broad spectrum of sectors or businesses or even, at the top management level, of overall bank management. Under any approach, improved information systems and public disclosure of its results are essential requirements which are not currently being met.

BIBLIOGRAPHY

Amoroso, B. and J. Xavier. 1988. "Adecuación de capital en empresas de inter-mediación financiera." Paper presented at Terceras Jornadas Anuales de Economía, Montevideo.

Banda, A. 1990. "Regulación bancaria, crisis financiera y políticas conse-cuentes: el caso uruguayo." In *Ahorro y asignación de recursos financieros,* eds. Günther Held and Raquel Szallachman. Buenos Aires: Grupo Editor Latinoamericano.

Banking Association of Uruguay. *Memoria Anual*, various issues. Montevideo.

Bucheli, M. 1992. "Diferencias sectoriales de salarios en el Uruguay." *Suma* 7 (12): 44–80.

Calvo, G. and C. A. Végh. 1992. "Currency Substitution in Developing Countries: an Introduction." *Revista de Análisis Económico* 7 (1): 29–72.

Central Bank of Uruguay. *Boletín Estadístico*, various issues. Montevideo.

de Haedo, J. and C. Sapelli. 1989. "Simplificación y modernización del sistema tributario en Uruguay 1972–86." *Revista de Economía* 3 (3): 79–114.

Dominioni, D. and D. Vaz. 1991. "Riesgo crediticio y concentración de cartera. Un enfoque de optimización." Paper presented at the Sextas Jornadas Anuales de Economía, Montevideo. Mimeo.

———. 1992. "El margen de intermediación bancaria en el Uruguay." First Mention of the Annual Prize of the Banking Association of Uruguay. Montevideo. Mimeo.

Fernández, W. and A. Pereira. 1992. "El margen de intermediación bancaria en el Uruguay." Paper presented at the Séptimas Jornadas Anuales de Economía, Montevideo.

Gagliardi, E. 1992. "El margen de intermediación bancaria en el Uruguay." First Prize of the Association of Banks of Uruguay. Montevideo. Mimeo.

Germidis, D. and Ch. A. Michalet. 1984. *International Banks and Financial Markets in Developing Countries.* Paris: Organisation for Economic Co-oper-ation and Development (OECD).

Grosse, R. and L. G. Goldberg. 1991. "Foreign Bank Activity in the United States: An Analysis by Country of Origin." *Journal of Banking and Finance* 15 (6): 1093–1112.

Hernández, L. 1992. "Financial Intermediation, Monetary Uncertainty and Bank Interest Margins." *Revista de Análisis Económico* 7 (2): 23–42.

McKinnon, R. 1973. *Money and Capital in Economic Development.* Washington D.C.: The Brookings Institution.

Milnitsky, S. 1989. *El holding bancario del Banco de la República Oriental del Uruguay.* Montevideo: Fundación de Cultura Universitaria.

Noya, N. 1988. "Ahorro, inversión y activos financieros. Los efectos de la liberalización." *Suma* 3 (5): 115–145.

———. 1989. "Orígenes y consecuencias del déficit fiscal." *Suma* 4 (6): 81–108.

Noya, N. and M. Rama. 1987. "¿Quién financió la reactivación? Cuando la dolarización tiene sus ventajas." *Suma* 2 (3): 105–50.

Oikos. *Panorama Financiero*, various issues. Montevideo.

Pérez-Campanero, J. and A. Leone. 1991. "Liberalization and Financial Crisis in Uruguay, 1974–87." In *Banking Crises: Cases and Issues,* eds. V. Sundarajan and J. T. Baliño. Washington, D.C.: International Monetary Fund.

Rama, M. and A. Forteza. 1992. "Indexación de activos financieros y ahorro privado: la experiencia uruguaya." In *Indexación de activos y ahorro privado,* eds. G. Held and F. Jiménez. Santiago: Economic Commission for Latin America and the Caribbean.

Roldós, J. 1991. *La crisis bancaria uruguaya de los ochenta.* Serie Temas Económico-Sociales 4. Montevideo: Centro de Estudios de la Realidad Económica y Social.

———. 1992. *Política fiscal, ajuste y redistribución: el caso uruguayo, 1985–91.* Montevideo: United Nations Development Programme-Economic Commission for Latin American and the Caribbean.

Savastano, M. A. 1992. "The Pattern of Currency Substitution in Latin America: an Overview." *Revista de Análisis Económico* 7 (1): 29–72.

Shaw, E. 1973. *Financial Deepening and Economic Development.* New York: Oxford University Press.

Stiglitz, J. 1992. "Capital Markets and Macroeconomic Fluctuations in Capitalist Economies." *European Economic Review* 36 (2): 269–396.

Torello, M. and N. Noya. 1992. *Las políticas de incentivos a la inversión privada.* Serie Informes de Investigación No. 23. Montevideo: Centro de Investigaciones Económicas.

Végh, C. A. 1992. "Stopping High Inflation. An Analytical Overview." *IMF Staff Papers* 39 (3): 626–95.

Index